About the Author

Bradley Rubenstein is a painter and writer who lives and works in Brooklyn, New York. His works are in the collections of The Metropolitan Museum of Art, The Detroit Institute of Arts, The Museum of Fine Arts, Boston, The Tang Teaching Museum, The Krannert Art Museum Teaching Collection at The University of Illinois at Urbana-Champaign, and The Teaching Collection at the Whitney Museum of American Art, among others. He has been the recipient of the National Endowment for the Arts Fellowship in Painting, the Pollock-Krasner Award, and a grant from the Emily Hall Tremaine Foundation. He has contributed interviews, essays, and reviews to *CultureCatch, Artslant, Battery Journal, M/E/A/N/I/N/G, The Brooklyn Rail, Sharkforum, ArtKrush, New Observations*, and *Art Journal*. Mr. Rubenstein is the author of *The Black Album: Writings on Art and Culture*.

Gennifer Levey is an editor and publisher based in Brooklyn, New York.

Nicola Tyson
Larry Krone
Inka Essenhigh
Mira Schor
Rodney Dickson
Ryan Steadman
Lucio Pozzi
Ajamu Kojo
Erin Smith
Dennis Kardon
Anna Ehrsam
Wesley Kimler
Franklin Evans
Gary Stephan
Pedro Barbeito
Susan Bee
Patricia Cronin
David Humphrey
Bjarne Melgaard
Deborah Kass
Allison Schulnik
Brenda Goodman
Rick Briggs
Scott Grodesky
Peter Williams
Millree Hughes
Pia Lindman
John Paul
Michael Rees
Michael Zansky
Liz Markus
Gina Magid
Hannah Kallenbach
Angela Dufresne
Joseph Nechvatal
Taney Roniger
Michael Lee Nirenberg
Alexis Nunnelly
Magalie Guérin

PRESS EJECT AND GIVE ME THE TAPE

Dialogues, Interviews, and Exchanges

2001–2020

Bradley Rubenstein

Edited by Gennifer Levey

Foreword by Michael Rees

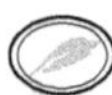

Published by Meridian Art Press, Brooklyn, New York.
www.meridianartpress.com
Printed in the United States of America.

Publisher's Cataloging-in-Publication Data
Rubenstein, Bradley.
Press eject and give me the tape : dialogues, interviews, and exchanges 2001–2020 / statement of responsibility.
Brooklyn, NY : Meridian Art Press, 2020.
LCCN 2019920697 | ISBN 978-1-7322219-4-9 (paperback) | ISBN 978-1-7322219-5-6 (ebook).
LCSH: 1. Artists--Interviews. 2. Art--Technique. 3. Art--Themes, motives. 4. Arts, Modern--21st century. 5. Creation (Literary, artistic, etc.).
BISAC: 1. ART / Individual Artists / Essays. 2. ART / History / General. 3. ART / Popular Culture.
LCC N85 .R83 2020 (print) | LCC N85 (ebook) | DDC 709.05--dc23.

Library of Congress Control Number 2019920697

Contents

Acknowledgements

The author would like to thank the following for their editorial contributions:

Andrea Alessi
Trong G. Nguyen
Mark "Dusty" Petracca
Steve Holtje
Christopher Elam
Natalie Hegert

Foreword

by Michael Rees

Why? Why on earth would anyone be interested in a book of interviews by artists? Because it's as good as interviews with anyone else? Artists really inhabit their lives. Usually they've started out thinking whatever "conformity" is, "I don't want it. I chose to explore." And explore they do. Arcane, occult, mystical, materialist, historical, formalist, psychological, explorative, theoretical, scientific, algorithmic, and on. They immerse themselves deeply in their business. It is deep immersion. Sometimes it means something to other people, or lots of other people. But artists, everyone I've ever known, are concerned with quality of life, immersion, and depth of experience. It's an unmistakable sensibility. Like comedians. They can't help it—they go there. They go again and again. Rumination, that's a typical quality of an artist too. For artists, and especially for those artists who aren't born yet, books like this are priceless.

Bradley Rubenstein's characters are not all on the A List, or maybe they are, or maybe they're fluctuating between the A and B and D Lists of art world hierarchy, shuffling constantly, in and out of fashion. I mean they've shown in museums, been written about, done writing and curating. Why choose them in favor of the just the A-Listers? The ones everyone knows? The ones you see in museum after museum, in art fair after art fair? The ones whose ossified quips are instantly graspable, or comfortably familiar.

Rubenstein casts a wide net. He doesn't limit his choice of subjects to what is fashionable at the moment, or what is going on in New York, or what is in *Artforum* this month. The people who he talks to are the strings that reach down and up into the communities of artists, writers, curators, collectors, and so on. They're in touch with others. They're growing out of the art historical past, the casual historical present, and into diverse futures, but they're also doing that in conversation, in practice, the original social practice, with one another. They are distinct personalities, and they blend with others as well. The interviews, dialogues, and back-and-forth exchanges in this collection span two decades, four continents, as well as a variety of art world styles that have come and gone in those 20 years.

In the 19th century the German playwright Heinrich von Kleist wrote a tiny little text that I hold to my bosom, the one above my heart. It is called *On the gradual completion of thoughts during speech*. I read this first in a small pamphlet conceived, designed, and produced by the designer Erik Spiekermann. In it, von Kleist describes an alternative to what I imagine to be the approach of the German educational system. In that system you speak only what you know and know thoroughly. You do and learn expert speak. You speak to inform others, to perform your knowledge. But in this essay he proposes an alternative: to speak out loud to understand something, to use speech to form it. He describes it so:

> The mind develops this confused conception into complete clarity in face of the necessity
> for a beginning to have an end—in such a way that, to my astonishment, my discovery
> and speech conclude together. I intersperse my sentences with inarticulate sounds, stretch
> connecting particles, perhaps make use of an apportion where one is inept, and use all
> manner of tricks to lengthen my speech, to gain sufficient time to proceed my idea in a
> workshop of reason. I find nothing is of greater benefit at such times than a movement
> from my sister as though seeking to interrupt, since my mind, already under pressure,

becomes still more excited at this attempt from without to wrest the conversation from its control, and, as a great general when events conspire, its faculties list still one degree further.

Later in the text he almost tosses off the most potent metaphor of this speculative type of speech, implicating the philosopher Immanuel Kant "as the true master of the midwifery of thoughts."

The midwifery of thoughts. Speech, a performative action in which things that were not previously understood are delivered. They are born, created, developed. Language is used not violently, politically, or authoritatively, not to command and control. Rather it is used to enlarge, to develop, to elaborate, to speculate, and to imagine. To improvise. The form of the interview gives this speculation free reign (a berth). At times you can see the artist speaking well within the bounds of their "message," and at other times you see them veering off in an unknown direction prompted by the strangeness of having to deal with another—someone who wants to know and who is asking the questions. Interesting questions formed out of the interviewer's experiences, knowledge, and research about the artist. The questioner can be an authority, or they can be a knowledgeable other, a familial practitioner. In this case, a fellow artist with similar commitments.

Rubenstein has been publishing these pieces since the mid-1990s, and the selection in this book covers the period 2001–2020, taking pains to step out of his art practice to develop the discipline of checking in with other artists. It is important that he is an artist. The artists give him a certain trust, and he is an adept raconteur. He demonstrates knowledge about each artist and their work; Rubenstein is someone who physicalizes his knowledge of the work by seeing the exhibitions in person, reading, and talking with other artists. It is often said, if you want to know what's hot and what's not, who's doing good work and who's developing, get it from the artists. Curators, collectors, writers, dealers, they can all "have an eye," but none are as committed to *seeing* like the artist. Mostly, for them, the artist is the object of their gaze; for artists, other art and artists are the subject of their gaze. Such a book as this enlarges the subject and, by extension, their subjects. This is a record, an historical document of a time and a place. A place at the end of history, or at least the end of American hegemony in the world. A few people living their brief lives through the commitment and practice of art.

Michael Rees lives and works in North Bergen, New Jersey. He is an n-dimensional sculptor who teaches and runs the Center for New Art at William Paterson University in Wayne, New Jersey.

"Ideal conversation must be an exchange of thought, and not, as many of those who worry most about their shortcomings believe, an eloquent exhibition of wit or oratory."
—Emily Post

"Most people in the world don't really use their brains to think. And people who don't think are the ones who don't listen to others."
—Haruki Murakami, *1Q84*

"I really don't care that much about 'Beauties.' What I really like are 'Talkers.'"
—Andy Warhol

Transience Is the Meaning: Gary Stephan + Bradley Rubenstein

Gary Stephan was born in Brooklyn in 1942 and currently lives and works in New York City, as well as Stone Ridge, New York. He has been showing his painting and sculpture since the '60s in the U.S. and Europe. He is on the faculty of the School of Visual Arts MFA program.

Bradley Rubenstein: I really want to talk a little about the new work, to begin with. Seems like these are the start of a new way of thinking about painting for. They appear abstract but also strangely concrete.

Gary Stephan: I see them abstracted from the world, but also concrete in that they are material objects. I try to make complex spaces. In fact they include three types of space. There's a cartographic space, where you look down on it as though it's a map. Then there is a conventional picture space, whether Eastern or Western. You're essentially looking at things sideways, with objects stacked up as they are in these particular ones where it is pushed up. But even in these, there are moments where the easiest way to read parts of them is sideways.

BR: So it's almost like an MRI?

GS: No, that would be the third one, the cross section, and an example of that is here, where you have this little tunnel that goes down into this chamber, similar to these. I can show you—this is Japanese.

BR: And this is Indian. This kind of contradicts my initial reading. These are very narrative pictorial structures. You seem to be playing with the idea that the visual structure that originally contained the narrative can be flipped, in a way.

GS: Yes, I'd like to make abstract pictures that go right up to the line, and sometimes fall over into representation. I'd like to load them with as much stuff as I can without having people say, "oh, a dog" or "a golf course." But I'd like to get that level of complexity, that level of world-like material. See, the problem for me with representation is—I love its complexity, its richness—but I am troubled by the fact that once you read it, essentially all the meanings are collapsed at that moment. Like when you see something in a bedroom, a shaft of light comes in the window and catches a wrinkle on the sheet, and for a split second you think there's a toy duck on the bed. That moment where it's open is great. It's completely open, then the minute you realize, "Oh, no, I know what it is," the whole thing collapses. You can never turn it back into a duck; it just won't go. The brain sees that as a mistake. So I'd like to see if I can make abstract pictures that have that kind of openness to them, where you can still find them highly suggestive.

BR: So it can always be a duck.

GS: It can always be a duck, or if you make a duck out of it, you know it's your making, not mine. I'm not making pictures of ducks. Although, oddly, people have complained that these pictures fail because they saw something they had imagined, and they were so convinced that I had willed it. They didn't realize their responsibility as constructors of the images.

BR: The pictures almost beg that, though.

GS: Yes, they do!

BR: Which, in a way, deconstructs the idea of you as an artist making an image that says what you want it to mean.

GS: Yes, but transience is the meaning. You've said before that the works looked very determined. I was thinking about how I make them and do things to them and then change them and then change them back. I found the word that best described this was "interrogate." I sort of interrogate the painting. I am making it and unmaking it. I keep adding gray, for example, until I block too much out, then I'll start carving it back by adding white again. I am interrogating that edge of, how much do I need to say? How much can I unsay?

BR: When I grew up, in my neighborhood, the guys always had these really nice cars, seventies cars, like Chargers or GTOs, and they were always taking the engines apart or customizing something. For them, the inside of the car—the making and unmaking it—was just as important as actually driving it.

GS: In a way I think it's the essence of the modernist argument that instead of the object being presented to the viewer as a closed set that reflects the authority of the artist—and indirectly the authority of the state—this is a set of elements that, if you'll contribute as a viewer, can be organized as a satisfying picture. But without your participation, it isn't enough. You have to help, like with a late Picasso. If you play with them, then they start to come together.

BR: Going back to some of your earlier works, there was the same sense of constructing a painting.

GS: Yes, in the early sixties, I began to say to myself, these aren't only pictures, but they're paintings. In the process, I began asking myself, what is a painting and what is a picture? I made a column for myself, and on one side of the column I wrote, "Stories are to books as pictures are to paintings." You know, in those days I wouldn't have said, "As software is to hardware, brain is to mind." In other words, every image manifests itself as matter. There is the painting, which is this real thing. So a lot of those material investigations were seeing how far I could push making a thing a thing, but also an image, and have them stress each other, without having one put the other into question. It would come back and forth; for a while it was the connective tissue, and at another time the connection was to these ways that, say, a Fra Angelico was painted in a niche—how site-specific they were. Oddly, sometimes he would have them miss the wall by six inches so. Maybe it was just that he got it a little wrong, so there would be a tearing down. I think it's an old thing that artists have always liked to do.

BR: Playing with the limits.

GS: Yes, what I call the picture painting discourse.

BR: So where did this take you?

GS: I made a bunch of templates, abstract elements. I said to myself, "I want them to have more properties than pure geometry, but not as many qualities as a thing." So I made these up. They were about as interesting as furniture. Furniture is about right because it's sort of halfway between geometry and bodies. Furniture always looks a little like people, because we use them. But they're also geometric, because they respond to architecture. So that was how I came up with the vocabulary of shapes.

BR: I read them like that, like they're elements of grammar.

GS: Yes, elements of grammar, perfect.

BR: They weren't objective enough though to seem really post-modern, like, say, Allan McCollum—you know, a surrogate painting.

GS: I thought of them as tropes rather than surrogates.

BR: Yes, that fits. They're sort of Rorschach, in a way. You're anticipating the psychology of the viewer by the shapes you choose.

GS: Well, that surprised me and still surprises me, because it continues to happen. You know the joke where the guy goes to the psychiatrist who gives him the Rorschach test, and the doctor says I think you're obsessed with sex. And the patient says I wouldn't want to work with someone who just showed me all those dirty pictures. The remarkable thing is the reason that's a joke is the patient fails to appreciate his complicity in the construction of reality. And that's the problem with doing things that have a Rorschach-like quality. Very often, people don't realize their involvement, and they put the entire burden on the artist. I had a psychologist in the studio recently, and once I'd given him permission, so to speak—of telling me how they worked, or how they could work—he began to completely free-associate. I pointed this out to him, and he said he could do this. It's true up to a point, but it's also *not* true. As an analogy, I said, "Look, you come upon an automobile, a brand new Lexus, and you've never seen a car before. You come up to it, and you like it. It's attractive. You walk around it. Then you realize, of course, that there's an inside to it. You open the door, get in, fiddle with the knobs and dials, and eventually you get the radio to turn on. You sit there for a while and you think, "This is sensational! Here I am listening to music in this very beautiful little room! You get out, you close the door, and you leave thinking it was great." Now, I say, that's not really what cars are about, and you could say, *they are to me.* In other words, whatever you make up about a picture is what it is about. But you shouldn't think that whatever you do with it is as good as anything else. It still has a specific nature to it, much like a car does. You can do other things with it, but if you don't drive it, you're missing what's most important about it.

BR: Half the fun of a car is taking it apart in the driveway; the other half is driving.

GS: Exactly.

BR: I want to talk about color a little. You spend the summer upstate, and your colors seem really connected to that for me. They look organic, which is interesting because they are synthetic, acrylic. But somehow this seems a part of your thinking, this dichotomy.

GS: Here is a perfect example: people upstate will, you know, smoke cigarettes, and they take the package at the end, and they crumple it up and throw it out of the car, and it's sitting on the country road. So when you are coming toward it, for a very long time you can't figure out what you're looking at. Your brain does a lot of things. It says, "flower," "button," whatever. Eventually your brain says, like with the wrinkle in the sheets, "Oh, yeah, crumpled cigarette pack." But it also has what I call cultural color. There are little passages in the paintings, too, that have this cultural color.

BR: Marlboro red.

GS: Exactly. Marlboro red.

BR: Coming back to the new work . . . When I first saw what you were doing, I was really surprised. I thought for some reason they seemed really streamlined, really tight, like Klee Bauhaus-period. You still have all the same elements, the same conceptual base to the work, but suddenly it all really clicks in a way that distinguished these pieces from the rest.

GS: That's interesting to hear. I feel that way about them now in a way that I haven't felt before about my work. In the past I've had the feeling there was something I wanted to do in the paintings, but for some reason I couldn't. Would be nice, I told myself, if I had a little more of some kind of experience, but, well, it's no big deal. What is nice is now I don't have that anymore; in fact, I have a sense of almost taking on the hardest way to make it happen and just seeing how I get from one place to the next place. I always felt I had to leave something out, but I don't have that feeling anymore.

BR: That's the sense I get. They're working, and you're not.

GS: Right. It isn't exactly like they're a breeze, but they constantly engage me. I have a feeling now, which I never used to have, that even if they're going badly, I always think, this is going to be fun . . . relax. It's almost like an intellectual puzzle: it's hard, but you don't feel hopeless. I think, for these to be good, the key is they don't cave in to style and design. There are a lot of people making abstract pictures who are stylists in the way they create. You know right away when you see the work. What I prefer to do is even if the viewer doesn't know exactly what something is, they know these things are legitimately like this. They're not just brand signifiers like the great little propeller on a BMW—which I like. However, a lot of painting, unfortunately, works like that. So instead of having some organic thing where it came out of a process in which you actually tried to make something real, they become sets of signifiers.

BR: Trying to de-stylize something that has become mannered and stylized, like putting tail fins on the Lexus.

GS: That's right. It doesn't strike me as a particularly good idea.

BR: Well, to me, what you've done seems the antithesis of that. You appear to have arrived here in a very thoughtful, concise way.

GS: I don't think I'm going to wear this out. It strikes me as a fairly protean metaphor for how things go together, so I think it will serve me well. You always fear when you start to get a language of elements together that at a certain point they stop being lived experiences and start getting into exactly what I was talking about. They start to become sets of signifiers that don't mean anything particular to you but mean something to the people who like them. And, with the template work, I thought, well, I really like them, but I'm not going anywhere, I'm not learning anything. This is just ridiculous, this is no way to live a life. They start to break down.

BR: So, in a sense, you are creating a space in your paintings, partly for the viewer, but also for yourself—place to explore something.

GS: The goal, the highest goal I know of in my analysis of what makes painting really interesting, is a term I've come up with: the expressive eye. At one end of painting you get pictures that are incredibly optical, like Bridget Riley, where they don't mean a thing but do a lot visually. At the other end, are things like Kiki Smith; they don't look like much, but they mean a lot. So they're emotionally charged, but visually they're just residual, you know, like a dead crow. It's metaphor that's so compelling. I want something between that literary end and the empty optical end—something that's both expressive by being visual, by visual means. The formal construct is the meaning. I think the best example is Cézanne where the paintings are both highly optical and highly expressive, but not in any way that you can pull apart. You can't say there's the part that means something, and there's the part that just looks like something. It doesn't work like that. They're seamless worlds.

Published Fall 2002.
ArtKrush

Game Symmetry: Lucio Pozzi + Bradley Rubenstein

The Proust Questionnaire has its origins in a parlor game popularized by Marcel Proust, the French essayist and novelist, who believed that, in answering these questions, an individual reveals his or her true nature. Lucio Pozzi and Bradley Rubenstein reinterpret Mr. Proust's concept.

Lucio Pozzi is an Italian-born American artist currently based in Hudson, New York and Valeggio sul Mincio, Verona, Italy. He studied architecture in Rome before moving to New York City in 1962. Pozzi is a painter whose painterly concerns extend to environmental art and actions. He also has created large installations, performances, and videos—one of the first single-artist exhibitions of the *Projects:Video* series at MoMA, New York. Pozzi also teaches, writes, and lectures.

What is your idea of perfect happiness?

I have no idea. Perfection is boring, but striving for it is great.

What is your greatest fear?

To be locked in definition.

Which historical figure do you most identify with?

Giordano Bruno.

What is the trait you most deplore in yourself?

Conformity.

What is the trait you most deplore in others?

Conformity.

What is your greatest extravagance?

Being myself.

What do you consider the most overrated virtue?

Success

On what occasion do you lie?

I try not to lie because then I forget and get caught.

What do you dislike most about your appearance?

My chest

What is your greatest regret?

No regrets.

What or who is the greatest love of your life?

Five women.

Which talent would you most like to have?

Quick repartee.

What is your current state of mind?

Permanently tense.

What do you consider your greatest achievement?

Having a curious view of life.

What is your most treasured possession?

Painting.

What do you regard as the lowest depth of misery?

Lack of love.

Where would you like to live?

If I have a minimum of food and shelter, anywhere.

What is your favorite occupation?

Probing.

What is your most marked characteristic?

Openness.

What is the quality you most like in a man?

Generosity.

What is the quality you most like in a woman?

Generosity.

What do you most value in your friends?

Trust.

What is it that you most dislike?

Hypocrisy and greed.

How would you like to die?

In my sleep.

What is your motto?

   "Why not?"

Published January 1, 2020.
Battery Journal

Unicorns and Terror: Inka Essenhigh + Bradley Rubenstein

Inka Essenhigh was born in Bellefonte, Pennsylvania, and lives and works in New York City. She is a painter and printmaker. Her paintings are richly colored, distorted fables peopled with archetypes, sprites, and anthropomorphized nature. The imagery is imbued with a sense of a collective unconscious and mischievous narrative that makes its way into landscapes, buildings, and figures.

Bradley Rubenstein: Your work combines a very sophisticated design sense with an almost teenage-like conception of surrealism—a smart mix I think. I picture you as the kid in high school who painted murals in the hallways or did the best copies of album covers. Did you have an interest in art when you were younger? And is some of that what you draw on when you work now?

Inka Essenhigh: Actually, when I was in high school I'd already had a lot of art training and was way too self-conscious to make anything really interesting. I'd say my best, *freest* period making art was between the age of three and maybe eight. I do draw on that stuff. It was all narrative work. I'd make lots of story books. I would re-illustrate the entire *Star Wars* story and make up friends and, you know, because I had a little bit of a lonely childhood, I'd make it into a book—the adventures of these people. It was a comic book-style thing. For example, my sister and I would have a houseboat, and the story would cover our life on the houseboat. It would be pure fantasy, illustrated for twenty or thirty pages. I've always been drawn to narrative stuff, and I do draw on that time period as being a really genuine time.

BR: One of the things I find most interesting about Francis Bacon's paintings is he had an innately *decorative* sense of color—especially his backgrounds—in which I think his previous career as an interior designer shows. You can almost date the painting by what was the color of the period—black in the fifties, orange and green in the sixties, beige in the eighties, and so on. Your sensibility is similar in a way. You use these shiny, Ralph Lauren colors as benign environments for your weirdies to play in. Where does this come from?

IE: Well, as far as color goes, I did fabric design for a year or two where I designed boy's and men's boxer shorts, and they were always trying to break it down—it was cheap fabric for Sears and stuff—and they were always trying to break it down to the smallest number of colors possible. I do think it played a part in my subject matter and freed me up, because at that time I was making these abstract expressionist paintings. It was probably 1995 and I was very miserable, but I just kept doing them, and I wished they looked a little more contemporary. Then I was making this fabric design, and it just looked so much more interesting and much more about culture and the world I lived in. The One Shot paint I used gave the paintings a specific look. There always has to be a solid color, and it just sort of leads you down a certain path where it becomes easier to use. It's just the way the color looks; it already looks like a robin's egg blue rather than a cerulean blue. It's solid so there's no transparency; there's no light. It's all decorative, and that was part of the content of the work, that it was this fake world, this design world where the weirdies, as you called them, were existing. But, yeah, it was all fake. It all looked like it was made out of plastic, but that is changing now. Some of it looks the same, but I have these arrangements where one color is the dominant color, and then there is the secondary color, which might not necessarily be its opposite, but one step closer to it. I like these off-colors; and I like grays and these muted tones, but now that I've gone to oil paint, it really does seem different. I can't help but feel that people who think my paintings have really changed that much probably weren't really looking at the work in the first place and didn't see past the shininess. I don't think it's all that different; it's just that the paint that changed.

BR: Let's talk about this new stuff. How do you feel about it?

IE: I feel great. Next question! When I start doing something new for myself, it feels as though I'm not really making art, and that's a good thing. When I see works of art in a gallery, I think of art as being not the part of the paint that covers up the raw emotion or whatever it is, but the part that funnels something—whatever you are doing or feeling, or whatever experience you're having. It funnels it through this system of what it is supposed to look like.

BR: Mediating?

IE: Mediating, right. And so when I first started the enamel paintings, it was fantastic because I was getting away from Abstract Expressionism, which is what I, at that time, thought art should look like. And these little cartoon guys would come up, and that was actually far closer to a more direct way to say what I wanted to say. I guess there is a time where, after a while, whatever becomes new just turns into what is expected of your work, and that's when it is like arthritis in your bones, and it is time to change. Sometimes it can be great because, for a little while—you know when you are making your first new paintings—the first ones might not be the best ones, but you understand a little bit more about what you are doing, and then you can represent it. I believe that I'm making art for other people. I'd be really depressed if I had to go to my studio and say, I'm making it for me. I would, actually! I want it to be for an audience, and I don't know who that audience is all the time. Right now it's the New York art world. If they didn't want me anymore, I would probably go and seek out a new audience. But right now I'm happy that I'm beginning a new body of work.

BR: This painting, with the Minotaur . . . you said before that you were trying to depict this emotional state—you called it "waves of terror." This piece, to me, is maybe the best example of your taking something, your genuine idea or emotion, or something you experience, and asking yourself how to depict visually something that isn't necessarily a visual thing—terror. That seems like where the art comes in for you.

IE: That I am making art—in a bad way or a good way?

BR: Art in a good way. I think that is what art does. Isn't it where you have this stylization—or finding a way to communicate to your audience? That's ultimately the role of the painter. I think what you are doing now is adding layers on top of layers and approaching how you are depicting your subjects from a significantly altered position.

IE: Yeah, well, I do feel like—when you said this is where the art comes in, when we were talking about the little red lines in this painting, where the people are trying to sort of dodge and miss the "waves of fear" or "arrows of fear" is actually what I think of them as—I feel that in some ways this is the dumbest and, at the same time, most sophisticated way I could paint it. It's something I have done a lot, in depicting forces of nature or weather, energy, things like that. Everything ended up being a solid shape with the enamel paint, so I took things that were invisible and depicted them as shapes. I feel like it is kind of like Futurism in a way—showing energy in a physical way. They do it in Warner Brothers cartoons all the time too, you know. Bugs Bunny will have this kind of thing . . .

BR: He'll see stars when he gets hit with the anvil.

IE: Right!

BR: There are a lot of disparate visual elements here that I think successfully convey the story, which is kind of important because your paintings usually have this one simple subject—fear, love, whatever—that isn't really that simple to depict.

IE: I do feel like there's a certain amount here—I've bitten off a pretty big chunk. How many multi-figured paintings do you see that aren't complete cheese? This is complete cheese too, but you know, there are a lot of academic paintings out there.

BR: But these, in a way, are more theatrical, in a Star Wars meets Looney Tunes kind of way.

IE: Yeah, right, because I wouldn't go to a gallery to see a lot of, you know, salon art.

BR: In a way, you are sort of reinventing that tradition though . . . Minotaurs, Moby Dick, vampires, and stuff. It's old subject matter that you investigate by filtering it through your own personal experiences. So they end up being very contemporary because of that. But in a way, when I look at these, I really think it's a kind of painting that people haven't done in a long time.

IE: It is interesting. I think it took a long time for me to get here. I think that, you know, growing up I always cursed myself like any artist, "Gee, what are my experiences? Are they really large?" You know, even at an early age I was disappointed that I was so suburban. And I'm not talking about country; I mean the deep suburbs. There's nothing romantic, it couldn't be more safe by comparison to everywhere else in the world. And so how do you translate something as fake and coddled as that into having raw emotions where you can relate to a lot of different things? And the answer is you can't. That means you have a choice—either you are going to make safe art or you are going to take chances. And I wanted to take chances. Here, I've depicted a terror scene, which I have never actually experienced before. But still I am giving myself permission— through surrealism in a way—by making the scene and in a way not meaning it, like it's a dream. I feel I am slowly stripping away all the reasons for doing something you feel you have done but maybe haven't experienced. There are lots of other people, like Kafka, who didn't leave his parents' house; he spent his entire life living in their front room right near their bedroom. But nevertheless he can go ahead and say whatever he wants to say and go and travel wherever he wants to travel in his novels, and it is ok because his voice sounds sincere. It just does.

BR: I don't think I would question the credentials of someone or where they came from necessarily if what they make is a compelling depiction.

IE: Right, if the voice is sincere, the picture is compelling. It took me a long time to let myself do this.

BR: One of the most successful portrayals of Vietnam, to me, is *Apocalypse Now*—but it was basically written a hundred years ago, and the movie was directed by someone who had never been in the war. But isn't that what you should be doing as an artist? You know, using a synthetic structure to get at a specific, authentic meaning or emotional experience? That is how I see these pictures working.

IE: To make it convincing, yeah. But it isn't like the space is actually convincing. It is almost like you have to convince yourself it is ok.

BR: [Eyeing *Arrows of Fear*] As I look at this one, I'm drawn to the figure at the top.

IE: That guy. Yeah, you identify with him because he has tripped and fallen, and maybe this guy on the right will help him, but you aren't sure—you know, he's not sure either. Is he going to get left behind? He's in a seizure of terror—you know, when you get so scared you can't even run.

BR: Simple depiction, complex idea.

IE: Unartfully done!

BR: It reminds me of this sculpture I like in the Met of this man holding a flayed skin. It's marble, but the way it's modeled, it's like the less information there is, the more it starts to look like skin—flesh—the more you can really put yourself into the artwork, imagine something. What do you think you have really arrived at now? You've been working on these for almost six months.

IE: I can't tell really because I want to go in so many directions at once. I want to make them more three-dimensional. I also want them to be more raw. I can also see the line separating from the painting a little more. These are all instincts of mine. The things I want to depict will probably go in this direction. Looking at this painting [indicating "Optimistic Horse and Rider"], most of the emotion is coming from the direction of the hair. It's knotting and flowing, and the whole thing is jumping out. That's where you are meant to feel how optimistic this is.

BR: But the horse is sinking in the water.

IE: No! He is coming out of the rainbow behind! What are you talking about? He's not sinking!

BR: You see the glass half-full.

IE: Well, yeah, ok! I don't know. When I made this painting I thought, well, now I'm going to make an optimistic painting! And you think he's sinking!

BR: I think it's really which character you identify with. If you go with the guy that is falling, then that's a pretty depressing painting too!

IE: Some people melt, some don't! The thing is, it's kind of an emotional breakthrough in some ways for me. Just like you have an emotional breakthrough in therapy, because actually I am always embarrassed by how they kind of come up in my paintings, and I don't know what they are about. At the same time I show them to my friends, and the thing I thought was really emotional they see as derivative or something. It's neither here nor there to me, but the important thing is not to go crazy. This might not be the best painting I've ever done, but it will lead to better paintings, and that is important.

BR: I don't think it looks derivative—mannerist in a way. You've taken all these styles and elements and tried to put them together to depict this really complicated scene—horror, the Minotaur, you know . . .

IE: They were just scared [laughing]. I think these paintings are close to what I did after college—before I started to become too self-conscious and self-aware and hate myself [laughs]. I hated myself for being a magic realist—for not wanting to say I liked to draw more than paint. There were all these issues, and before I could make these paintings, I had to draw and render each figure perfectly, and of course you learn you don't have to. I don't have to do anything. I can go home and go to bed. This work is what I am doing now, and this is what I have gotten the most from.

BR: You are arriving at the point where there aren't any rules.

IE: Right. That is something you have to realize again and again every day.

Published Fall 2001.
ArtKrush

Let's Get Lost: Rodney Dickson + Bradley Rubenstein

Rodney Dickson lives and works in New York and Vietnam. Born in 1956 in Northern Ireland, Dickson grew up during the troubled years of civil disorder that engulfed that country. Having drawn and painted since a child, he reacted to his early experience by considering the futility and hypocrisy of war through art. He said that he witnessed the aftermath of conflict in its indiscriminately brutal form, and it is from this point that his work proceeds.

Bradley Rubenstein: Let's go back a few years, first, and touch briefly on the paintings of yours that I first saw: pictures of Tanya Roberts. They evolved out of a complex system of sending off fan shots or pap shots, which were faithfully, more or less, reproduced. In retrospect, though, it seems that you were really interrogating painting via an intercontinental telephone game—seeing how others saw American culture. How did you see the project, and how, in a larger sense, did this have anything to do with your personal painting practices either before or after those works?

Rodney Dickson: The show was about the fascination many people have with celebrities. The gallery director, Magalie Guérin, and I thought of a lonely man living alone and obsessed with a sexy actress called Tanya Roberts. I got images from the internet and emailed those to Miss Nguyen Hoang Bao Ngoc, my assistant in Saigon, Vietnam. She had them copied by local artists and mailed the finished paintings back to me in New York. I liked the international collaboration and having no control over the finished paintings. Some were highly accurate, like a photograph, and some were not at all. In some of them, Tanya looked Asian. I found them all to be interesting and made no judgment about good or bad copies. I like the element of chance, and I am ready to accept it in my own paintings, too, if it works.

I approach painting from all angles and consider it as research to develop my way of seeing. I have been working on a performance type project since 2009 called *Entertainment*. It came out of my current paintings, although I imagine that viewers of the show would not be aware of it. The show is in a series of parts, building up to a final show some time, and so far it has been in New York, Beijing, Hanoi, Rangoon, and Mexico City. In this project I am trying to create chaos to represent the chaos in the world by having the local people come into the gallery and do their everyday job, many of them doing different activities in the same space at the same time. I think of it as a moving painting with sound and smell and real everyday things. I think it feeds back into my painting—at least I hope so.

I don't consider there to be boundaries in painting and have worked in figurative, sometimes highly realistic, ways. Currently my work is abstract. I am constantly searching for any way to develop my paintings. Not all of these ways may appear logical, but there are no rules and no formula for creating worthwhile art, so logical or not, if it works it is okay.

BR: Your frequent flier miles must be off the chain. That is a very peripatetic working method. In some ways you are combining elements of Joseph Beuys with painting. Interrogating it from both inside, by doing it, and outside, by seeing how others approach it. Before we get further into that, though, tell me a little about where you are from, when you first became interested in painting?

RD: That's funny—I don't even have frequent flier miles. I keep forgetting about it. Thanks for reminding me of it, though. I must get hooked up for that.

I was born in Bangor, Northern Ireland in 1956 and grew up in a nearby town called Newtownards. It is a small rural town, a kind of quiet place more or less—a bit boring. At the worst time of The Troubles (a period of political strife in Northern Ireland), I was a teenager. It was a dangerous time to be that age, surrounded by violence, and many young people got drawn into that. Instead, it gave me a critical view of society and is possibly why I became an artist. I became curious about the psychology of people and how seemingly ordinary people could do terrible things when put in extreme situations. It seemed to me there might be something more to find in life than that, so through making art, I guess I am constantly searching for it.

It would be too romantic for me to say I was always compelled to be an artist, even as a child. Well, not even too romantic; it would be untrue. I could say I always enjoyed to draw, though, and was maybe the best in art class at school. It was never really in the cards for me to be an artist. In the kind of ordinary place I grew up, no one became an artist; people became terrorists, alcoholics, or maybe car mechanics, or a teacher if they did well at school. However, I went to art school in Liverpool, England in 1979, and from the first day there I knew I would be an artist. Suddenly I felt at home and not like an outsider, as I had felt previously. I had always been interested in painting, but I guess I became seriously or professionally interested in painting from my first days at art school. I found it very difficult, though, to do anything I liked and had a tough time in the first years at college. It was a good beginning, though, as it taught me to not be complacent with my work and constantly battle to find a way forward. I still do not find painting easy at all; it is the most difficult thing I do in my life, but that is okay. No one said it should be easy. I am never satisfied with my work, and I'm always trying to make the next one better than the last one. I think it is very strange when I hear artists say their work is great and everything is going well. I never think like that. I think it is always a struggle; I'm always on the edge, always fighting for a way forward. Each day is a new day, and starting again to try to paint, it never seems to get easier. No matter what I learn, there is always so much more I have yet to discover. It is endless, and because of that it is fascinating. I am excited every day to continue working to find something new.

My teacher from Liverpool Art School, Mike Knowles, said something like this: "Painting is easy; thousands of people do it every day. But in order to make good painting, one must create a universe within the space of the canvas, and that is almost impossible."

I graduated from Liverpool Art School in 1983 and immediately moved to live in Amsterdam, Holland. From my degree show at college, I was taken on by Murdoch Lothian Fine Art, Liverpool, the only commercial gallery in Liverpool at that time. I did my first show with Murdoch in 1984. In Amsterdam I worked with Kunst Handel Van Der Have. He later changed the name of his gallery to Torch Gallery. Sadly Adrian Van Der Have died not long ago from cancer. He was a nice guy, and I showed some early work with him in 1983. Those were my first experiences of showing my artwork professionally.

BR: How do you see all of this traveling affecting your painting, particularly as it stands today? Has it been a process of interrogating it from the outside, that is, seeing how others work on projects you designed, or has it been an investigation leading up to something?

RD: I live in New York; it is a wonderful city. There are not really more interesting places than this, and having said that, I am going to the countryside in China soon and will paint outside in nature. I enjoy traveling, and I'm always fascinated to see other cultures. Asia is the place I like most, and Vietnam is the most interesting country I have been to there. The way of life is quite different from the West, and I have been sometimes amazed by things there. Travel has affected my work in a number of ways. In a direct way, there are some artists I have met whose work I like, but I've also been affected by an Asian sensibility that is different from ours in the West. I don't think this is always and directly from Buddhism, but probably it has a connection. There is sometimes a different idea about time; for example, an appreciation that if things happen slowly this may be a good thing, whereas in the West we often want things to happen immediately. I think similarly about my paintings; they take a long time to finish, but this is good and necessary to develop the work—to get an experience of life into the work.

I am constantly looking for ways to move my work along, and I could not pinpoint one thing that is more important than another. Certainly travel is important, but in the end, the work is done by me in my studio, which is a very familiar place for me, and there is no one else there at that time. So ultimately it comes down to working through the paintings, day by day, relentlessly creating and destroying until something emerges that is unfamiliar to me and works in some kind of way that excites me. Therefore I could say, the investigation comes from the inside, from somewhere deep inside me, but that core could be fed by everything that has happened in my life, including traveling.

BR: In your show last June in Gasser Grunert Gallery, New York, you could see a lot of this reflected in the paintings. They appeared to be well-traveled, collecting bits of imagery and layers of paint; they had a sense of being accrued rather than designed. There was a punk feel to them, like they were put together out of a sense of urgency. Very powerful. The works that I just looked at in your studio seem to have taken a lot of those ideas and really solidified them. They seem a little tamer—not necessarily in a bad way—just more solid and assured. Inevitable, I believe is how I described them when we were chatting. Can you talk a little bit about the show last year and then give me some of your thoughts about how those works manifested themselves into the new body of paintings?

RD: I have worked in many ways as a painter, never feeling the need to make a distinction between figurative or abstract, realistic or expressive, and not responding to fashion or any particular style. I am only in search of the best way to make my next painting and will approach that from any angle that seems to work at that time. I believe it is open-ended, and there is not one way to do it; there are an infinite number of possibilities.

You could have seen some of those possibilities in that show . . . figurative elements—some of them hyper-realistic and abstract too. The paintings that were more figurative were kind of issue-based, dealing with the legacy of the Vietnam War and The Troubles in Northern Ireland. How people survive in such circumstances and how that affects their lives, even long after the conflict has ended.

I specifically referenced my own experience and that of my former assistant and good friend from Saigon. The abstract paintings in that show were approaching this in another way, a more general way, and although the paintings don't have a story, there is a sense of struggle in the work, as in all of my work. I feel this represents the struggle in life. My favorite painter is Vincent van Gogh. You can see that in his work; it is timeless and reveals so much about the human race. It is necessary to have his paintings in the world, and it is a better place because of them. Art, or painting in particular, should be as vital as that; it should not just be for entertainment or to decorate a wall.

In retrospect, I now feel the paintings in that show were very direct, which I prefer, but a little too simple. When I did them, I wanted them to be like that, but after the show I felt I could go further. So I am now being more ruthless, painting and wiping out day after day, and the work has become more complex because of that. I am trying to learn how to paint better, and day by day I do learn. Every time I paint I learn something, so the work changes and develops. It never gets easier, though. Maybe it becomes more difficult, but I think the current work goes deeper. I don't want to use words like "transcendence" or "spiritual" or phrases like "coming from the soul." I think they sound a bit too romantic or hippy-like for me, but I do believe I am constantly trying to unearth something, and I am certain art has a meditative ability to transport the viewer to another place, which may be out of this world. It needs to be pretty good art, though, to do that, and I am trying.

BR: It is interesting to even bring up something like "transcendence" or "spiritual." The connection to van Gogh I get, but I also see a lot of Milton Resnick and Eugene LeRoy—very concrete painters. Maybe there is a way that painting can redefine our ways of looking at "transcendence" by showing us a reality, a history of one person confronting a futile activity, like making a painting and constantly facing failure, that provides a spiritual experience that no other art form can? I mean, there is almost something Beckett-like about the whole fucking process, no? We've talked a lot about the Leon Kossoff show, how he has been struggling for years and years to capture a moment on canvas—a painting of a tree. Now even the tree is dead, and he caught something enormous in his last show in New York—the dead or dying tree propped up, like a crucifixion.

RD: Have you seen the video of the Buddhist monk burning to death as a protest during the Vietnam War? How could he do that? The power of meditation, I guess.

The concentration and solitude of working on paintings is a special experience. I work in very intense sessions, which can be quite physical, especially when working on the large paintings. The focus required for this kind of effort is kind of meditative, and I know when I am very much into the work; I am unaware of anything else around me. My best work comes during these periods, and it is a time when I can finish a painting. I search for it, but it does not come every day.

You mentioned some good painters there. I can see why you mentioned Milton Resnick and Eugene Leroy. Some of their paintings look similar to some of mine, but I don't think we are on the same track. They both look more comfortable than I hope I do. I don't think I am trying to make a beautiful painting. When I paint, it seems like a battle to me—like I am trying to do something and there is a force working against me. I think this is evident in the work, and for that reason I don't feel a connection to those painters. Leon Kossoff is a better example, and as you have said, his focus for years on painting the tree in his back garden is something I can relate to. Trees are pretty common things, but he has painted it to have a strong presence, like a living thing in the gallery. The struggle of his relentless working practice is evident in the work, and the colors he uses are not chosen to make a pretty picture; they are essential, inevitable, to use a word you used earlier. From somewhere he brings forth something magical by constantly working through the unnecessary possibilities to find something vital. This goes beyond merely good painting; there are many good painters in the world, but only a few who can find that magic. Those few people make something that is indispensable.

BR: I meant to suggest that there is both a collective memory or consciousness to painters and painting, which in many ways is contra-indicated by the solitary nature of the work. I see that in those guys, and get a strong sense of that in your work too.

That collective nature of art making is summed up in a famous *mot* of Guston's that, appropriately enough, he attributed to a friend: "I believe it was John Cage who once told me, 'When you start working, everybody is in your studio—the past, your friends, enemies, the art world, and above all, your own ideas—all are there. But as you continue painting, they start leaving, one by one, and you are left completely alone. Then, if you're lucky, even you leave.'"

RD: That is very interesting, and I agree. There seems to be a collective consciousness, as artists who have no contact with each other and live far apart sometimes do something similar at the same time. I guess this is not impossible to understand because whatever is happening in the world at that time may have a similar effect on more than one artist. Although as artists we pride ourselves as being individuals, as people we likely share similarities.

I also like very much the words you have here by John Cage, and it is true. This is kind of what I have been saying in the previous part of the interview, about finally getting into gear in the studio and doing your best work. You have to focus and build up to that. I guess Cage would consider his friends, and he would have left the room at that point.

BR: Yeah, this seems like it is really the point at which you have arrived in your painting. It seems like you are really focused on attaining a very personal connection to your work. Yet, the closer it seems that you get a bead on that, the greater your connection with a whole tradition of painters is coming through. I think that that is where all of us really want to arrive at some point, so it must feel very exciting to you to be getting there. Is that just my interpretation? Or is it more like, in your head you are thinking, "Oh, fuck, what next?"

RD: Hmm . . . good question. I think I am doing my best work now, but at the same time, I always think something like, "Oh, fuck, what next?"

In a way I could have done these paintings at any time in my life. It could have been twenty years ago, as even that long ago I had a mental image of paintings a bit like these—something I really wanted to do. For some reason, though, I never exactly got around to it then. I don't really know why, but it has something to do with time and age and working through many other ideas to sort of come back to the beginning. When I was a student, I painted a bit like I am doing now. I have some old landscapes from the early eighties that are surprisingly similar to my current work. I think, in a way, I would have considered these paintings to be a bit too conventional then, as I was dealing with some hardcore subjects, such as war, sex, religion, politics. These were things I wanted to confront in a direct way, so my work had to be different then. Ultimately, it is all about learning to paint better, and all of those approaches have given me the experience, confidence, and ability to do what I am doing now.

Yes, my work has more connection with the tradition of painting, and certainly I spend much more time looking at the old masters than I ever did before. I realized the thread of art history is vital in developing my work and don't any longer consider the connection to be trite. On the contrary, my work is more radical now than before. I have to say, these are the most difficult paintings I have worked on, both mentally and physically. I find them to be almost beyond me, but because of this they bring out the best.

Getting back to the "Oh, fuck, what next?": I know that every day I paint I learn something new and become a better painter, but at the beginning of every new painting, I feel like I am starting to paint for the first time. If there have been any good paintings I have done in my life, at the beginning of a new painting, I always feel the good ones were just a bit of good luck and unlikely to be repeated. Also, when a painting is going badly, which is most of the time, I feel lost, desperate, and I am convinced I will never do another good one. I feel it is over, and whatever there may have been has gone. This is what I meant when I said something about working on the edge, but I would not have it any other way, as I don't want to make comfortable paintings. I am not that kind of chilled painter. David Hockney seems to me to be a confident, highly talented painter who does cool and confident work. I like his work a lot, so I will leave it up to him to do that. I guess I always need to push to the limit and make life difficult for myself.

Someone asked me a few weeks ago if I "like" my paintings. That should be a simple enough question, but I found it difficult to answer fully. Truth is, I don't "like" my paintings. I like other peoples' paintings, but I cannot say that about my own. I am "interested" in the one I am working on at that time, and when it is done I sometimes feel some sense of achievement at getting to that point, but I have little interest in them when they are done. All I am thinking of then is going further with the next one.

BR: There is a great little passage in Irving Stone's biography of van Gogh that somehow seems really relevant to your whole project. Van Gogh is looking at his drawings at the end of the day. Stone writes, "They are bad," he said to himself with a curious grin, "very bad. But perhaps tomorrow I shall be able to do a little better."

RD: Yes, that sounds quite appropriate.

I had read van Gogh's letters when I was in a Foundation course in Liverpool, England in 1980. They were very helpful for me and a "good read." I would recommend to anyone to read them, whether they have an interest in art or not. I have read some of them several times since then, but I have not read the biography you mentioned. That's funny—I can imagine Vincent would say his drawings were bad. He was pretty hard on himself. Actually, his drawings are as good as anyone has ever done, but maybe he did not feel that way about them.

I don't judge my work as either good or bad. I don't compare myself to other artists, I mean. I don't go around looking at shows and saying to myself I am better than that artist. I prefer to have respect for everyone. I think everyone should do their own work, and I wish everyone the best with it. However, much of the stuff I see holds no big interest for me, and I am only focused on what I need to do in my studio. I have my own ambitions for my work, and especially at this time in my life, I feel a definite path I am trying to move along. I am not wanting to paint a picture or show how clever I can be with drawing or in handling paint. I don't choose colors to look beautiful, for example; they come to me when I know they are necessary. There is something I am trying to show, to uncover. I am searching for the essence of something. It is more vital than painting a good or bad picture. Maybe, hopefully, I have achieved something in some of my work so far, but there will always be more and better to come. I will find the path to dig deeper into myself to bring out what needs to go into the work. This is what keeps me striving to paint better day after day.

Certainly I am not comparing myself to van Gogh, but maybe that is what he meant when he said his drawings are bad.

BR: I enjoyed going to the Met with you yesterday.

RD: That was a good day. Thank you for asking me along. The de Kooning paintings are great—also the early Baselitz. Of course, the Met is amazing—room after room of the best paintings imaginable. Too much to comprehend, really, but good to have a quick look anyway. Overall, it is Courbet that has remained in my mind this time.

I got up early today to paint, starting a new big one. Of course, it is going very badly, so I am a bit worried right now. I will take a break, I think. Maybe a short ride into Chinatown to pick up some food and then resume in an hour or two . . .

Published July 11, 2011.
CultureCatch

The Poetry of Space: Scott Grodesky + Bradley Rubenstein

Scott Grodesky was born in 1968 in Warren, Ohio. He moved to New York in 1989 and now lives and works in Ridgewood, Queens and teaches painting at SUNY Albany. His most known works are reverse-perspective paintings—a space where objects are larger the further they are from you. These paintings are usually of intimate family or personal experiences rendered in translucent colors with color pencil lines.

Bradley Rubenstein: Scott, I've been looking at your work for a very long time. We talked a little before about the "explosion" paintings from the nineties. I found them quite impressive at the time and still do. You said they were a beginning of an exploration of perspectival systems. Can you elaborate a little on that? Give us a little background on where they came from—what you were thinking of when you began them.

Scott Grodesky: Prior to the explosions of 1991, I was working with this idea of reverse perspective (RP). My problem at the time was that the RP paintings lacked focus, and I was looking for a solid way to depict the space. It was in 1990 that I threw out all of my materials. I reduced my materials to graphite pencil and powder graphite suspended in acrylic medium on canvas. Keeping in line with this, I reduced the images to simple structures that represented the expansive system of RP. Concentric rings and explosions were those basic structures for me, so I set about trying to rebuild my language from a new standpoint. The goal was to keep things simple and then add materials and elements over time to make more complicated works. It was the beginning of a longer-term project. I was surprised at how I became enamored of the explosions and spent a couple of years working on them. I was influenced at the time, and still am, by Agnes Martin and Roy Lichtenstein—throw in Tibetan thangka paintings and these comic books I would buy down in Chinatown.

BR: That is interesting; you really went from one kind of Minimalist way of working—simplified pictorial structure—and combined it with simplified materials, like Brice Marden or even Robert Morris. How did that work for you with such narrative influences like thangka painting or Lichtenstein?

SG: It didn't work! I had to narrow the narrative to really ambiguous situations. In a way the thangka paintings had narratives that I didn't really understand or connect to. I was just curious about the structure and how it was so otherworldly to me. Lichtenstein had the narrative in a simple form, or in some cases removed like in the *Mirror* series. I was really responding to a coolness in the structure and approach of these artists.

BR: To me, these works, what you started doing in painting, was kind of concurrent with what a lot of artists were doing in other mediums at the time. I think of Matthew Barney's *Cremaster* films. He started out with video, then silent film, then sync-sound, and so on. Do you think that what you were doing was part of a larger zeitgeist, for lack of a better term, or were you off on a really idiosyncratic trip?

SG: In some ways it was both a zeitgeist and a personal trip. I was interested in a bunch of artists at the time: Cady Noland, Olivier Mosset, Karin Davie, and Peter Halley. Mathew Barney was a catalyzing force at the time. There was this feeling of change in the early nineties, with the eighties still a heady spectacle. This idea of reduction and reconstitution of what the formal construction of a work could be was in the air. But at that time, I was still working alone, so to speak. Later in 1991 I began to meet these heroes of mine, and that was when the whole thing began to coalesce.

Barney is interesting for me; in 1990 I was an art installer for Gladstone, and I worked on Barney's first show. In a way, that show helped solidify the ideas that were bumping around in my work.

BR: Yeah, I agree that that time was kind of a watershed moment, especially in painting. I remember it as a great time to be painting, if you were really interested in coming up with ideas that were personal or approached picture making in an oblique-strategy kind of way. Strangely, I have always thought that Barney may have had a greater impact on painting and photography than he did on sculpture. His sense of color has always impressed me, and I've often viewed his performances as a form of travel photography. He goes to different places and interprets them into his own narrative.

SG: I love the color in those early Barney works. I remember his use of the first fluorescent coil bulbs and how that really affected the color of the show. I think that Barney was a great influence on the next generation after the early nineties. Most of the artists working in the early nineties had been working out their ideas even before or concurrently with his debut.

BR: So, basically, at that point you reached a kind of ground zero in your work and manifested these really iconic images of explosions. Let's stay in that moment for a bit, and tell me how they fit in with what was happening then. How were they received at the time?

SG: I did reach a ground zero. It was very satisfying to reduce to rebuild. The explosion paintings were well received, That surprised me. I was very young and not completely prepared for the interest. This all happened at the beginning of the new direction of the work. What I had planned to do was build on the way the explosions had the cool effect that I admired in other works, and I was going to add in elements to generate the RP paintings. I suddenly was making explosions for a while—well, a while in young-artist terms. I could have continued, but it was brought to my attention that Halley was making explosion prints, and I was more interested in the concurrency of multiple ideas forming simultaneously. I built up the explosions to a real crescendo using silk screens and gunpowder. They ended in a more pictorial space.

BR: Now I am remembering that about the explosion pieces; you took the literal elements and made them pictorial. That was really interesting to me. Looking at the arc of your work, then, you can see how you went from a minimalist, concrete way of working into something more theoretical and abstract over the years.

Not to beat a dead horse, but I do want to ask about one more connection to your exploration of RP. There's a really interesting David Hockney painting in the Met, an interior done with RP. It relates strongly to a later Braque. Both of these painters dipped a toe into that river, but they were mostly one-offs. Hockney went on, though, to do a lot of research into perspectival systems, particularly focusing on Vermeer. Getting back to your work, you pushed on after the explosions and started a painterly exploration. Give us the impetus behind this changing direction in your work.

SG: It wasn't my intent to go from a minimalist to a more pictorial way of working. I wanted to follow the leads that the painting gave me. Each group of work showed me a new place to go. I was really into experimentation and advancement in the way the paintings were made. I moved into the new RP space in order to clarify it. That painting of the interior space by Hockney was always interesting to me because I thought it failed at the idea of RP. There's a chair in the painting that shows a reverse space, but the rest of the painting is kind of goofy. I love it! When I think of Hockney and RP, I think of his photo works and the way that he nailed it with all of those shifting small photographs.

BR: Was there a psychological element to what you were doing? For example, by turning things inside out, are we seeing into how you perceived things, or was it purely on a mechanical level?

SG: As I was following the paintings' cues to make the next work, I began to notice that the works that depicted friends had a stronger psychological thrill. It was at that point, at about 1998, that I began to paint people I was close to, mainly my wife Sara. In the beginning I wasn't interested in psychological spaces, but I ended at that place.

BR: Yeah, the work from that period seems like the big turning point. To me, it is where you really begin alluding to a whole lot of ideas, whether intentionally or not, that give the work a great deal of depth. When I look at the figurative pieces, particularly of your wife, I really like how, even though she is the thing that should, in traditional perspective, be closest to the viewer, in your work, she recedes. The picture with you and her together is wonderful; you loom very large over her. It's like some Renaissance *Pietà* or Madonna and Child kind of thing. These works call to mind so many styles and concepts.

So, having reached this point with the work, you began doing more complex scenes. In some ways these seem so overwhelming visually, it's hard to imagine how you laid them out when you painted them. Did the more elaborate compositions present more problems for you, visually, technically, or in any other way, or was it a seamless progression for you?

SG: The idea of a seamless progression is great! That never happened for me. I had plenty of paths that led in directions I felt were dead ends. My main goal was to open up the world in the paintings. I love the challenge of making a complex painting with all of its brain-hurting choices. Basically I used, and still do, a way of working that is additive. A start is made, usually with an eye or ear, and the painting is grown from that point. Any quirky compositional situations are welcomed. I find it interesting that RP space is too complex to pre-envision, so as the painting is constructed, all kinds of accidents occur. In a certain sense, this is imprinting an abstract way of thinking onto a figurative system.

BR: Looking at the arc the paintings took, you can see how the working space of the painting became limitless. These paintings basically took you to the series of still lifes, the most recent work?

SG: The space really opened up for me around 2005. That's when I started to make a series of large paintings, 6' × 14'. These paintings were based on earthquakes, war, city planning, and domesticity. I could put a lot into a large work, so the space in the paintings became wonderfully complicated. It was after making this work that I settled back down to the still life. The still life became a form of closure for the works. Skulls began to appear in the paintings, signaling an end to the whole period. I'm in the process of rebuilding now, and the new paintings have more symbols intertwined within them: floating eyes and skulls. In these new paintings, RP is also now a symbol for memory. The latest paintings are constructions about memory, love, life, and death.

BR: When you're working that way, plotting out the space of the painting by starting at point A for creating the RP, how do you factor in lighting and such?

SG: When I work I have a tumult of ideas for the painting. As the initial drawing progresses, the ideas become clearer and more focused. Issues like lighting and color begin to take shape partway into the work. The color choices are often the last to be made. I like that part of the painting process when the decisions become binary; a simple yes or no to the problem is all that is needed to continue the work.

BR: Are these paintings going to be the last of the RP series, then? Where do you see your painting going next?

SG: I don't know if these are the last of the RP works. There have been a lot of new elements filtering into the paintings, causing me to think the end of the RP series was soon. I can never tell where I will be next. I have been playing with abstraction, and that's the reason I pronounced the end of the RP project a year ago, but it just will not die.

BR: So, rumors of RP's demise are greatly exaggerated! In some ways you are going full-circle, taking it from the abstractions of the explosions, through the various degrees of representation, and then back again.

SG: Ha! I don't know if they're exaggerated. It's just a long metamorphosis. I like to think of change as having a corkscrew shape; you go around the circle, but you end up in a different place. Hopefully a notch above.

Published December 16, 2011.
CultureCatch

The Thing Itself: Mira Schor + Bradley Rubenstein (Part One)

Mira Schor, born in 1950 in New York City, is an artist, writer, editor, and educator, living and working in New York City and Provincetown, Massachusetts. Schor is the author of *Wet: On Painting, Feminism, and Art Culture*, *A Decade of Negative Thinking: Essays on Art, Politics, and Daily Life*, and the blog *A Year of Positive Thinking*. She is an associate teaching professor in MFA Fine Arts at Parsons The New School for Design.

Bradley Rubenstein: You grew up in New York City. Your mother was an artist; your father was an artist; you were exposed to art at an early age, both at home and in the museums. Can you remember when you decided that you were going to be an artist?

Mira Schor: The precise moment was during a nineteenth-century art history class in college. I majored in art history at NYU. The professor was saying something like, "Monet wanted to . . . ," and I thought, "How do you know what Monet wanted?" I realized then and there that I identified with the "wrong" side of the slide projector: the artist, not the art historian. So that career choice fell away, and the only one that was left was to be an artist. I had shown interest and talent for drawing, painting, and sculpture all through my childhood. I was always serious about it and worked rather like I do now, in series, in which I would work a subject, form, or style until I was bored with it. I did many very lively little clay figurines when I was about ten. I was influenced by the Ashanti weights and pre-Columbian art my parents had collected. For a while in my teens I thought I wanted to be a fashion designer, so I filled sketchbooks with ink and wash designs, imitating the style of the *New York Times* "Women's Page" fashion reporting, which was all done with ink sketches in those days. I got pretty good at it, but when it came time to think of designing as a career, I realized I just liked to draw (and to own beautiful clothes!) but wasn't interested in learning how to actually make clothes.

I received encouragement from my parents and a lot of exposure to art through their work and their love of art. I was brought up in art and to some extent in the art world. I sensed then that there was a distinction, and I still operate under the terms of that distinction today. Making art and thinking about art, art ideas, art history—that's one thing. The art world and career—that's another.

On the door of my father and mother's small studio in our apartment in New York City is an antique metal shield on which my father had painted in oil the tools of the goldsmith's trade, a saw and hammer. The tale of the goldsmith's floor was one of the foundational metaphors of our family: In the workshop of a goldsmith, gold dust is husbanded carefully, but it sifts into cracks in the floorboards. When the goldsmith moves, the floor is burned to recover the accumulated gold mass. My parents, Ilya and Resia Schor, would often say, "We have gold on the floor, and we don't know how to pick it up." That can be understood as a metaphor for the precarious finances, career disappointments, and the frustrations of creating something fine and not being able to capitalize on it into material prosperity, which are all part of an artist's life and were certainly part of what I learned as the daughter of artists. But most importantly, this story speaks of artwork that is not concerned with commercial exploitation. My parents often did work on commissions, from private collectors or religious institutions, but they each pursued the truth of the work rather than its marketability; indeed, they could never figure out how to mass-produce or design for mass consumption, or how to market themselves and their biographies, even though necessity often indicated that they should try to do so.

On the other hand, we did live in a house filled with treasures. When my father would finish one of his Torah Crowns, for example, he would come out of the studio wearing the human-sized, bell-laden crown on his head, its bells tinkling. He had a remarkable face with high cheekbones and wildly upslanted eyes that would be alight with joy at his wondrous creation. I had seen the work made; the work had deep religious meaning, and it was an art object filled with joy and generous with visual and narrative pleasure that even a child could enjoy and appreciate. What a wonderful introduction to art and art making!

I think I was always going to be an artist, but I still had to make the decision to be an artist for myself and take the consequences.

BR: What was the most significant experience you had at CalArts? Looking back, do you think your experiences there really defined how you approached being an artist?

MS: CalArts was the most significant experience I had at CalArts! The total atmosphere of that school at that time in the L.A. of that time. There was a unique multiplicity and parity of avant-garde positions all freely available and in the air. I had a dual experience at CalArts, and both aspects of it are equally important and deeply formative. I was in the Feminist Art Program my first year, and that was certainly the single most important experience in terms of determining much of my political involvements and critical focus since. But I am also very influenced by the Fluxus movement and the conceptual art movement that, with their anti-object and anti-market orientation, were very strong at CalArts. People like Allan Kaprow, Emmett Williams, Alison Knowles, Simone Forti, and John Baldessari taught there. I also had a wonderful advisor, the sculptor Stephan Von Huene, whom I worked with after I left the program. He was then doing sound sculptures that were beautifully crafted wood music-making machines with piano roll type of movements. He was really supportive of the intimate personal revelation I was trying to put into my small gouaches. One didn't necessarily have to work with each artist; they gave a "flavor" to the entire institution. You could pick up the Fluxus ethos on the way to lunch, passing Simone Forti doing something blindfolded in a hallway. Their conceptual yet playful and somehow whimsical attitude toward art made a great impact on my work.

There was a goofy spirit at CalArts then that is best expressed in *Pee-Wee's Playhouse*—subversive but in a sweet, slightly anarchic rather than nihilistic manner. Paul Reubens, then Paul Reubenfeld, was at CalArts at the time I was there. Later the school became more earnest about conceptualism, more dogmatic about theory, and ever more savvy in terms of careerism, as the times changed in those directions and the history of the school was rewritten to make the success of some of my contemporaries, such as David Salle, seem like manifest destiny. And, surprise, surprise, the very existence of the Feminist Art Program was erased almost totally until, after the Northridge earthquake, a student was assigned to go over some books that were being junked. Lo and behold, she found copies of the catalog for the *Womanhouse* project from 1972 about to be discarded. Students researched the existence of the program and organized a major conference. Now, the history is surely forgotten all over again.

BR: Your working method has changed a lot since then. You are concerned with issues such as the materials and craft of painting . . . also the idea of tradition and the history of art. What changed your direction or focus?

MS: I am not sure that my working method has changed as much as the way my work looks. If you look at one of my "story" paintings from CalArts and a recent painting of the word "trace," you might wonder if the same person did it. The first is a narrative painting in which a personal story is set out through self-figuration. The scene is set in a landscape whose forms are distillations of landscape and nature forms but whose forms are also related to the way the figure is drawn. I was skinny, and I liked to paint skinny cypress trees and pointy cacti. The second is of a word retraced a few times on a flat white ground, but basic characteristics of form and material are there in both: narrative, whether depicted or literally written; small scale; water-based media; and a certain way of using line. It is like the gloves are different, but the hand is the same.

There has always been a strong narrative and discursive impulse to the work. I first started using language as image in my work at CalArts. The language was more poetic then; I chose words I thought were beautiful. Later the language was autobiographical. Now the words are less personal and, in a sense, I let them choose me. I just wait for the right ones.

I was always interested in tradition and art history. I think that what has changed is only the illusion that I understand more than I did before. But I've thought that at every stage of the game. The biggest change is perhaps in what oil paint can do.

BR: The images of words or phrases that you paint seem perfectly logical to me. You write, you paint, you paint what you write. But your earlier works, which I also like, for example, "the penis paintings," are more image-oriented, figurative. Did writing and editing *M/E/A/N/I/N/G* have an impact on your painting?

MS: I'm glad that my painting of language seems logical to you! You know the typical conversation: "What do you do?" "I'm a painter." "Oh, what kind of paintings do you do?" (abstract or realist, figure or landscape?) "I paint language."

I had used language as image before I ever wrote about art, and at the same time, the critical writing and editing had a great impact on the image paintings you're talking about. The penis paintings were done at the same time as I was researching and writing "Representations of the Penis." At this same time, a book review piece I wrote called "Researching Visual Pleasure," in which I reviewed Barnett Newman's *Collected Writings*, was simultaneous with and instrumental in my beginning to simplify my painting surfaces toward a flatter surface. This is also the moment when I began to shift from representational images to handwriting as the image.

The biggest impact writing as a process had on the work is that I learned that writing must be edited. The need for editing is imbricated in the text itself and springs out at you even if you didn't intend to do it. All you need is to set a text aside for a week, and what needs to be done to it jumps off the page. The media I had painted in and worked with until that point were immediate and didn't allow for much reworking: gouache, dry pigment on paper. But finally by the early '80s, I was pushing gouache to its limits, doing very large gouaches on 36" × 72" rice paper sheets and painting it to the limits of its capacity for impasto. The fragility of paper and the various media I used were no longer a proper metaphor for self, so finally oil, which I had avoided up until that time, was the necessary medium. I made my way into it through about a year of pushing the sculptural aspects of the paper objects I had been working on. Then I started to paint in oil, and I had started writing and editing at the same time. I found that writing's organic necessity for editing gave me the patience and courage to use the capacity for alteration that is unique to oil. So just in the sense of process, my writing and doing *M/E/A/N/I/N/G* led to my ability to engage with oil.

The "penis" paintings were part of the last works that contained recognizable figural imagery. I sometimes miss having that kind of representation in my work, but I worked through those embodied representations over about seven years and moved on. The penis/ear/breast/language/ punctuation mark paintings were part of a time when I was learning a lot about psychoanalytic theory and when the body was the arena for political discord, over abortion and AIDS. Gender was topic A. I am not convinced of any similar subject at the moment—or any that would take the form of a figurational representation.

You can't imagine the shit I had to deal with, doing those penis paintings. People would read all their inner conflicts about masculinity and femininity into the paintings but never give the paintings or me credit for provoking such strong emotions. I experienced the downside of using controversial imagery; some people get famous, I just got told I was doing something wrong. The work would remind someone of how much they hated their father, and then they would tell me it wasn't well painted. And they were just looking at a slide! On the other hand, I really had fun seeing men roll their eyes back when I would talk about "my penis paintings." A woman saying "my penis," that really got people going, but actually I felt very happy and optimistic when I did that work, evidently characteristics that I ascribed quite positively to masculinity!

I see certain things in popular culture that I might want to interact with, things that relate to my "story" paintings—the spiky forms of some of the strange dark cartoons on afternoon TV or something like that. It seems that every few years or so the art world produces another woman artist doing small autobiographical personal paintings with a surrealist touch. I moved on from that kind of work, so I tend to think of it as a stage. I don't feel the same need to put myself physically into a painting as I did then. My work doesn't serve the same purpose for me. Then it was necessary for me to use my art to tell people what was going on in my life. The work was a form of ventriloquism. Now the work is the work. It is not so personal, or, rather, what is personal has changed. I can't quite envision a way to represent myself as a figure in painting. And I don't really see myself doing that or going back to the tight painting techniques that calls for. Right now I want to move toward a looser, wilder, more entropic approach to painting.

BR: I view art making as an essentially social, not political, activity. As I see it, social is how you function in the world with other people, political is how you function in the world with other people to get them to do what you want.

MS: That does make political sound sinister. Actually I think all art has political content or valence, whether intentional or not. I think of my work as political not because I want people to do what I want, but because it is done in response to the political content of other art, and by that I include, for example, the political meaning of the pure aesthetics of modernism. I find it possible to get sustenance from art for its "purely" aesthetic qualities and at the same time to function in art with a political perspective.

BR: You published your second book with Susan Bee, *M/E/A/N/I/N/G: An Anthology of Artists' Writings, Theory, and Criticism*. What else are you working on besides your painting?

MS: I'm working on the book I mentioned and on a whole group of paintings that are intimately related to the book, just as the book is intimately related to my painting. I've written about half, but the writing has been extremely difficult, very slow and tortuous. I'm trying to write differently than before, more personally, and with a much broader theme—two themes really, painting and the role of the past in an ahistorical time. I've written one chapter essay called "Modest Painting," and I'm working on a really ambitious essay that examines the affectlessness chosen by much contemporary art and embodied in some familiar visual strategies, like blurring, by tracking these back to Gerhard Richter and then tracking the sources of his aesthetic decisions in the Holocaust and the Second World War. One of my works on paper related to this essay is a gray blurred text that "says," *"Why does the Past always have to be grey and out of focus?"*

BR: When I first moved to New York in the mid-nineties I thought it was a really great time and environment—there was no style or movement to follow, the money was pretty much gone, and galleries opened and closed pretty quickly. The celebrity-ness of the '80s was kind of out of vogue for a while, and suddenly it seemed that you could try to do anything you wanted. You really anticipated that way of thinking in your career, allowing yourself to change style, developing other aspects such as teaching and writing. Was this something you set out to do from the beginning, or was it just the "zeitgeist," like it was for me?

MS: I never have had the belief in the art world that it demands. The art world I was brought up in had its careerists and even its youthful stars, but nothing like the 1980s commodity culture notion of career, professionalism, big money. Anyway, I had a run of beginner's luck in the early '80s with a couple of shows, and then all of a sudden I didn't have a gallery, and a friend of mine said, "Now you can do anything you want because no one is looking at you." The rhetoric of Western individualism is that the artist does what he wants, but often artists lose sight of that, or have their sight narrowly focused on what they think the art world wants. I thought that I already was doing what I liked, but it is true that my dealer had liked to think of me as someone doing quaint mystical landscapes, whereas I wanted to pursue the sculpture and was going back to the more feminist aspect of my work. So my friend's advice was very good, and I really did go through a lot of changes in the next few years. *M/E/A/N/I/N/G* was the biggest other thing I did, and that was both against the zeitgeist of the great big hype art world of the '80s and part of the zeitgeist of the interest and excitement around critical theory in the '80s. Susan and I could do it because we had nothing to lose; we weren't interested in wielding power or in commodifying our critique or in growing into an institution. We also had the tradition of small magazines and poetry journals behind us.

BR: This year has gotten off to a difficult start, and I understand that your older sister, Naomi Schor, died suddenly in December, but what are your plans for the coming months?

MS: I want to finish writing the expository text of the book and then develop the presentation of its visual content. I want it to have a high visual quotient. I'd like to produce it in several incarnations, from straight text with pictures, to an artist's book of the drawings of elements of the text, to a CD with enhanced visuals including video clips. After September 11th, people wanted to know if it would affect my work, and I felt that my work was already about loss. But the death of my sister has made me question art making in a more profound way. At the moment, human relations seem more important. But I have begun to get back to work. She had wanted a painting of mine in which the word "joy" is painted with a very gritty, fleshy, and shitty-brown paint, but it was in fact the last painting of a larger multi-canvas installation, so I substituted another *joy* painting. Now I am painting the word *joy* in as dark and contingent a manner as possible. That is the only way I can think of to re-enter art making after the loss of such a primal figure in my life.

Published December 30, 2011.
CultureCatch

The Shape of Color: Pia Lindman + Bradley Rubenstein

Pia Lindman was born in Espoo, Finland. Her art practice revolves around the themes of social context and space, as well as the performative aspect of making and experiencing art, using video, drawing, and performance. Her interest in social space stems from her studies in architecture, which led her to study art as a Fulbright scholar at M.I.T. She has lectured at Columbia University, Yale, NYU, RISD, and Institut Française d'Architecture in Paris.

Bradley Rubenstein: Tell me a little more about your background. I know you have moved around a lot. Where are you originally from? What made you decide to become an artist?

Pia Lindman: I am originally from Finland. After high school I studied architecture in Helsinki, and in six months I realized that neither my fellow students nor the professors were concerned with making environments more livable or with simply facilitating happiness. I switched to fine arts, thinking naïvely that I could share these goals with artists. Now, after a few years of experience, I realize I cannot "build" happiness and then impose it onto people. I am still concerned, though. So, I try to be in dialogue with other people, to understand what I can facilitate—more dialogue, I guess. I have also found artists and architects who are concerned with the same things that I am. Thus far, I have chosen to continue to function as an artist rather than an architect, because I feel I have more free range as to what I can do.

BR: You have worked in the United States and Germany for many years now. Do you still think of yourself as a Finnish artist?

PL: This is a complex question. If with Finnish artist you understand the common stereotype often promoted by Finnish cultural personalities and institutions themselves as THE "Finnish" artist—one that finds inspiration solely in (Finnish) nature and his or her own subjectivity— then I am not a Finnish artist. However, my ethical grounding for any work that I do has clear connections to me growing up in Finland. Growing up in Finland can mean a lot of things, also things that are similar to someone growing up in another part of the world. So, even though I experience my background as particularly Finnish, I do not think that "Finnishness" is a unique condition or propensity. Yet, I have a knowledge and sensibility that originates from there.

Another stereotype about Finland that Finns like to define themselves by is in design and architecture: the purity and beauty of the pristine Finnish nature is reflected in Finnish design and architecture. The natural purity of Finnish form makes the design livable and beautiful for everyone. This is why Finnish design is so world-renowned.

I spent many years struggling with issues of aesthetics and ethics—building an argument for my own approach, which is based in social context and interaction. My own naïveté in the beginning of my architectural studies reflected the utopian ideas of purity and beauty purported in Finnish design and architectural discourse since the turn of the century. My reactions against this discourse, as well as my own initial naïvety, have been formative for my art practice.

BR: You seem to have moved from pieces that focus on yourself and your body to works that are primarily about social constructs and relationships. Is this a fair assessment? Why this direction?

PL: Before, I moved toward work that involved the audience in my "events," rather than just me performing. There was a time for me when I sorted out my take on feminism. This is why in my art I focused on my body, partly as a cultural artifact and partly as a tool or organism over which I could take command. I was looking for ways through my body to alter cultural codes. This bodily investigation has been another important part of the grounding of my current work. Assessing the importance of culture in human interaction, I also realized that architecture participates in giving the premises for this interaction. So, it has been clear to me since then that my work situates itself in the intersection of architecture, social context, and culture. The form follows this equation.

BR: Some of your work involves an investigation into the relationships of different cultures to physical hygiene. What is it about this subject that interests you?

PL: Body and gender politics for one. Even more than just that, I am interested in how these politics are played out in spatial arrangements—architecture. Also, politics of leisure and pleasure interest me. They are always part of our cultures of corporeality.

BR: As a painter I am reasonably aware of when one of my paintings is finished—either it looks like what I had in mind, or I stumble upon an image that I find interesting enough. Your work usually involves constructing an object of some sort, then there is an activity or performative element, and then sometimes the piece lasts for months during an exhibition. When is it "done" for you? Is that even important?

PL: Usually, when I start working on a site—that can be a social situation, or a specific place, or both—I do a lot of background research. I find out what discourses about the site or in the site would be something I want to work on. It is important to me to decide to realize a project under the specific conceptual premises that I work out. That is the beginning. The ending may or may not be defined. For my mental health, it is sometimes good to close a chapter, but it may not be necessary for the piece itself.

I engage and live somewhere, and that will always result in learning about that place. Oftentimes, it will also lead to projects. I learned about Joyce Kilmer Park on Grand Concourse in the South Bronx because I participated in the AIM seminar at the Bronx Museum of the Arts, visiting the museum and park weekly. That is why I decided to do a piece there, relating to the specific situation in the park. Of course, making a piece is a continuous learning process regarding the place.

BR: You made the *Mastress* project in an investigation into sexual practice—more or less an attempt to find a tool for better girl-on-top sex; and your *Hybrid Sauna* was your attempt at recreating a traditional Finnish bath in the United States. Is a component of your work an attempt to build something for yourself because of a personal interest that then turns into something larger in scope or concept?

PL: I have to have a personal relationship to the site or situation that I am working with. Taking my point of departure in my personal reactions, I develop concepts further in an effort to engage a larger context, before I actually take the step to realize something.

BR: We have talked about books and literature before. I know you like to read a lot. Have you read anything of particular interest to you lately?

PL: While on vacation in Finland this summer, I read a novel titled *Minä, Olli ja Orvokki* by a Finnish author, Hannu Salama. Hannu Salama wrote this book in 1967, after he had served a year in prison for his earlier book *Midsummer Dance*. He had been sentenced to prison for blasphemy. Both novels contain some swear words and snappy remarks about God, but what must have been most difficult to swallow for many Finns at that time was his direct depiction of the life and bitter sentiments of the disempowered working class in Tampere. *Minä, Olli ja Orvokki* has a crude atmosphere of acerbic class war, including a devastating Civil War. It is an atmosphere I recognize from my childhood and growing up. I think about it now as a traumatic social condition in which bloody murder was hushed up by a whole community, in shame of murder ever having been possible. What affected me the most in the novel, however, was the pervasiveness of a macho culture embedded in Finnish society in the form of alcoholism and misogyny. I wonder how much this machismo must be part and parcel of the trauma. Reading this book reminded me of my past as part of a society with its own specific past. It was insightful but painful.

Currently, I am reading Margaret Atwood's *After the Flood*. I have just bought an old farm in the South of Finland together with some friends, and we have started to build an ecological village. Fully aware of the risks involved in an enterprise such as this—that is, forming a company with friends, building together, sharing an ideology about sustainable living, and community building—I thought I should learn from Atwood, who seems to have mapped out some of the pitfalls.

BR: What usually inspires a new idea for you?

PL: For instance, reading Salama or Sassen and pondering over the issues they bring forward to me causes the accumulation of a body of knowledge, including emotional knowledge. Of course, the knowledge builds up in various ways: lived experience, news, other peoples' accounts, or simply observations. When I have a site, that is something more specific to attach this knowledge to, I will start having ideas. A site may come to my attention by my own accord or by someone else. Many times an institution invites me to do something on premises defined by them. I do a lot of research about the premises, and I usually find a site there that I can relate to.

BR: After *Public Sauna* you created an exchange program for museum guards. Can you tell me a little more about it?

PL: I worked a year at P.S.1, earning minimum wage guarding my own piece there, *Public Sauna*. During this time, I came to know many of the guards there. I noticed how the specific culture of guarding varies from country to country, even museum to museum.

Cultural exchange usually is a privilege of the educated classes. Cultural exchange among the working class seldom happens other than as a necessity, which is the result of displacement by labor markets. Yet, cultural exchange among academia is quite free of radical renegotiations. The languages of academia are usually shared among educated people. Knowledge and ethical standpoints, however different, are still usually based on certain shared premises. Talk of a harmonious global village is a redundant dream as long as we only promote cultural exchange on the levels of academia.

BR: Along the same lines, it seems that your teaching has taken a more forward position in your activities. Can you talk a little about that as well as what role it has in your work as a whole?

PL: Ever since the first sauna projects (*Hybrid Sauna* in Cambridge, MA, 1999, and *Public Sauna* in New York, 2000) my work has often taken on forms resembling workshops. With *Poison and Play* I worked specifically with the idea of workshop as an artwork. Hence, for instance, *Lazy Climbers*, a workshop I created together with an acrobat, Katja Echterbecker, to teach adults to climb trees.

In August 2011 I started as Professor of Site and Situation Specific Art at the Finnish Academy of Fine Art. I love teaching and I thrive on the two-way feedback I have with art students. I take it as a great opportunity to develop further ideas of art as workshops and research.

BR: International curators travel around the world. Art travels. Can you give a little backstory to your recent project *Poison and Play*?

PL: In 2006 I discovered I was poisoned. It was a horrible experience, but it pushed me to pay attention to parts of my body that I had previously ignored. I was able to feel organs in my body that you're not supposed to feel, such as my kidneys, my liver, and I still feel my pancreas. My intestines were so irritated that they cramped when someone lit up a cigarette. I was really sick and couldn't eat anything sensual in food: no salt, oil, or sugar—just white rice, boiled carrots or beets, and water, and sometimes not even that, for two years. I also smelled and sensed everything acutely, for example, someone frying an onion miles away.

This experience put my body and my mind into a hyper-sensitized condition, forcing me to make very clear choices in my life. Suddenly it wasn't so important to be a famous artist any more. It was more important to survive and be happy. I also learned that happiness is not hedonistic, but the very key to life. If you are unhappy and sick, you are not going to get better. Happiness sustains life, which is why we need to play, hence the title. It's for this reason that we bought the farm in Finland.

BR: You were also interested in color theory—an interesting tie-in to an otherwise conceptual piece.

PL: My healer told me that exposing myself to the color green, either by seeing it or through my skin, for example, green light on my skin, would help my body to heal. I also heard about a study that was published in Germany about how people in the countryside are happier than people in the city, because they are exposed to the color green. This news was hilarious, because when I was sick I was drawn to the color green. I bought green sheets, green shirts, green cups and mugs, everything was green, green; I couldn't resist it. And this was well before I visited the healer.

I am interested in the effects that color has on the human mind and physique, and the colored hammock provided a perfect color chart. In researching for this project I looked at Paul Klee's fascinating color chart. Klee was a visionary who saw color as this hugely sculptural space, where the blue becomes a cone that curves—very spacey and futuristic. The idea is that in the middle the cone is thick and dense and at the edges it gets thinner and narrower until you have three colored shapes, the yellow, the red, and the blue, chasing each other in this wild circle of motion. When you create the cross sections anywhere on that circle, you get a certain color. The other part of the three-dimensional model was the white and black with the gray in the middle. I was intrigued with the shape of these colors and thought, "What if this shape was a hammock, twisted, into a parabolic shape?" I wanted to make it physical with a model. But, if I were to exactly replicate the Klee model, then these hammocks would be suspended in the air in a way that you couldn't actually lie in them. There would have to be a centrifugal force to throw you into that horizontal movement. So I took that idea and developed it further.

BR: You yourself have become something of a healer with your most recent performance, *Kalevala* treatment. That seems to relate to a lot of what has interested you in the last decade.

PL: I passed my first exams given by the Finnish Folk Medicine Association, moving from a novice to an apprentice in *Kalevala* treatment. *Kalevala* is the Finnish epic. It's the unwritten story of Genesis conveyed through songs, orally transferred from generation to generation, as was the Greek, the Icelandic, and the Native American Genesis. This oral tradition of *Kalevala* had songs that were entire descriptions of human anatomy, of medicine and herbs used for certain diseases, how to farm, when to do what or how to find certain things in nature, and so on. These songs contained all the knowledge of that society. This is why this treatment is called *Kalevala*, because it is a tradition transferred by generations through practice. It's not one type of massage. The long translation of the name is: Finnish traditional limb correction according to *Kalevala*. If you have problems in your spine or knees they can be treated in a very soft way, manipulating the body to correct itself. Osteopathy is similar, but, in addition, *Kalevala* invigorates the metabolism and deals with the meridians and the neural system, so it works on multiple levels.

Last summer I decided to work with other people's bodies, but I didn't know what form it would take. I had a dream where I saw living people's bones through their flesh. I immediately knew this was what I had been looking for.

Published February 24, 2012.
CultureCatch

The Thing Itself: Mira Schor + Bradley Rubenstein (Part Two)

Mira Schor, born in 1950 in New York City, is an artist, writer, editor, and educator, living and working in New York City and Provincetown, Massachusetts. Schor is the author of *Wet: On Painting, Feminism, and Art Culture*, *A Decade of Negative Thinking: Essays on Art, Politics, and Daily Life*, and the blog *A Year of Positive Thinking*. She is an associate teaching professor in MFA Fine Arts at Parsons The New School for Design.

Bradley Rubenstein: I feel that the art and the politics of the artist come together pretty seamlessly in your work, but in your most recent paintings there is more of a sense of introspection, despite the use of language, etc. They are really contemplative self-portraits. Am I far off the mark on this one?

Mira Schor: It's true. The work I've done since my mother Resia Schor died in 2006 has been deeply marked by that loss. It is an individual, private grief within a world where terrible loss is a constant, as we look at events in Syria today and around the world. Mine is a private individual loss, underpinned by larger historical forces. I'm the last of my immediate family on a family tree that my mother and sister composed in the 1990s. That piece of paper has been a major driver of the work I've done since 2007, beginning with my thought-balloon paintings. My mother remembered about eighty named or specific individuals from her family and my father's, going back to the nineteenth century. I counted that nearly half had perished in the Holocaust. At the bottom of the paper, at the end of this chain of human beings, my sister placed her name and birth date and mine. I feel a responsibility to all these lives, to my parents' artwork, and to the stories of their lives, which include the war and the *Shoa*. So this is cause for introspection, which in itself for me is a kind of joy.

At the same time I'm a politically minded person, always drawn to oppositional ideologies and polemics. Interiority and exteriority occur sometimes in the same work, or works in a series shift from one frame to the other. I speak of two "politics": what's happening in the world, and art politics—examining which definitions of art are hosts for different types of power. So in one painting I did last summer, a figure lies under a tree and looks at words hanging from the tree, words on time and space: "here/then" and "there/now." I was reflecting on the question posed by an e-flux book I was reading, *What is Contemporary Art?* I felt that the real question suggested by the book was "*Where* is contemporary art?" and that the answer is that the contemporary, the now, is not *here*, where I am—in the West, in the tradition of painting but *there*, in new global sites and new media. But I can only continue to paint, in the place I occupy, "here." Another painting in the series represents the same figure asleep with only the word "time" hanging from the tree, so now "time" is not just historical time or timeliness, but also the time one has on Earth to work and express—the temporal sword of Damocles.

In another new painting, the same figure sleeps under a series of cartouches that spell out the words "the dreams of all of us." I was trying to figure out how to express in my newest work the effect of Occupy Wall Street. This gets at some of the basic problematics of political art: Do you represent? Do you illustrate? Do you perform? I already was painting these sleeping dreamers, and then I was touched by a comment made by the student of a friend, which she posted on Facebook. The student (whose name I don't know, but I'm grateful for the eloquence) wrote, "In abstraction, one might think of Occupy Wall Street as a 'Sleep-In.' What fascinates me about this particular conceptualization is that it implies using the body's faculties for repose and rest(oration) in an artistic form of activism. The use of the shutdown of the body to attempt a shutdown of the system is not only a startling symbol (metaphor), but also a deployment of the one thing that capitalism has not yet fully infiltrated: our sleep. It metonymizes sleep with resistance."

This was such a beautiful idea. I have a lot of trouble sleeping but love to and need to sleep; one of my favorite scenes in the movie *Orlando* was the long sleep from which Orlando awakens as a woman. As he sleeps on, doctors are summoned, they examine him, and finally, with great and deliberate pomp, they declare, "The Lord Orlando is sleeping." I often think of that line with longing for such an epic and transformative sleep. Meanwhile the tents and all the apparatus of sleeping at OWS was the unglamorous (and courageous) nitty-gritty basis of what they were doing and maybe what drives authorities craziest. They are (they were) lying outside at night, vulnerable, *for us*, and collectively they were *dreaming for us*.

BR: It is interesting, when we started this interview, you were talking about doing figurative work again. How do you see what you are actually doing now as being different from how you pictured it would be?

MS: It was funny to read now what I said in our earlier interview, "I can't quite envision a way to represent myself as a figure in painting." Now most of the recent paintings are inhabited by a sketchily drawn figurative avatar of self, wearing glasses. I think I couldn't imagine it because all my earlier figurative work had been pretty tightly painted one way or another, and my goal was to move toward a more painterly expression in oil paint. For example, my figurative and narrative *Story* paintings from the early seventies were painted really differently than I do now; then, I literally filled gouache color into line drawings. And the body I represented at age twenty-two was a lot differently imagined than the one that appears in my work now: then it was that of a girl growing her sexuality; now it is a barely gendered, barely embodied person walking around, sleeping, watching, reading. Some people have read my current avatar with its blocky head and large glasses as a walking camera rather than a human figure. But, in fact, there's a chain from narrative drawings I did in childhood to the current figuration. And painting language, which remains central to my work, is in part another form of figuration, though with a certain objectivity and power derived from the power of "speech" over "voice" or embodiment.

When I started painting in oil, in the eighties, I was as scared as any intro-painting student by the uncontrollable aspects of oil paint, the fear of "mud." At first I couldn't figure out how to achieve the freedom that I had gained using pastel and dry pigment on rice paper in my work from the early eighties, but once I gained some control over oil, the goal has been to *lose* control. The process is sort of a throwback to Abstract Expressionism's ethos of "finding the painting" or of the painting as an arena for an action, though that ethos is grafted to a conceptual program. Desperation is a good motivator—when you really feel you have nothing to lose because the painting seems so bad. A work needs at some point to become unmoored from intentionality, and the path to that is engagement with materiality, even if you have a conceptual frame.

BR: When we talked in your studio while you were working on these pieces, I mentioned Plato's Cave—which you had already written about—but maybe Walter Benjamin is closer to these works. He wrote about the Truth content with regard to art: "The transformation of material content into Truth content makes the loss of effect, whereby the attractiveness of the earlier dream [of Renaissance or Medieval art] diminishes decade by decade . . . in which all ephemeral beauty is stripped off." It sounds contradictory, but your paintings are both very beautiful and steeped in the arcana of painting, but they seem to be in the process of shedding a tradition of painting, getting down to the elements of what makes a painting a painting.

MS: Thanks for that perception, both parts of it, but particularly the idea that I'm shedding a tradition of painting while trying to get at the elements of what makes a painting a painting—sounds good to me. But what you are seeing and saying is something that must be said by others than myself. What I can say is that my identity as a painter has always been caught, in a generative way, between the traditions of painting and the proclamations of the death of painting, of the object, of the individual artist, of private studio practice—everything that has become the *doxa* of contemporary art.

When, in my late teens and early twenties, I first declared that the works I was doing were paintings, they were absolutely not accepted as such because the work was small, gouache on paper, figurative, and autobiographical; early on what I was doing was dismissed as illustration. This was at the tail end of the dominance of Greenbergian formalism. So right off the bat I was propelled by rejection of my claims for my work, into a place outside of "painting." Feminism clarified the underlying ideologies to me and made me understand more clearly what I had intuited before, that what I was doing was a political act, was artwork with a political valence, even when it did not have the overt markers of "political art." Then, conceptual art's use of language helped release me from a bond of admiration to the great traditions of painting and from a bond to figurative representation; it provided a portal to language as image. These shifts all took place in my earliest years as an artist.

A bit later the work was really more sculpture made of paper than painting, but I still called myself a painter. It got more complicated when I went through a phase of saying that I was a painter for whom sculpture was at the heart of my work and then that I was a conceptual artist who was a painter. But all these identifications really do exist simultaneously. I'm always bringing something from one faction or identity into the other, in ways that have generally made both sides uncomfortable and that give my paintings maybe a sense of, as Mike Minelli recently wrote, "not resting easy on the wall." Maybe that's what you are picking up on when you say I'm shedding the traditions of painting while trying to get to the heart of it.

In a number of the paintings I've done during the past year, my little avatar of self contemplates the displacement of pictorialism to other media than painting. "The Displacement of Pictorialism" was the title of a piece that was going to be a chapter in *A Decade of Negative Thinking*, but I never finished it. Whenever I find myself in a darkened gallery or museum space looking at a large video projection on the wall, I think of how the painting that once would have occupied this space has been displaced because it is no longer seen as a contemporary interlocutor; its physicality is cast aside, only to be replaced by a projected image on exactly the same square footage. The only change is the displacement of faith in one medium to another, not the circumstance of pictorialism. What's the diff? Or, what the fuck? I think that's why I'm so interested in the objectness of painting—painting as a "thing." So my little figure sits under a tree and looks at two cartouches hanging from it: one says "sociality"; the other says "The space where painting was," and a heavy ball, like an overloaded wasp's nest weighing down the tree branch, contains the word "matter." Meanwhile, the painting itself is a small oil sketch/

ink drawing, so it is itself barely a painting—somewhere between an oil-assisted drawing and a cartoon.

BR: We spoke about Ad Reinhardt's cartoons and what if Reinhardt had tried to merge his passion for satirical art commentary, in his cartoons, and his reductive passion for painting, into one highly contingent work. But maybe that's stretching it; you may feel that the work itself is closer to Guston in style and spirit, with a touch of Indian miniature painting, and some of Florine Stettheimer and Remedios Varo thrown in, in your diffident and studious figures. But my take is a little different: with Reinhardt and Guston there was a definite separation between text and image; I see your painting and writing concerns becoming synthesized. There isn't as great a distinction between where one begins and one ends.

MS: At this point I feel I just have to get to whatever I want to, and that means disregarding artificial distinctions imposed by others. I see that too in the way I approach writing now. For a long time I felt I had to write to a certain academic standard so that my arguments were solidly enough grounded in research and theory that they might be taken seriously in the arena I aimed them at. It was a necessary discipline at the time, but I don't feel I have to do that now. In my blog, *A Year of Positive Thinking*, I develop an idea in a kind of pressure-cooker method, and there's a free flow between research, politics, artworks, and some of my own photographs and drawings related to the subject at hand. I try to be as thorough as I can, but I'm working to the speed and range of the web.

Similarly, in the recent paintings I'm really speeding up the relations between theory and practice, reading and painting. A number of key paintings have been done in the following manner: In the summer I lie under my favorite tree and read books on contemporary art and theory. Usually I look for books that articulate views seemingly oppositional to my own. I thrive on the resistance they offer, though last summer, in addition, I read some writings and lectures by Philip Guston, as well as a book on his late work, and also the wonderful writings of Morton Feldman. I always keep a notebook near me when I read because I find it useful to engage in a kind of parallel thinking: reading makes me think and write, but not necessarily directly to the specific text (those annotations go directly into the margins of the book). I also have a pile of small sketchbooks, ink markers, and pencils next to me (and some chocolate chip cookies and ice tea—as you can see, I'm describing Paradise). I sketch to the readings and against them, responding as immediately as possible to my embodied sensations as I lie there, to the text as to the unseen birds chirping loudly in the tree above me. I try to capture the sense of myself lying there, reading and thinking without regard for any kind of representational correctness, in the aim of a more important accuracy, like an internal gesture drawing of a state of mind/body. Then I spring up, run into the studio, and as quickly as I can, I transfer one of these drawings to canvas in what I call oil-assisted drawings, Then these produce the further challenge of how to keep the spontaneity of drawing intact while continuing the conversation in paintings that begin and end with oil on linen only.

BR: You've given your upcoming show at Marvelli Gallery the title *Voice and Speech*. I see layers of meaning in it—voice is to speech as seeing is to looking. However, one must also master speech in order to have voice.

MS: Yes, exactly. A couple of paintings feature those words. I was inspired by an idea put forward in Michel de Certeau's *Practice of Everyday Life*. His theme is that there exists a knowledge that precedes theory and that retains "voice" even when "speech" attempts to subsume it. It is the same knowledge that causes the city dweller to inscribe living patterns of usage onto the fixed grid of the planned city; it's the knowledge of the folkloric, of craft. He writes, "In turn, 'the voice' will also insinuate itself into the text as a mark or a trace, an effect of a metonymy of the body a transitory figure, an indiscreet ghost, a 'pagan' or 'wild' reminiscence in the scriptural economy, a disturbing sound from a different tradition, and a pre-text for interminable interpretive productions."

I may be creatively misreading de Certeau—other writers from this period reverse the meaning, giving "speech" the meaning I'm giving to "voice"—but "voice" and "speech" are what I do: the feminist project of bringing the "voice" of living inside a woman's body with a mind into the "speech" of art, as co-editor of *M/E/A/N/I/N/G* with Susan Bee giving visual artists a public space in which to participate in "speech," as a writer bridging the gap between the "voice" of painting and the "speech" of art theory, as a painter of language bridging the gap between two systems of knowledge and returning "speech" to "voice." I'm always seeking to valorize "voice" while giving "speech" to "voice."

BR: I am looking forward to seeing your show. I am sure you are too. I think that seeing your new pieces is going to be quite an event, especially in New York, at a moment when painting, serious painting, is really needed. Any thoughts?

MS: It feels like an interesting moment for me to have this opportunity to show my work, when the art world may be reconsidering or reflecting on excess, and values may be shifting. I hope my work's mix of materiality and thought, interiority and politics, has an emotion that is tuned to the time.

I'm looking forward to installing the show. The works are small, and the space is imposing, with long walls and high ceilings, so right now I'm thinking about how to present the individual paintings while establishing visual rhythm and narrative structure. My work always has a narrative and discursive aspect, so I'm interested in my shows having an underlying narrative, though not at all an overt one, but one that somehow is communicated to the viewer as a subtext that may be intuited: each painting is an individual work, and represents a thought, yet is part of a larger thread of thought.

In this group of work there are a few major themes or progressions along an idea: the idea of contemporary art, painting and theory; the idea of time; the idea of the dream of social change. There are a couple of connections I want to make to slightly older paintings of individual words. Having some sense of sequencing and chronology matters, though it's possible that a less narrative or more metonymic sequencing will work best in the space.

But I'm most interested in the narrative I don't know about yet, in what will become apparent when the work is up. I'm interested in what the paintings will tell me about what the next paintings will be. The world and my daily life will always suggest "subjects," but the works themselves suggest directions in investigating painting itself.

Published March 10, 2012.
CultureCatch

The Architecture of Noise: Joseph Nechvatal × Taney Roniger × Bradley Rubenstein

Joseph Nechvatal was born in 1951 in Chicago. He is an American post-conceptual digital artist and art theoretician who creates computer-assisted paintings and computer animations, often using custom-created computer viruses. He studied fine art and philosophy at Southern Illinois University Carbondale, Cornell University, and Columbia University and obtained his PhD in the philosophy of art and new technology concerning immersive virtual reality at Roy Ascott's Centre for Advanced Inquiry in the Interactive Arts (CAiiA), University of Wales College, Newport, UK. In 1999 Nechvatal developed his concept of the viractual, which strives to create an interface between the biological and the virtual.

Taney Roniger is a visual artist, writer, and educator based in New York.

Bradley Rubenstein: We really want to get into the new book, as well as the upcoming show, but can you take a minute and give us a little backstory? You have always slipped in and out of categories: actions, painting, sound art, writing . . .

Joseph Nechvatal: Well, when I was going to undergraduate art school at Southern Illinois University (SIU), I was making drawings and little gouaches and smaller-type paintings on paper, generally. And they were well received. I was not so interested in painting on canvas at the time. You have to put it in the perspective of the post-minimalist period when people were doing a lot of installation and process-based activities—often anti-illusion type things. But I was more interested in poetic imagery and explicitly spiritual imagery. I really was into working on paper.

When I went on to Cornell I started painting on canvas for the first time, and there I was very influenced by Jasper Johns. So I started getting into stencils and maps. I really found the stencil and cut-out and spray paint dynamically interesting. Already I was interested in spraying paint, the way I paint now with robotics.

Taney Roniger: But very physical, it sounds like . . .

JN: Yes, you know, it was a period of action and process. That went on for about a year. Then I moved to New York City—to TriBeCA. And then I started making more minimalist paintings. I was very influenced by Fred Sandback and Mel Bochner. I started doing rather large, white canvases with very small indications of shapes—this is partly because I was studying Ludwig Wittgenstein's picture theory in his *Tractatus Logico-Philosophicus* with Arthur Danto at the time. I was trying to figure out how we recognize shapes that come towards us and shapes that go in—that kind of optical reading of reality.

So the Wittgenstein picture theory kicks in, which I picked up initially from Jasper Johns, because I had read that Johns was really interested in Wittgenstein. And, happily, Danto was doing this course on Andy Warhol and Wittgenstein, and it was extremely important to me. And at the same time I started doing some minimalist paintings.

Just before that I got into combine pieces using pieces of wood and stone in relationship to a white painted field. I remember I was using a lot of white oil stick at the time. So you'd get this kind of physical, textured surface that for me became a kind of a representation of white noise. You know, it had a kind of energetic feel, a kind of suggestivity to it of physics. I was interested in quantum physics and Albert Einstein and Fritjof Capra's book *The Tao of Physics*—all that was really important to me that year. So we're talking 1976 now.

That was my biggest hand painting period. At that point I had quite a nice little loft situation, but all of that went away in 1980. I ended up living in an abandoned methadone center on Canal Street where I did a show called *Methadone Median*. For that I started making tiny collage/paintings—and drawings. And that's what led me to making the all-over gray, networky, palimpsesty drawings that I first was recognized for.

At the same time—I can't leave this out—I was doing performance dance work. I had a dance-performance art group with Cid Collins and Carol Parkinson. We went to Europe with Carolee Schneemann on an art performance tour. That was very interesting.

I found my own language, my own vocabulary, with the gray, over-all, networky, superimpositional drawings.

TR: Which are not fully abstract, in any sense. Have you ever done anything that was really abstract? It seems like you've always retained some kind of representational element in your work.

BR: Or at least the process lends itself to some concrete reading.

JN: Yeah, I think that's safe to say. I've never thought of myself as a pure abstract artist. I don't think I have done anything that's entirely abstract. I love working between polarities—between representation and abstraction. Just as I love working between the ideas of Dionysian chaos and Apollonian order. I think to accept these dichotomies as given is a mistake. And really, it's where they interact that it gets interestingly adroit. So . . . from the little drawings, I got into media. I started photographing these drawings, blowing them up—as photographs mounted on board. I was doing posters in the street and taking these very intimate, difficult, obscure drawings and trying to force them into the public space, which was paradoxical, of course. But that was my interest, in attacking the logo—the political and social logos of the times.

That developed into the first *Computer Virus Project*. That's when I had my first residency in Arbois, France, and I said, okay, I'm going to start all over. This is at the height of the AIDS crisis and all that suggested—broadly and to me personally. I uploaded onto a big computer at the Saline Royale, Arc-et-Senans, my body of work and made that the subject of the first computer virus attacks that Jean-Philippe Massonie at the Université de Franche-Comté worked with me on.

BR: I found that work to be quite interesting in that you were anthropomorphizing the digital process, which was quite new at the time. Now technology seems very friendly; we have talking phones and whatnot.

TR: You were also deeply affected by the AIDS crisis, but it seems to me that your interest in viruses has less to do with actual, biological viruses than it does with the virus as metaphor.

JN: Yes. I think art is for me deeply symbolist, and I think I can trace that back to my youth. My first real interests in any kind of artistic expression were the French Symbolist poets Stéphane Mallarmé, Comte de Lautréamont, Paul Verlaine, Charles Baudelaire, and Arthur Rimbaud, of course. I used to read them in high school after smoking a joint, and they took me out of my suburban box. So I think symbolism is an important component in my appreciation of art. Which could be seen as passé, or due for a comeback. I think art has to be conceptual, but it also has to be poetic with a metaphoric component.

TR: A lot of artists refuse to talk about metaphor these days.

JN: Well, it was a taboo, to be purged under the Greenbergian paradigm. I mean, that was to be avoided like the plague.

TR: Because then it was all about pure opticality, pure formalism . . .

JN: Pure materiality, pure formalism.

TR: Noise is decidedly anti-purist.

BR: And a more open-ended paradigm. You involve sound, visual thinking, literature . . . all the Wagnerian elements.

TR: Joseph, in your previous book, *Towards an Immersive Intelligence*, you explored the shift in ontology that you saw emerging as a result of a nascent immersive consciousness connected to virtual reality. How did your interest in immersion come about, and how did it come to focus on noise, which is the subject of your new book, *Immersion Into Noise*?

JN: It started, first of all, with my ideal for looking at most painting: that you enter the painting. Like Wassily Kandinsky said, he wanted the viewer to enter and sort of exist in, and explore, and be, and travel in a painting. So already I was on board with that. I just think it's the total use of your imagination as an artist or as a viewer of other artists, to give all and just get into it, and drop what you're doing and go there. But then it got more specific with my research with Roy Ascott for my PhD. There I wanted to take that immersive use of the mind and see how it could apply to new technology. So I started to study virtual reality and its ideals. And the idea for virtual reality is that you're immersed into a virtual world that you can navigate. I did my thesis on that topic, and I revisited art history and the history of architecture and ritual and different cultural manifestations through the wide lens of immersion. What I call the immersive impulse or desire for immersion. So that was where it became concrete, with the head-mounted device. And then I applied immersion to audio aspects when I created the viral *symphOny*.

I did quite a bit of research on audio and sound art, and anything that was non-musical in terms of audio experiments, and that's what led me to the book about immersion into noise. So then I could use some of the lessons I learned from the VR research, and that idea of environment, of ambience, of surround sound, and apply it to a noisy surround vision. Pushing our sensibilities behind our head as well as in front of our eyes. Trying to use the full instruments that we have available to us to feel.

BR: Including music.

JN: I have to say, I'm very excited about the re-mastering of the audio piece, my viral *symphOny*, into a 5.1 surround-sound concert. Because I think when we're talking about immersion, and we actually physically re-master something into an immersive environment, we're getting closer to the book. Again, how form and content are trying to come closer together. I thought of this when you were talking about my method of writing the book. Because I think I brought my music closer to the book also, oddly enough. I realized some of the ideals in the book through this re-mastering of the symphony.

TR: And we will hear that soon?

JN: We will hear it as an audio concert, the night of the opening on the 12th of April at Harvestworks. You can take the same data that's being produced, and you can output it as a visual or as an audio production. It's easy to convert signals into whatever you want. You just change the parameters. It's very, very easy to do. The question always comes down to: What are you doing? Why are you doing it? And not so much how you do it, but the fluidity part. So, of course when we think of the digital age, the fluidity of the internet, the networked connectivity, we think of flows of data. But for me it's an interest also in human potentiality, which is one of the reasons I got interested in cyberculture in the early '90s. It seemed like the platform for transformation. And that folded me back into my interests in Classical Greek poetry—Ovid's *Metamorphoses* in particular—where things become other things, and flowers become people, and people become clouds, and this kind of super-fluidity, which we do experience in dreams sometimes, if we're lucky. But it has to do with a symbol, a poetic metaphor, for realizing our human potentiality and our full sensibilities towards our real life, the real people in our lives, our real politics—how we live our lives economically and the decisions we make in the real world. So in that sense I'm a materialist. Actually, that's why I became interested in Speculative Realism because they don't shy away from what they call transcendental materialism, which I really think kind of nails what I've been feeling and groping for. And it sounds of course oxymoronic, and certainly paradoxical—but maybe not! You have to dig in and dig around. Anyway, that kind of idea of human potentiality interests me. And I think that's the reason we have great art. I think art is to change consciousness.

TR: What I see underlying your whole project is a kind of syncretistic vision in constant search of destabilizing rigid polarities. But it's not like you're bringing the two poles together in order to form some third neither-here-nor-there thing; you're putting the two together in a kind of dynamic tension.

JN: Dynamic tension! Beautiful! That's the noise aspect. It has to have a tension, a kind of provocative element. It's not trying to say "Everything is everything." That may be true on one level, but we don't live on that level. I think it's more intellectual to perceive the minute differences, and that's what a connoisseur does.

TR: I think that's a really important distinction to make. It's not the unification of the two; it's the tension between them.

JN: I do think that's the real payoff for this—the knowledge that things can be contradictory and true simultaneously. If you've got that, then your life opens up and you're far more tolerant and understanding, and a better human being and a wiser human being.

TR: Another thing that I definitely want to ask you about is digitization. You've called it "the universal technical platform for networked capitalism." It's also your chosen artistic language. Can you talk a little bit about what makes it the ideal language for you?

JN: Okay. It's the idea of the Trojan horse. If you're going to be an agent of political consciousness, of resistant awareness, of non-acceptance, you still have to work within the language of the power. Otherwise, you're immediately marginalized and cast aside and have no subsequent contribution that's recognizable. So I think, again, you have to be driving a Trojan horse; you have to enter the dialogue, the vocabulary, the system, the semiotics, and then from there subvert. In other words, you can't subvert from the outside. You have to subvert from the inside. This is Jean Baudrillard. And I don't like a lot of Baudrillard, but I do think he was right in this case. Yeah, it's subversion from within. And that's really why I started doing the big blow-ups and got into the computer. If you read my artist's statement from *Documenta 8*, it's all about this subversion. Yes, I'm using the computer because the computer *is* the dominant language of military economics, and we have to confront it head-on. So it is a kind of realism. Of course, you have to be very careful with that, but that was my intension. I mean, it's easy to make like an avant-garde stance and then end up just being swept up inside of some kind of slick production that plays along with the themes, so that all of your criticality is glossed over. And it's hard enough already to maintain criticality in cultural production, but once you're inside the slick game, you have to really be subversive. For me, of course, it really comes down to the imagery. I guess that's really why I decided the anus was an important image. It wasn't to be a sexual or provocative or funny image; it was to be a key portal to poke into the post-industrial information age.

BR: There is that element of subversion there, but do you think that it ultimately has to be perceived as subversive, or does it have greater implications in the long run. Looking back over the last two decades, when it comes to things like CGI or RP work, that has kind of become the norm now.

JN: We are always in need of perceiving the act of multifarious and allusive searching for something antithetical to the established norm. I see that possibility in the digitals morbid deviation and subversion of the concept of individuality and authorship. It plays well upon today's desire to egregiously delimit signification through art and magic. Digital forms can enmesh and contravene, alter and disrupt the mundaneness of communications in an inexorable, unrecognizable, and chimerical way.

TR: You've talked about things like "digital fluidity," which is in some sense an oxymoron. You know what I mean? Because digital language is binary. So it strikes me as curious that if what you're after is in some sense exposing the fallacy of rigid binary thinking that your chosen language is itself binary.

JN: The string of zeros and ones underlying everything—you can't get more binary than that. I totally agree. But then it is like water. Water is made up of two kinds of atoms, but what we do with water varies drastically. We swim in it, we brush our teeth with it, we paint with it, we drink it, and we pee in it. It's undeniable that zeros and ones make up the structure of the digital medium, but I think it's almost not important because the medium is so fluid. The human spirit is being tapped down and down and down. We must strive to overcome the bullshit. It's a metaphysical battle. And each person, each woman and each man, is a soldier, and we all have to fight. And art I think is the domain for that.

TR: And you feel that—this potential to change—when you're with not only your own work, but when you have a profound experience with another work? You feel that it's changed you in some way?

JN: I do. Almost chemically. And it stays with you. And not that we don't outgrow our appreciation of certain artworks, particularly when you're young. In my case, I had a passion for Jasper Johns. I just couldn't get enough of him. I was in love with him, you could almost say. But then I outgrew it, you know? So that's part of the maturation period, I guess.

TR: Let's turn back to *Immersion Into Noise*. I just want to say that I found the chapter on Paleolithic cave art, where you describe your descent into the Lascaux cave (among others), so moving and so powerful.

JN: Thank you. I do think that's sort of the core of the book, and I try to make the case for the art of noise visually based on that, because I think it was the most concrete example—in immersive terms—that I experienced and that I could write about firsthand. I mean, as you can tell in the book, I tried to write about visual noise from my travels and experiences. But yes, the cave of Lascaux was a transformative moment.

TR: One of the things I was struck by in this chapter was the element of danger inherent in making the descent into those caves. I mean, it wasn't exactly like stepping into the studio for a day's work for these early artists. I wonder if there's something of that element of danger, or fear, or incomprehensible enormousness that attracts us to the internet. I think you've touched on this somewhere.

JN: I have talked about how computers stimulate us almost like sublime vastness, which is both enticing and scary. Your typical sublime reaction to enormity is a mix of attraction and fear. There is a reinterest in sublime art, as you might know, in Brooklyn with the metal group Liturgy and the movement called transcendental black metal music. I like what they do, as well as Wolves in The Throne Room. They're connecting music back to the vastness of nature. I find that very moving. They are an influence on my *nOise anusmOs* show at Galerie Richard.

BR: In terms of Black Metal, those are pretty recent, more granola-based groups. Did earlier bands like Bathory or Mayhem have any influence on you? I can see how the reductive aspects of the music achieving maximum effect might . . .

JN: No, I was much more influenced by Merzbow and industrial noise groups like Current 93, Hafler Trio, Throbbing Gristle, Coil, Laibach, Steven Stapleton, Thee Temple ov Psychick Youth, Smegma, Nurse with Wound, and Einstürzende Neubauten.

TR: What were some of your other influences? How did you come up with the theme for this show?

JN: I was also listening to a lot of Rahsaan Roland Kirk, Pharoah Sanders, and late John Coltrane—all this avant-garde sax. I was reading Manuel da Landa's breathtaking book *Philosophy & Simulation: The Emergence of Synthetic Reason* in which he explores simulations of emergence in systems of different scales, from the atomic to the social. He goes into the cellular automaton as a general principle as the basis of geology and tribal organizations and much, much more. A whole historical re-analysis through the cellular automata principle, which is, again, using simple elements with enough frequency that emergent properties pop up. I was reading that as I was listening to the music while I was in the south of France staying in a house in the country. So I would look at the flowers and the seeds all around at the same time.

TR: And Speculative Realism? Did that play a role?

JN: Yeah. I'd already been reading Speculative Realism well before because my neighbor Lauren Sedofsky had brought it to my attention. Actually I mention Quentin Meillassoux's *After Finitude*, which is the book that got me started into Speculative Realism, in a couple of footnotes in *Immersion Into Noise*.

TR: It seems there is, with Speculative Realism, a reintroduction of metaphysics into a climate that's been hostile toward it for some time now . . . Metaphysics is now okay again.

BR: Or Steampunk.

JN: Yes. I think that's the key thing. It's a hodge-podge. And in fact, Ray Brassier, who is the translator of the Quentin Meillassoux, says that it's not a real movement and that you can't lump these philosophers together. I've read Brassier's *Nihil Unbound: Enlightenment and Extinction*, a book on new nihilism, and his piece on noise music called *Genre Is Obsolete*, and I think he is right. With Speculative Realism you have speculative materialism, object-oriented ontology, transcendental nihilism, neo-vitalism, transcendental materialism, and you have an interest in music, art, and science fiction—which I think is just grand. But depending on how rigid you are as a philosopher, people could be put off by that. I was prepared for this by Deleuze because for him philosophy is the creation of new concepts.

Their whole jumping-off point is refuting Kant. Correlationism is the big thing they're trying to escape—where we can only understand the world because we have this human spectrum of perception, and so that's Being. And they say no to that, that being is post-human—it's much bigger than us. Again, that brings us back to the sublime and transcendental metaphysics and all that. So, in a nutshell, they basically say: We have to explore philosophy and being—ontology— outside of the Kantian strictures.

TR: And that we can do that; it's not beyond our capacities.

JN: And science fiction and speculation and art are all part of that. It's highly inspirational to an artist like myself and to some scientists because we are all into linked systems, like the body, the environment, a-life, the cosmos. That's why I named my show *nOise anusmOs*, as in it anus and cosmos are linked to other systems.

TR: I see so many parallels between what you're talking about and your working process. Here's my understanding of the process, and correct me if I'm wrong: You and your programmer, Stéphane Sikora, author a piece of viral code, which is then inserted into a selected image from your database of previous works. As the viral code transforms the image by altering its colors and configurations, you select captured stills from the process and play with them to make final compositions from which paintings are made. During the painting process, your hand does not touch the canvas; rather, the application is made by a robotic device acting on commands issued by the computer. The whole thing strikes me as a sort of wonderful dance—a dialectic, perhaps—between human agency and non-human processes. You don't seem to privilege one over the other; it's just this back-and-forth.

JN: I would not ever say dialectic, because I don't believe in dialectics. Deleuze does away with dialectics. It's too limiting. You have all the little differences in between the polarities—all those micro-areas that are far more rich and interesting and complex. So I would say: dialogue, but not dialectic. A conversation or dance.

TR: When you're selecting your host images for a viral attack, is it significant that they're always your own images, your own prior works?

JN: Yes. The only other example I used in an attack was two paintings of Andy Warhol's money paintings, which I just did for a short little YouTube thing because that was a specific thing for the Occupy Wall Street blog that I was happy to participate in. Otherwise, no. It's got to be within the family. It's not applicable for all things, in my mind. Or it would lose its meaning, it would dilute its usefulness.

TR: You mean if you took an image from . . . well, from anywhere out there in the culture. You could conceivably do this to any image, right? And interesting things would happen.

JN: Absolutely. It could be any image. And then the question is why. That's why when I talk about losing focus and the impact getting lost, that's exactly what I'm talking about. If it's any image, then why any one image? So I'm trying to maintain its function as art. I think I talked about that in the introduction of the book, that it's important to maintain this—even if artificially constructed—definition of art as something other. As a form of ideology. That's what artists are supposed to do: challenge ways of thinking.

BR: But you get two different metaphorical situations, one is you attacking culture; the other is more an interrogation of your own history.

JN: That would be creative destruction.

TR: In either case—whether it be directed outward or inward—thinking about thinking is really important to you.

JN: I think so. That's why I try not to make too much of a division between my philosophizing and my artistic creation. I mean, I'm not a philosopher, hard-core. But even Nietzsche himself said that the ideal philosopher would be an artist. And I'm trying to live that out on a mini-scale by keeping it moving back and forth between categories. Again, not looking for mush, not looking for homogenization, but looking for those differences which make for creation, that suggest new avenues of creation. Difference is novelty. I believe that art should try to be something novel, and I believe in innovation and invention. And I don't fall prey to these postmodernist myths of stasis and decay and repetition and simulation. That's a trap you can fall in if you want to, but I don't want to go there.

TR: You clearly traveled a lot while doing research for *Immersion Into Noise*. Travel is incredibly immersive.

JN: Yes, it's inherently immersive. Couple that with reading about what you're doing, the history of where you've been. I think that's true knowledge: having physical experiences in space, and the cultural things—the wine and art. The art is key for me. Looking at this painting here [points to a painting in the studio], it's easy for me to wrap it around my head. It's very easy. It's like this rectangle becomes a bubble that goes behind my eyes. And that's what I'm hoping that people can project when they look at the work—is to get into it.

TR: That's the thing. It doesn't have to be an installation environment for you to experience immersion.

JN: I don't feel it has to be. It can be, and that's obviously the most literal. But the literal way isn't always the only or the best way. For me, I tend to use all-over compositions—not always, but often. That suggests that it could go on forever. I think in the chapter on Jackson Pollock I tried to make that clear, with the two museums that were proposed of his work—one by architect Peter Blake and one by Tony Smith, a hero of mine. But they took that idea—the derogatory comment that Aldous Huxley made about Pollock's work at the Museum of Modern Art, saying, "Oh, but it's quite a bit like wallpaper. It could go on forever!" You know, disdainfully. That's what Allen Kaprow saw in Pollock's show at Betty Parson's gallery, where he said, "Okay, I understand. It goes around the whole room, meaning it's all the world, meaning it's the street, meaning it's a happening." That's where he got his idea to create the happening; it was from seeing this exhibition of Pollock's. So this idea of expansion, of distribution, of availability all around us is really a suggestion that has many applications.

BR: Can you talk a little about the work in this show?

TR: Yes, to what extent is it important that people know how the paintings are made—your process, your involvement with artificial intelligence, etc.?

JN: Very important, and then I hope they'll forget it. I want them to go to their own place with them. I don't want to over-determine the interpretation of the work. At the same time I don't want to deny where it came from or how it's done—the viractual materiality it's embedded in. But it's more than that, so I don't want to be self-limiting, and I don't want to limit the viewer. It's complicated.

TR: I see such a consistency across all your various media. Your prose style in *Noise*, for example, is characteristically syncretistic, non-linear, "allover"—in other words, it's noisy.

JN: Yeah. I thought it would have been silly to do a strictly academic style, when you're exploring something that is the opposite of that.

TR: It's not like it's stream-of-consciousness, with no punctuation. There's certainly a structure there, but the voice is ecstatic, personal, mercurial, even. And the text moves in unexpected directions.

JN: I think it's my allover approach to life that provides a moveable aspect that we're talking about.

TR: You make it explicit that your subject matter is ideology.

JN: Yeah. That started back with the early drawings. And that's why I started to draw these cliché images. When you look carefully at some of those—most of those—early gray drawings, they're pile-ups of biblical imagery and *Playboy* imagery and military or "macho man" cowboys because I was trying to work on cultural ideology and the visual language in which it's spoken.

I think we're talking about our own upbringing, our childhood, our relationship to our parents. Our relationship to our church, or synagogue, or whatever. Whoever—our Boy Scout master, baseball coach. What else is there? All the adults that teach us how to live. Which is not a bad thing, obviously, but it's something to be scrutinized. Particularly when you reach maturity. That's just the power of scrutiny, of self-reflectivity. That's how you can get to reprogramming yourself. First you have to get to what you don't want to do and stop doing that.

TR: So that's what self-transcendence means to you—moving beyond our unreflective cognitive habits, our conventional notions of the self, our utilitarian consciousness . . .

JN: Yes. And a kind of connection to the immanence of nature and materiality, the full vibratory spectrum. That is where it gets back to Speculative Realism, to understanding the limits of our perceptual spectrum and at the same time acknowledging that reality and being are beyond us while we still try to understand.

BR: Is it important that the viewer experience that transcendence the same way you do, or are you leaving that open-ended?

JN: I think that's an important understanding, particularly in urban life, for people to reflect on. I hope that's what they'll get from this show. That's what my intention is: that urbanites, sophisticated art viewers, will for one instance think about what is grander beyond that and have appreciation of it. The great outdoors, indoors, inside them. Yeah, connecting the anus to the cosmos is for that purpose. To place an extremely personal, sensitive, human aspect in a poetic marriage to that divine humongous "beyond us."

TR: Huston Smith comes to mind: "The larger the island of knowledge, the longer the shoreline of wonder." Always expanding, but with full knowledge that there's always that "magnificent more," as you say.

JN: I see it in some young artists who are really trying to work with getting back to respecting the enormity of nature. And of course it has everything to do with a kind of dialogue with cyberculture. The insufficiency of cyber-interactivity and networking and all that. No one ever said that would be the be all and end all.

Published March 29, 2012.
CultureCatch

Little Q + A: Michael Lee Nirenberg + Bradley Rubenstein

Michael Lee Nirenberg, born 1978, is an artist and filmmaker living in New York. He wrote and directed the documentary *BACK ISSUES: The Hustler Magazine Story* (2014). He is the author of the book *Earth A.D.: The Poisoning of the American Landscape* (2020).

Bradley Rubenstein: Your most recent action, *Redacted*, involves overpainting your past works black, repeating this performance from canvas to canvas. Has the result of this performance series turned it into something like a trademark, a signature style based in old Suprematist methodology, a non-dialectical negation that might once have been witty but ultimately only guarantees its own recognition? A gimmick? Has it replaced your work as a filmmaker and documentarian?

Michael Lee Nirenberg: Originally the project began with the immodestly modest premise that, while my earlier paintings might not be worth preserving, the *idea* of my past history as an artist was. Therefore, by removing the imagery, as such, from the work, I was maintaining its conceptual integrity. In many ways I believe that this conceptual conceit keeps the paintings from becoming iconographic—in fact denying to some extent the very idea of "recognition" in as far as what is recognizable is only the result of an extended painterly activity. With the exception of the audience who saw me perform the first *Redacted* action at the Hamburger Kunstverein in 2010, and certain video and photographic documentations, like the performance I did last month in New York (2012), it is impossible to see the work as a totality. Philosophically, I think that Mikhail Bakunin's quote "the urge to destroy is also a creative urge" comes closest to summing up my approach to this project. Ideas can't become a gimmick, only artworks can. I use every means I can to make something that will last—that will speak for itself. Because I think that before I get the other kinds of recognition, like "hanging in a museum," I'd probably see the museum directors hanging in a museum. And I don't think that's gonna happen.

BR: The video reminds me of Joseph Beuys's statement "truth must be found in reality, not systems." I know that he has had a great influence on your work. Do you think that statement applies to this project?

MLN: Beuys, of course, is important, as is Andy Warhol, Carl Andre, Buckminster Fuller, and Yvonne Rainer, all of whom also influenced me very much. Kippenberger, too. Like Beuys, I think that any system ultimately contains the seeds of its own destruction. It is only when the inherent vice of the system, whether in art, science, politics, or philosophy, makes itself apparent do we find the truth.

BR: By obliterating the images, then, while retaining the historical weight of the artwork, do you see that as a way to reinvent yourself and the work? Is it a statement about personal history weighing an artist down?

MLN: This relates to the question about Beuys. There was probably no artist in the twentieth century who was more buried under the weight of his cultural and art historical history, to say nothing of his own past! Yes, getting rid of the imagery is a way of lightening that baggage. Just look at some of these journals and sketchbooks [shows documentation of past projects]. These are notes about paintings I was making, sketches, photographs I copied into artworks—copies of German tourist postcards, newspaper photos from *Paris Match*, a sketch of a Thai girl from a massage parlor in Amsterdam, the lion monument at New York Public Library, a portrait of the Marquis de Sade, a baked Florentine, a picture of Helen Keller, a plate of German sausages, two "glowing cigarettes," designs for cd covers for my old punk band The Mohels, a coke mirror and razor blade on a table, my mother's fifty-seventh-year birthday cake, chopsticks and Chinese food, my old Ducati motorcycle, lightening bugs on a back porch . . . the list goes on and on [closes book]. Wouldn't you eventually want to "clean house"?

BR: The performative element owes something to Pollock, in particular his film with Hans Namuth. Was this something you intended?

MLN: Definitely Pollock—in the Namuth film you have the collision of art and fashion. No artist before Pollock had so carefully stage-managed his career and image so well. Tom Savini (who did the costuming and makeup) was very influenced by this film. Pollock influenced a lot of artists this way—happenings, Andy Warhol, a lot of performance art in the 1970s. Maybe Duchamp or Dalí came close. But it was really Pollock with that film that changed everything. There is also an element of Absurdist Theater and Artaud's Theatre of Cruelty. This passage from Yarostan Vochek is applicable, I think.

> Then the strikes and demonstrations ended, when most workers realized the carnival was over and returned to work, our group continued to perform a show. We were still printing posters, gluing posters that read 'Factories to Workers' on recently cleaned walls, shouting about the worker's commonwealth. At that point we had become dangerous, because at that point people like us elsewhere saw that at least some had meant what they said and that the performance of a play had not been the only possibility. Only at that point did we begin to act on our own, but we weren't aware of this. We were so carried away with our performance that we failed to see that the curtain had fallen and the carnival had ended.

I mean, this is really what art should strive to do, right? And a performance that essentially is nihilistic in nature can become a metaphor for reality in a way that only art permits. There is an element of meta-appreciation that you can have in a situation like I am creating.

BR: Okay, beyond art historical influences, what about books? Music?

MLN: J.G. Ballard, *Running Wild*, definitely. Also *Hunger* by Knut Hamsun, Musil's *Three Women*, Huysmans's *Against Nature* and *Là-Bas*. Kafka, *Amerika*; Gogol, *Taras Bulba*; Goncharov, *Oblomov*; Baudelaire, *Paris Spleen*. Also Robert Caro, *The Power Broker*; Rigaut, *Suicide*; Vaché, *War Letters*; Lewis Carroll, *Alice in Wonderland*; Vischer's *Auch Einer*; and de Laclos, *Dangerous Liaisons*. Lermontov's *A Hero of Our Time*; Babel, *Red Cavalry*; Proust's *Swan's Way*; Diderot, *Rameau's Nephew*. Makarenko's *The Road to Life*, also. Music? The Misfits.

BR: You are also working on a follow-up project called *Index*. You are basically redacting the work of other artists, à la Rauschenberg's *Erased de Kooning* (1953). How much of that is *homage*? Is there an element of doing away with the competition?

MLN: [Laughter] There may be some element of truth to that, but that is for the psychiatrists to figure out! There is an apocryphal story about Picasso painting over a Modigliani when he ran short on canvas. Everyone claimed that he was out to get Modigliani or something and was destroying the work, eradicating it. But he said that he was *preserving* it. The *Index* pictures are like an archive; the artists are freely giving me a work to overpaint, leveling the aesthetic value of the artwork. The only signifier left to determine those works' value or importance relative to each other is based on the aura of the artist. Their aura, not mine. Stephen Prina's projects have involved something of this. John Baldessari burning his early work . . . Sherrie Levine's art "replicants." Looking at these non-images is kind of like that old question, "If a tree falls in the woods and no one was there to hear it, would it still make a sound?" Except here there is no tree, no woods.

Published July 18, 2012.
CultureCatch

Game Theory: Michael Rees + Bradley Rubenstein

Michael Rees is a New York artist originally from Kansas City, Missouri. His first New York show at 303 opened in the early '90s. He has worked widely, developing animation, sculpture, installation, and interactive media. As of late, his interest in the object grows through collaboration, humor, and language examined through a collision of medias. Rees is currently professor of sculpture and digital media at William Paterson University, and director of the Center for New Art there.

Bradley Rubenstein: Can you talk a little about the early pieces and how they have turned from performance to the rapid prototyped works and to where you are now?

Michael Rees: Yeah. Those early pieces (*Studio Performance*) are so open. The body in the earlier pieces becomes a locating force, whereas these newer works are further out; the body is only dimly available. These newer works are actions, continually evolving in some other space. The project is a kind of heterotopia. And we were listening to King Crimson. In this sense, both projects are performative. Robert has a history of developing a philosophical framework for the performative in an exhibition he curated in St. Louis called *Performance and Performativity in Contemporary Art*. Our experiences with performance brought us to work together

BR: In the past, your sculptures gave priority to the internalized, subjective representation of the body—a form of very subjective portraiture for lack of a better term—what might be seen as akin to Freud's Imaginary Anatomy. You were following a line that started perhaps with Rodin or Giacometti. There was a real haptic quality to the work, which is interesting considering how it was generated in the no-space of the digital world, but one gets a sense that you weren't simply distorting something already in existence, like, say, Francis Bacon would, but that these works exist *because* they were manifested by your process. Is that a fair assessment?

MR: I think there were a lot of contemporary influences as well: Burden's performances, Kiki Smith, Bob Gober, David Wojnarovic, Cindy Sherman, Matthew Barney, and so on. But for me, there is no doubt of a psychological reification in the act of making. It's not everyone's agenda, but it certainly was mine for a long time. That way of making continues from the *Studio Performance* photographs into the *Ajña Skull 1, 2, and 3* from 1996–98. They're actually pretty gory and grotesque—for example, the uterus in the skull—but they're mediated and represented in amber plastic accretion, laser-hardened goo, faceted impression. It's interesting that all of your examples belong to an older existential aesthetic. The newer works no longer partake of the gore, the slime, the choice. They are transformed. They are endless surfaces and endlessly pliable. This is our contemporary condition. Media representation in a real-time, 24-hour, 7-day, 24-time-zone world. There is no end nor beginning to anything. I think the older *Imaginary Anatomy* in my work is struggling with the newer mediated tendencies.

BR: Your work has been rather a frontier-like response to a very modern apprehension of reality as mediated through new concepts of understanding the "actual" world. I see it as related to psychology. How do you see it fitting in historically, as well as art historically?

MR: There are artists who are keenly aware of their project within an historical continuum. I am of a different sort. Although I have my precedents and my antecedents, more and more I tend to float things out there into the world to see what will happen. I think it's a notable exercise to close your eyes and try to visualize your body—not the one you see in the mirror but the one you feel. It's a strange concoction. As we become increasingly extended I think we identify less with the look of the body and more with the surface alterations of these concoctions. This still places me within the psychological. I didn't quite get the memo about the mediated control of experience. I keep looking for leaks, fissures, the edges where the utopian systems of representation break apart and new possibilities emerge.

BR: There is a line of sculptural thinking too: Eva Hesse, Bruce Nauman, Joseph Beuys . . .

MR: I think as a younger artist these artists were of great concern to me. As I get older I think Nauman is the gift that keeps on giving. I think his early experience with math is way underplayed in the reception of his work. And of course he's there with the deep investigation of body space that so many people would pull from. But tactical play exchange keeps Gordon Matta Clark in mind. Ours is not an exterior space but more of a heterotopia. I feel the most kinship to him. When I saw his show at the Shitney, I think I was overcome by waves of nostalgia for New York in the seventies and eighties. Dangerous razor New York. So long gone.

BR: The collaborative process seems to have opened up a lot of doors for you. I get the feeling that it gave you license to go to places that you might have shied away from. Humor, for instance, plays a role to a great extent.

MR: Ahhh humor—what a joke! William Shatner says he always goes for the joke. He describes laughter as rare and delicate. I have so much in common with him!

Humor's new for me?!? My first show at 303 was chock full of jokes. There was *Do Be Do Be Do* actually based on that joke that "To be is to Do – Sartre, To Do is to Be – Camus, DoBeDoBeDo – Sinatra." *Stud Study* was dark and sexual and by extension funny. When people explained my work they often used the joke about the guy who goes to the psychiatrist and gets a Rorschach test. Viewing picture after picture he responds to the doctor, "That's two people making love!" Every single one, he says that. Finally the doctor's diagnosis: "You're obsessed with sex!" Our patient exclaims, "Obsessed with sex?!? Hell! You're the one showing me the dirty pictures!" A show I did in Houston in 2009 was self-curated by my humor response to the pieces. If they didn't crack me up somewhere along the way, they didn't make the show. Weirdly, but of course, the show ended up having a dark streak through it. And with the current pieces, Robert and I watched Ernie Kovacs's YouTube videos as we were working. Enough said.

BR: Were there any influences that you can recognize, or precedents, for the collaboration? It seems like Martin Kippenberger and Albert Oehlen's back-and-forthing produced something similar—not an equivalent, just a similar tone in the sculptures they did in the eighties.

MR: It's funny, this kind of play has been around in so many places and ways, like Robert Morris sharing videos in the seventies, then of course Kippenberger, Oehlen, and so on. Tim Rollins and KOS. Andy Warhol and Basquiat. Lots of people play around with it at some point. I think I take my clues more from music in this regard for this project—dubbing and sampling, for example. But also the sense of working off one another. It's interesting to think of the virtual object as an expression of energy that you act on and that is always in play. It only becomes physical when you print it. Otherwise it's in a dormant state of energy, a strange artificial state.

Digital media gives the collaborative a flavor too. What is the material of the work? It's kind of immaterial material. It's low-hanging fruit to talk about the way computers have learned from biological systems—to talk of how the iterative and the generative have become part of everybody's process. What may have been probable and likely in video and sound for many years, we're just getting to in terms of objects because of the technologies. I've been working with sampled objects in 3D space since the *Ajña* series in the middle nineties—spines and so on—so it seemed to make sense to enlarge this. I've worked back and forth with James Stewart on Digiplasty projects at various points. As a teacher I brought this kind of practice into my classroom to work with students around collaborative practice and digital media. I've lectured about this here (https://vimeo.com/9634047).

Remember, too, that I've done a lot of collaborative work starting in the late nineties with my project *Sculptural User Interface (SUI)*. I worked early on with Chris Burnett on the show *Artificial Sculpture* and then notably with Don Guarnieri on the interactive software installation *Social Object: Sculpture and Software*. Even so, many people have also contributed alphabets to the project and participated in exhibitions around it. The *SUI* was firmly built on Beuys's idea of social sculpture but tweaked up with a retool of the ready-made made ready, synthesized from Kosuth, and fed through the digital machine in a kind of turntable, open-source assemblage.

I don't want to go all geek on you, but our practice of sharing models has a kind of transparency to it too—a total surveillance. As we further work the objects manually, after they become reified by rapid prototyping and CNC milling, this faithful print of the interaction between us becomes strained. At the end of our process we almost removed this transparency and began to have conversations upon and within conversations, noted and marked on the pieces—obsessive transparency, giving way to veiled convoluted activity. I think you feel this when you're in the work—the sense of the transitory, the shifting, the changing. Each piece or show is a frame of an animation. I think this is important. It starts to allow for the space of an individual in the machine but shielded from its panoptic gaze.

BR: Epochs or paradigms?

MR: Eeekk. I like *Atemporality for Artists* from Bruce Sterling. He's trying so hard to nail a new aesthetic, but I think he got close to something in that talk. We're in the extraverse where one thing is mashed with another and another, paradigms on each other; epochs present and lost and mapped to paradigms and so on. It's a mess. I guess I'd have to go with paradigms for the simple reason we can replay epochs at will.

BR: Lines of force or aesthetic caprice?

MR: You'd think I'd be willing to be so binary, but I'm not. I feel both present in every aesthetic act—always unresolved and unresolvable. A kind of breath in and breath out (not unlike my project *Um and Ah*).

BR: Rules or chance operations?

MR: You set up systems, brutal workflows, extensive labor, aesthetic machines, and the coolest thing to emerge is that serendipitous shit right there, some grotesque utterance.

Published December 16, 2012.
Artslant

The Order of Things: Pedro Barbeito + Bradley Rubenstein

Pedro Barbeito was born in La Coruña, Spain in 1969 and lives and works in Easton, Pennsylvania. His artwork is based on images of war taken primarily from the world news media. For Barbeito, these works address the formative role of violence in contemporary life, from a political ethos driven by "terror" and deception, to the aesthetics of visual assault prevailing in popular culture. They draw on the anxieties of an age when we are afforded, primarily through the Internet, unprecedented visual access to the violence of war and political strife.

Bradley Rubenstein: The paintings in the show at the Aldrich Museum are from around 2006 and deal specifically with depictions of war and violence—media depictions and whatnot filtered through painting. This is a kind of subset of your larger interests. What drew you to this subject matter?

Pedro Barbeito: It was around the end of 2005. I had been working on my cubism/digital imaging series for a couple years, and the imagery I was representing in my paintings (my relationship with my wife) was getting more and more tempestuous to the point where I realized the paintings weren't about us anymore. Maybe I was responding to all the imagery I was seeing in the media. Abu Ghraib had just happened, and I discovered ogrish.com (a now defunct site that revealed censored imagery in the news media in its original form). I was looking at a lot of new video games that dealt with violence and war imagery—*Gears of War*, *Call of Duty*, *Grand Theft Auto*, *Medal of Honor*. That was when I also discovered that game developers in the 1990s worked with the military in developing a lot of cross-platform (military and gaming) software and hardware, so facilitating a move from flying a fighter jet on a game console in one's bedroom after school to a few years later flying a drone aircraft in Iraq . . .

BR: That is interesting. I don't know if you ever saw the movie *The Color of Money*, but Tom Cruise talks about that happening—video games training teenagers how to fly planes and launch missiles—in one scene. There is a sense in your work of it being somewhere between a critique of media and being a part of the media. Your painting methods in some ways are a reflection of how we look at things now, like HD television, iPads, 3D film. Do you see your process as evolving out of this relationship with pop culture?

PB: I've also always enjoyed looking at Golden Age, early superhero comic books—*War*, *Captain America*, *Fighting Yank*, *Captain Marvel*, *Superman*, *Daredevil*, *Bullet Man*—all of which, back in the early 1940s, were used as propaganda to create a pro-war mentality. Today the U.S. military publishes Iraqi superhero comic books and distributes them to Iraqi and Afghani youth to similarly turn them against the enemy (Taliban, Al Qaeda) while building nationalistic pride. All these things—as well as my affinity for horror movies, particularly zombie flicks; George Romero I've always appreciated for his mix of politics and camp—further involved me in this content. Romero's crew of bloodthirsty, stop-at-nothing, we-need-viscera, consumerist Zombies are fantastic. Once I started researching all these popular forms of depicting violence, I was hooked.

The similarities and contradictions that emerged in response to what I was watching in the news were fascinating. I was also intrigued with how digital technologies were being used to capture these events in the news. Abu Ghraib was documented by the propagators themselves in a reality television, look-at-me-I'm-a-superhero kind of way. The seduction of performing, of fame, outweighed any potential repercussions. The ease with which we can upload imagery to the Internet allows for anyone to make news, even at the expense of one's freedom. The media use digital technologies to censor—lower the resolution, pixelate, blur, make the images smaller—all to protect us from the horrors of war. Media in other countries do this to varying degrees. The BBC edits and censors less than CNN and Fox News but more than Greek media (I'm half Greek). Al Jazeera censors even less. The media in the U.S. censor and edit these horrors, yet they remain ubiquitous within our culture.

The paintings in their fractured, multi-layered compositions also reflect the access to and speed at which we are seeing and processing this imagery. Depending on our choice of media outlet, the representations are similar; the message, though, is different. The censored or uncensored imagery is used to promote outrage toward the shown atrocities, to minimize the outrage, or even to promote the rationale behind the atrocities. The paintings in the Aldrich exhibit represent popular cultural images of horror in ways analogous to how the news media reveal wartime atrocities. The viewer is protected from these cultural horrors—the imagery is beautiful, candy-like in color, simplified enough so that all is okay on the surface; our youth and innocence remains intact. A recent painting, *Zombie Parts*, that's in the Aldrich exhibit, references the recent imagery from Afghanistan where U.S. soldiers posed with blown-up, dismembered enemy body parts.

BR: Pedro, you said, "Painting, since the beginning of history, has been the representation of the world through pictures; as such, my paintings represent our current world, exploring the relationship between digital imaging, culture at large, and the history of painting."

A lot of your work draws upon very contemporary visual theories and ways of seeing, but a close look at one of your paintings shows a very sophisticated, very craftsman-like working method. Can you talk a little about your process? It is a rather complicated way that you arrive at your painterly destination.

PB: For the past sixteen years I've been working on five distinct series of paintings, each investigating different meeting points between a painting history and digital imaging in culture today.

The various themes I've been working on reference astronomical and scientific imagery, primitive representations of figures as representations of the universe, art historical images in conjunction with video game imagery, war imagery, and cubism—all seen through the lens of the digital and translated to paint on canvas.

Currently I'm working on three of these series, the Aldrich Museum exhibit being one of them. In each series, the tools used in making the works reflect the theme and content of the works. Over the years I've developed ways of applying paint (developing my own tools as well as different processes of application) in order to best define the content and keep each painting series unique. For example, in the science- and astronomy-themed works, I fabricated a tool to apply the paint to achieve the thin web-like grids that I use as a matrix for the paintings, to mirror the endless space of the universe. Due to the relative smallness of the paint marks in relation to the size of the canvas, these paintings can take up to four months to complete.

The works from the series I'm exhibiting at the Aldrich are quicker to make because of the tools I use. The paintings are primarily made using an airbrush, a tool I don't use in the science-informed pieces. The airbrushed representation is thin, lacking physicality, similar to the media images I download as reference material.

The third series I'm currently working on is the primitive-informed series. These paintings are more expressionistic; the paint is brushed, poured, dripped, and splattered on the canvas. The physicality of the medium and its looser, less controlled application references the Boli sculptures and other figurines I've been looking at as reference material. Conceptually, these paintings are a counterpoint to the scientific series and science's assuredness and exclusionary stance in understanding life and the universe.

BR: In the paintings at the Aldrich, there are a lot of references to historical precedents—*Guernica*, for example. Do you see these works as being political or primarily aesthetic explorations?

PB: I'm not sure I separate the two. One without the other would be meaningless as far as the paintings are concerned. Once I decided on what subject I wanted to paint and why, I had to and wanted to take ownership of both the political and aesthetic aspects of making the work. The pleasure for me is finding a perfect coexistence between the content and the medium. In a way that's the challenge: how to keep the painting vibrant and alive—good composition, good color, good drawing, intelligent use of the medium—while bringing across a narrative that's specific yet mysterious enough to unfold at a slow speed that is similar to how the painting visually unfolds.

Guernica is one of the greatest paintings ever made because of its footing in both these terrains. It's not more political than aesthetically beautiful; one allows the other to exist. The choice of, or lack of, color and the forms and composition help define the content and vice versa.

BR: There is a great line in Zola's *L'Oeuvre* where he describes the protagonist Lantier's working method (Claude Lantier is a painter based loosely on Cézanne) that reads: "He neither ignores nature or reality, nor imagines scenes or stories that are not readily apparent—but consumes them into the painting, freeing them as a new image." This is kind of how I see your process; you are starting with these categories, then combining the categories into different pairings—building little worlds in paint.

PB: The idea was to create various series or categories of paintings that would investigate, through the lens of art history and the painting medium, new imagery and approaches to making and finding imagery that were appearing due to technology and digital imaging. For millennia painting has been the form we have used to document the world, and so it holds the most variable approaches, both visual and conceptual, to visualizing an image. The digital realm provides painting with new ways of finding source material, new ways of processing the material (a job held by drawing for centuries), new aesthetics, and also new ways of physically making the work. In my opinion, digital imaging is the perfect tool to expand on the rich history of painting.

BR: You have some more recent work up now in Chelsea . . .

PB: The last of my series, science/astronomy, is currently being displayed at an exhibit in Chelsea at the C24 Gallery. The paintings depict scientific imagery that has only been visible over the last twenty years through the use of technology. The paintings in the exhibit look abstract, yet all the "information" in the paintings is derived from scientific representations—it is, in fact, all factual. All of these paintings, as well as the prints, also have a direct link to technology: the oval centers are pigment printouts. Also, the center of *Tracking and Imaging* is made of a laser-engraved and cut oval piece of Plexiglas with a laptop computer positioned behind it.

I'm interested in how the painting medium can interact with new media. I see these works as homage to science and its accomplishments, as well as its failures, in its quest to uncover the great unknowns. The painting *James Webb1*, for instance, represents the satellite that is due to replace the Hubble telescope in 2018. Its ever-growing budget ($10 billion+) in relation to its potential benefits has fueled controversy over whether the project should move forward. This public debate inspires the content of my painting. How much is too much money when it comes to scientific innovation?

In conjunction with this body of work (though not currently on exhibit), I'm making another series of paintings, the primitive series. These speak to how we understand the universe and our existence through religion, superstition, and the occult. I was interested in painting in a completely different way, a fluid, organic, expressionistic use of the paint versus an ordered more predetermined application. This is allowing me to investigate alternate forms of understanding that try to answer similar questions to science. As the title of Gaugin's masterpiece goes: Where Do We Come From? What Are We? Where Are We Going? These are the questions that both religion and science ask and attempt to answer. With the paintings from the science and primitive series hanging next to each other, the viewer will be able to consider which holds the greater truth.

Published August 26, 2012.
Artslant

Psychosexy: David Humphrey + Bradley Rubenstein

David Humphrey is a New York artist, born in 1955, Occasionally called a Pop Surrealist, his work hybridizes a variety of depiction schemes and idioms to make works charged with psycho-social content and narrative potential. He is a senior critic at the Yale School of Art. An anthology of his art writing, *Blind Handshake*, was published in 2008.

Bradley Rubenstein: The last time I was at your studio, we were looking at an empty landscape in progress. You said, "This one is just waiting for a protagonist." You were thinking in terms of storytelling—a part of the picture was the character, another was the set.

David Humphrey: Yes, sometimes the location scout gets ahead of the casting director, who still hasn't received the script. I like thinking of my painting process as an ill-coordinated collaboration, so that more than one role is present within the work, and there's the possibility of a disaster. But that's a different narrative than what appears in the picture, which tends to be relatively simple: owners hang out with their pets, two friends go shopping, a horse lusts after a snowman. Habitat and protagonist, though, is a good working binary for me (like figure and ground) from which meanings can be generated and terms reversed; location becomes protagonist, and characters are displaced from other contexts.

BR: A series that you are just beginning is one of abstracted trees. You said that these started from a children's drawing. You were making studies from that, kind of stripping it down until it began to look like a Mondrian. It was becoming a kind of armature that you could hang a lot of other stuff on—very tree-like, conceptually.

DH: Well, you caught me in the early process of developing an image. I wanted to use the madly beautiful engineering of the child's tree as a way into modernist abstraction. I've already made a few small paintings that simplify the geometry and minimize the kid's multicolored foliage blobs, but my itch is to import some narrative possibilities. Working with a source is a way to let others into the work—to cook up a sense of collaboration.

BR: When you say collaboration, it has a kind of double meaning here: it is in some ways a split-personality thing—you are playing the exquisite corpse game with yourself. But in another sense, you are collaborating with the materials as well.

DH: That's true, and the risk would be that the so-called collaborative process is a ruse—that mastery and dominance over the materials is masquerading as openness and sociability. Either way, skill is folded into the content along with a quantity of socio-historic associations. I've been introducing more spills, over-diluted paint, and reckless gestures to complicate the meaning of the labor while using quotation, citation, and allusion to thicken that meaning.

BR: You are also referencing a lot of art historical figures, painters as diverse as Churchill and Eisenhower, as well as de Kooning. There is a little irony in these choices, but on some level I sense a certain amount of sincerity too. In using their work you are not simply appropriating their styles; it seems like homages to the work.

DH: Each case is different. I started one series of paintings by making loose copies of Eisenhower's nostalgic landscapes that I would use as locations for my narrative additions. His paintings were sometimes copies of Hallmark greeting cards, so the images already had a life before Ike or I got our hands on them. The Supreme Allied Commander of the invasion of Europe was such an odd softy in his paintings. De Kooning is another story. I've taken his ways of developing and breaking down images very seriously. My recent use of large gestures is a slightly comic way of saying, "Me too!"

BR: Before we get more into the new paintings, I wanted to touch on some of your other activities: you teach a lot, write art criticism (recently anthologized in the book *Blind Handshake*), and are in a couple of bands. Is all of this feeding into the paintings?

DH: Teaching and playing music with other people are both formalized ways of having a conversation. I like to think of it as an extended series of dialogs in which established artists and students are trying to sort out what matters by looking at art from many perspectives. Teaching affects my work the same way that seeing a lot of exhibitions does—by sharpening my sense of what to avoid, but also by introducing unexpected things to care about. Music is also a very efficient antidote to looking at a lot of other people's work; it can clear a cluttered mind and restore a vivid sense of the unfolding present.

Writing about art is related but more fraught. Crafting words into sentences that make sense and go somewhere is not like painting and way more unpleasant. The anthology is an attempt to nest the writing into a turbulence of other people's work and my own to suggest that writing can be an extension of the studio.

BR: What about books and film? Considering the deep narrative qualities to your work . . .

DH: I'm tearing the plastic off of a new book called *Crackpot Poet* by Jeremy Sigler as I type these words. I'm reading a few poems at random while answering your question and realize that I'd like the images in my paintings to sneak into people's brains the way his jabbing poems, like jokes, are sneaking into mine right now. I've also been practicing my bass guitar at night before going to bed, and it's been very helpful to screen a film while my sluggish fingers perform their strengthening repetitions without nagging eyes and meddling brain.

BR: One gets the sense that you actually seek out other interests, not as a distraction to painting, but as an extended part of the process.

DH: Maybe I'm triangulating, or polygonulating. I need to find other perspectives to both orient and disorient what I'm doing in the studio.

BR: You work in Pennsylvania in the summers, the rest of the year in your New York studio. Is there a difference in what you do in each place? Or does the juxtaposition of quiet and away versus loud and New York add some element of discord to the paintings?

DH: Being in the woods recalibrates my senses—the quality of my ability to notice changes as soon as I get out of the car. Being in a world of plants shifting in the wind under the changing light is great. Making sculpture makes a great mess and more sense in the country. I'm in love with roadside vernacular sign structures and scrap wood.

BR: There is an interesting "found" quality to some of your sculptures. I'm thinking of things like the snowman installation. It makes sense that having a roving eye to that kind of thing would help shape your sculptural work.

DH: I want my sculpture to balance and sometimes confuse the relation between what is found and what is made. I like to think that incorporating a manufactured object into an artwork is a way of responding to its rhetorical solicitations. I made a series of sculptures that are paper-pulp and hydrocal layered on top of oversized stuffed animals purchased at Kmart. The original's plush asks to be touched, and that's what I do with a transformational vengeance.

BR: Bringing it back to the paintings—can you talk a little about how your work has developed? Can you sketch in a little background about where you started?

DH: When I finished art school in the late seventies and started to look around at the art world, I found it hard to connect my Beckman/Picasso/Guston figurative painting with the avant-garde work being shown then. But the picture changed quickly as the eighties got rolling. My work, over time, assimilated aspects of pop and photo painting and became charged with psycho-social content in the context of that moment's feminism and identity politics. I took a Freudian film theory class with Annette Michelson at NYU that energized and enabled my painting, even though the studies were applied exclusively to film. Because I was an artist among academics, I felt free to bend the concepts to serve my work. I was a heavy-handed neo-surrealist in my twenties, a post-modern idiom hybridizer in my thirties, a born-again amateur in my forties, and now I don't know what the fuck I am.

BR: I think maybe something of a hybrid! Makes sense when you look at the way you assimilate things into the painting. One of the most striking aspects was how you were using the photo-derived images in a way that was kind of like Photoshop but in paint. There was also a tremendous psychological component to the way the figures interacted. Everything seemed kind of nice on the surface, but you sensed a tension underlying the image.

DH: The emergence of consumer-level imaging software was not just a great tool for constructing images, but also provided a working metaphor (albeit limited) for how memory, perception, and imagination dynamically interact in the mind. I made a lot of digital prints but was most interested in how the computer's logic could be absorbed in the emphatically material practice of painting. The computer might have operated as a prosthetic mind, but I wanted to see what happened when output was through the body and stinky wet paint. I made a series of paintings called *Love Teams* that pictured embracing couples derived from very different sources, mostly beefcake and cheesecake. The computer could help enact my deranged dating service: naked guys from period physique magazines could be joined to nudes from student figure paintings; a George Quaintance toreador could tangle into a calendar pinup.

BR: There is a great picture by Picasso at the Met called *At the Lapin Agile* (1905). It's a self-portrait of Picasso as Harlequin sitting at the Lapin Agile. Next to him is Germaine Pichot, his girlfriend, painted in a totally different style. Then in the background, the Lapin's owner, Frédé Gérard, is just roughly sketched in. The way all these styles overlap is visually grating. They don't really connect, but that was the point. Similarly, during the nineties, there were discordant elements in your pieces, but if you added them up correctly, you got into the psychology of the painting. You were arriving at a new way of telling a story in pictures. How did the work develop after that?

DH: Everyone in the Picasso painting is in a crafted role that seems partly their doing and partly the artist's. Thank you for connecting *At the Lapin* to my paintings! I've always tried to use the labor of representation as a way to inflect my imagery. The mark-making produces a fiction of the artist as skilled specialist or manager, devotional noticer or anarcho-regressor. It doesn't seem like there is as developed a language for the authorial voice or the unreliable narrator as there is in literary criticism.

Inhabiting more than one roll is especially useful. I switched to acrylic paint around 2001 as a way to disorient my craft. I used to say that I wanted to paint like the sort-of talented niece of an ice cream store manager who needs an image of a triple scoop cone to put out on the sidewalk. That was when I made my first paintings of kitties. Greeting card companies use adorable images as a way to make money from people who want to subcontract their exchange of feelings. I wanted to conscript those rhetorics into my paintings for other purposes. The pastoralism of my mismatched *Love Teams* evolved to include twin kitties, puppies, and other companion species. Amateur paintings can be heartbreaking, in the way earnest striving coexists with awkwardness and failure, but also interesting for the way historic picture conventions devolve into vernacular. I was hoping to mine some of that goodness in my paintings and sculpture. Still do.

BR: When you say you are "inhabiting the role," you are bringing the act of paining into a theatrical vernacular. A kind of Method Painting. It allows you to make these jumps in style and painterly syntax while keeping everything unified by contextualizing it under the idea of it being a "role." When you made the change-up to acrylics, your work, in my opinion, really opened up. You did that show about Walt Disney. You used Churchill and Eisenhower as "characters." You really created a whole painting world to roam around in.

DH: I hope it's possible for painting to engage socio-historic subjects in unexpected ways. We are so habituated to see a painting as a reflection of the artist and his or her intentions that it still seems exciting to unsettle them, perhaps at the cost of losing a stable, branded status. Still, I'm happiest when I make a painting that cracks me up, where I half recognize myself in the new object.

BR: In some ways you have arrived at an approach to painting that goes beyond a kind of tried-and-true deconstruction of the artist as author. You are sort of approaching a meta-appreciation of painting—in these recent works you aren't just quoting from an historical index of sources, you are getting into, say, de Kooning's head, when you lift his brushwork.

DH: I try to make paintings that are lively interpretive playmates that invite or stimulate a variety of perspectives. Is it possible to believe that the language of painting in this current state of belatedness or post-post-modernity is evolving a richness and depth in which layers of citation, irony, criticality, and heartfelt directness can coexist productively? I'd rather not have the fiction of the artist produced by my work, or its author effect, be Mr. Meta, the super detached, knowing employer of slippery signifiers and strategic gambits. I'd prefer to be the crying clown.

Published September 22, 2012.
ArtSlant

Theater of Painting: Susan Bee + Bradley Rubenstein

Susan Bee is a painter, editor, and book artist who lives in New York. She has collaborated with Susan Howe, Johanna Drucker, Charles Bernstein, Regis Bonvicino, and Jerome Rothenberg on several art books. Her art is a mixture of Expressionism and Pop. She is co-editor, with Mira Schor, of M/E/A/N/I/N/G: *An Anthology of Artist's Writings, Theory, and Criticism,* with writings by over 100 artists, critics, and poets, as well as *M/E/A/N/I/N/G: A Journal of Contemporary Art Issues* from 1986–1996, and *M/E/A/N/I/N/G Online.* She teaches art criticism in the MFA program at the School of Visual Arts, New York.

Bradley Rubenstein: Susan, I just saw this piece by Roger Denson in the *Huffington Post:*

> Mira Schor and Susan Bee, the Thelma and Louise of the Feminist Painting and Crit set, pose the biggest threat to male domination of the medium and criticism of painting in that they are critics as well as painters, and editors to boot, whose joint imprimatur has been pulsing out the feminist-left political art journal *M/E/A/N/I/N/G* since the mid-1980s.
> (May 1, 2012, http://www.huffingtonpost.com/g-roger-denson/nomads-occupy-the-global-_b_1464387.html?ref=tw)

I thought that was really great. It ties together your importance as a painter and the relevance that your work with *M/E/A/N/I/N/G* still has today as intellectual currency. In some ways it seems that it might be a little daunting to be seen as such an historical figure. I wanted to bring it up as we start, since we are going to be talking a little about your past work as well as the things you are currently working on for your upcoming show.

Susan Bee: I was pleased that Roger included us in his "Left Political Art Timeline, 2001–2012" and also that he cited my painting with the caption: "It was a decade of ANGRY painting, and nearly all of it was by women painters." I am feeling more like an historical figure lately, especially with the 25-year anniversary of *M/E/A/N/I/N/G* in 2011, and my own work as an artist going back over 40 years. I guess that feeling is a product of growing old and continuing to make art—against all odds. I have seen many other artists quit, as they became discouraged and just couldn't keep up the fight to make their art. It has been a struggle for me to continue. I sometimes talk to my students about the sixties and seventies and the beginnings of the feminist movement and Woodstock, about politics and living in the rainforest in British Columbia, and so on. They seem fascinated with this period of experimentation and often want to know more about my artistic and political beginnings and why and how Mira and I started *M/E/A/N/I/N/G.* The other aspect of my life that has become daunting to me is just the fact that I have had so many shows, worked on many collaborative book projects with poets, edited and designed numerous publications, and produced so many art objects. At some point, I realized that I was having trouble just keeping track of it all.

BR: Let's go back a little bit, get a little of your history in general. I know it is a lot of ground to cover, but can you pinpoint something of a real beginning of when you knew you were going to be a painter? Was it a slow discovery, or was there a real "aha!" moment?

SB: I seem to have been literally born into this profession of painting. Both of my parents, Miriam Laufer (http://writing.upenn.edu/pepc/meaning/Laufer) and Sigmund Laufer (http://

writing.upenn.edu/pepc/meaning/Laufer-S/index.html) were artists. They had emigrated to New York City from Berlin and Palestine in 1947, five years before I was born. I was brought up in the hub of the bohemian New York City art world of the 1950s. We spent our summers mostly in Provincetown, or we traveled to Mexico or Europe. I had the chance to meet many artists and see many artworks as a child. I grew up in Yorkville, at 85th Street and Lexington Avenue, very close to the Metropolitan Museum of Art. My public elementary school was just a block away from the main entrance. The museum, the streets around it, and Central Park were my turf. I would hang out in the museum on weekends and after school and regarded it as a home away from home. This was before the museum was spiffed up and gentrified. In those days, it was dusty and unpopular. I remember it as a quiet place for art lovers and eccentrics, as well as the perfect meeting place for moody, arty teenagers like me and my friends. I also took painting lessons at the Museum of Modern Art as a child. When I was quite little, I would accompany my mother to her studio and sit in the corner, making my own oil paintings. Later I went with my father on weekends to the Pratt Graphics Center and worked on small etchings. I went to the High School of Music and Art in Harlem (now LaGuardia High School), which was a wonderful experience, because I could spend half the day painting and had great teachers like Sherman Drexler.

My parents were opposed to my going to art school and following in their footsteps. They wanted me to be a professional of some sort—perhaps an architect—but art turned out to be my calling; I couldn't escape its grip. By the time I was 13, I realized I was committed to art. But I was also good at academic subjects, so I ended up going to Barnard College, where I had gotten a scholarship, rather than an art school. I also got involved with Charles Bernstein in high school. We met when I was 16 and he was 17. That relationship continues. At Barnard, which is an all-women's college, I got an education from major feminist thinkers like Catherine Stimpson and Kate Millett, who were teaching there. It was a time of turbulence with many protests, and the campus was often shut down. I also studied art and art history with Brian O'Doherty, Adja Yunkers, and others and continued to paint there.

After college, Charles and I went up to Vancouver in Canada, where he had a fellowship for a year. We lived in the woods in the rainforest. I drew and painted, and he started to write poetry. This work was recently published in *The Capilano Review* (http://www.thecapilanoreview.ca/issues/issue-3-12/). We then lived in Santa Barbara for a year before we returned to New York City in 1975. I got married to Charles in 1977 after living together for many years. I had my daughter, Emma Bee Bernstein, in 1985. She died in 2008. My son, Felix, was born in 1992; he just turned 20.

In 1975, I went to Hunter College to get an MA in Art. I worked with prominent minimalists, such as Robert Morris and Ralph Humphrey, and I studied art history with Rosalind Krauss, who was my thesis advisor. At that time, I was doing altered photographs and paintings, and I published my first artist's book, *Photogram,* in 1978 (https://jacket2.org/commentary/susan-bee-photogram-1978). My MA thesis was about Man Ray, Moholy Nagy, and photograms.

I designed Charles's and Bruce Andrews's poetics magazine $L=A=N=G=U=A=G=E$ from 1978 to 1981, which I also wrote for. I became very involved with a large group of young poets, filmmakers, and artists in New York at that time.

Around the same time, I became reacquainted with Mira. I first met Mira as a child in Provincetown. Her parents and my parents were friends and colleagues and were in the same milieu of Jewish American artists. At one point, my father told me that he and Mira's father, Ilya Schor, collaborated on a book before we were born. My father designed it, and Ilya illustrated it. Mira and I met again as young adults on the beach in Provincetown in the late 1970s and found we had a great rapport. This led to us working together on *M/E/A/N/I/N/G*, which we started in 1986 (http://www.writing.upenn.edu/pepc/meaning/).

BR: I think it's so interesting that there were these connections between your family and Mira's. Almost like you two were predestined to work together. Both *L=A=N=G=U=A=G=E* and *M/E/A/N/I/N/G* were very influential to me starting out as an artist in the Midwest in the eighties. It may seem kind of strange, but journals like that, as well as Chicago's *New Art Examiner*, were much more important in terms of keeping up with art than, say, *Artforum*. When I moved to Detroit, especially, *M/E/A/N/I/N/G* was the journal of record. George and Chris Tysh were always talking about this or that article. I think the design of it, too, had something to do with how seriously it was taken. In Detroit there was a longer history of painters and writers putting together magazines, like *Meat City* or *Destroy All Monsters*, but you two were combining art theory and politics in a way that was also very straightforward.

SB: We knew and admired the *New Art Examiner* and felt very involved with the poets, artists, and theorists that ran most of the small press publications. We set out to be an alternative to the glossy art journals, but we also were well aware of the other political and feminist journals that directly preceded us, such as *October* and *Heresies*. Our decision to exclude pictures was financial—it cost too much money to have images, and it made our journal different from the glossies. I was interested in creating a design that emphasized readability and legibility. You had to read *M/E/A/N/I/N/G*, not just look at the pictures!

In the meantime, I worked as an editor and designer for many other publications. For a year from 1979–80, I was the editor of *Women Artists News*, which I also pasted up and designed. I also designed and edited many small press poetry publications, including many Roof books from 1980–1992 (https://jacket2.org/commentary/susan-bee-segue-and-roof-books). But mostly, I worked for commercial publications such as medical and legal journals. I also worked at Lincoln Center designing the programs, including the playbill for the original *Einstein on the Beach*. I continued doing my artwork and tried to get it shown with little success. I brought my photograms and altered photographs to galleries, but most dealers weren't interested in this type of experimental approach to photography. I also had difficulty getting my paintings seen at that time. I did have a solo show of the altered photos in 1979 at a small local gallery and participated in many group shows. It wasn't until 1992, at age 40, that I had my first solo show of paintings at a commercial gallery, the Virginia Lust Gallery in Soho.

BR: I remember that show. She was also showing June Leaf's paintings around the same time. I don't think I had seen any of your work before that. I saw Mira's work in Provincetown, where I was spending the summers, but I remember being excited to finally see your work in that show. Can you talk a little about what you were doing then, about the work, how it fit in to what was happening at the time?

SB: I am amazed that you saw my first solo show. At that time, I was making collaged paintings with paper dolls and plastic animals and fake jewels embedded in the surface. These were dense compositions with a fractured narrative. Some of the painting also included dripped enamel paint layered over the entire surface as an homage to Jackson Pollock. I was interested in exploring the gender relationships as played out by the male and female paper dolls and also, at the same time, was using a lot of imagery derived from children's books and toys. No doubt, I was influenced by having young children around. In fact, I used to borrow their toys to use in the paintings. So this show had a lot of children's imagery. I was also interested in kitsch and in addressing high and low imagery, so I was combining oil painting with collaged Victoriana, postcards, vintage ads, and other sources. The results were layered and weathered and somewhat comic and surrealistic, yet faintly nostalgic for my own remembered childhood. I played with paper dolls and small plastic toys as a child and would create imagined worlds and fantasy situations, so this reimagined play was reflected in these paintings.

However, shortly after my show there, the gallery closed, so I was left to look for another gallery again. A few years later in 1996, I decided to join A.I.R. Gallery, the first women's cooperative gallery in the United States, now 40 years old, which presents a real alternative to the commercial system. I am still a member and have had six solo shows there.

BR: Yeah, I remember that there was a quality that hovered between a kind of high and low art, a combination of "abjection" and kitsch, which was something I found compelling when it was combined with high-art painterliness. Can you talk a little, in brief, about those six shows—how the work developed? Looking at the work in retrospect, do you see an arc, or storyline, in the development of your style?

SB: My first solo show in 1998 at A.I.R. was *Post-Americana: New Paintings*. It had images of American icons and kitsch elements, such as the Liberty Bell, Molly Pitcher, Big Ben, the Pilgrims, turkeys, as well as various small objects, such as plastic snakes, butterflies, shells, insects, and fake flowers. The figures were embedded in encrusted, paint-saturated surfaces. These paintings were a comic and surrealistic exploration of American history.

My second show at A.I.R. in 2000 was *Beware the Lady*. The paintings revolved around appropriated figures from movie posters and pulp fiction covers of the 1940s and '50s, as well as paper dolls, postcards, and advertisements. These paintings and the subsequent ones in my next show, *Miss Dynamite* in 2003, dealt with the themes of love, imprisonment, female rebellion, and punishment, alongside childhood innocence and the passage from girlhood into adulthood.

Color is a major element in these paintings—bold, splashy, and expressive. I am attracted to images of the strong, sexy, and somewhat dangerous dames that are endemic to film noirs, pulp novels, mysteries, and B movies. These bad girls seem to represent the underside of the innocence of childhood. In these paintings the women are strong figures emerging out of the morass of the paint to assert themselves and their sexuality.

In 2006, I had a show at A.I.R. titled *Seeing Double: Paintings by Susan Bee and Miriam Laufer*. This was a two-person show of paintings by my mother, Miriam Laufer (1918–80), from the sixties and seventies, and my *Philosophical Trees* paintings. This series of collaged oil paintings use the motif of the tree of life as a structure for cultural references to everything from Blake, film noir, and pin-ups to mystical traditions, such as the Kabbalah.

In 2009, my fifth solo show at A.I.R., *Eye of the Storm*, opened just two months after my daughter died in Venice and a year and a half after my father died in October 2007. The paintings explore an expressionistic, apocalyptic vision in the form of imaginary seascapes, floods, and storms at sea. The themes are reflections on the aftermath of disasters, such as Hurricane Katrina, September 11th, and the Asian tsunami, as well as more personal losses.

My sixth solo show, *Recalculating*, opened at A.I.R. in 2011. I showed mostly small oil paintings, which dramatize the relationships between male and female characters through the lens of the dark, violent films of the 1940s and 1950s, engaging psychic dislocation, trauma, and incongruous mystical and religious iconography. In contrast, natural elements formed the basis of some of the other paintings I showed, which were inspired by Caspar David Friedrich and Charles Burchfield.

Looking back on the trajectory of these solo shows, I can see that my approach to the subject matter and painting changed over time. In my last show, I was creating smaller paintings without collage and with a simpler palette and a flatter style. The paintings were tighter and more focused on the interactions between the characters. Meanwhile, my landscapes have become more romantic and expressionistic, more oriented to fantasy and religious and dream-like visions. I am now less interested in a decorative surface and find myself creating narratives with an emphasis on the inherent painterly composition. In my first solo show at Virginia Lust's Gallery, I was using paper dolls in a similar way. But the paper dolls were static icons and did not have the emotional force that the more expressive figures I am using now have.

BR: You spent part of last fall at the MacDowell Colony. Did the change from being in the city have any effect on your new work?

SB: I appreciated the time to develop some challenging new paintings. I was at MacDowell for three weeks and started four paintings, which I finished in New York. Two were related to compositions by Caspar David Friedrich, but they were influenced by the colorful autumn foliage, which I could see from my studio window in the barn where I was painting. Another work was a based on a film still of two girls in a car, but the fourth one, *Ahava, Berlin*, was the most complex and different.

Ahava was inspired by a trip Charles and I made in the fall of 2012 to Berlin. We stayed near the former Ahava Kinderheim, located in the Mitte, which was the Jewish ghetto, and is now an arts district. It was a politically progressive Jewish children's home. My mother lived there from 1927 to 1934. This is painfully personal material for me, since both my parents grew up in Berlin and were exiled in their teens to Palestine. I based this painting on a melancholy snapshot of me standing in front of the war-scarred, graffitied building, which remains standing as a testament to the suffering of the Jewish population in Germany. Lucky for my mother and for me, the orphanage and most of the children were transferred to Israel, where Ahava (Hebrew for love) continues to this day.

Raphael Rubinstein wrote the following, which is part of an essay to be published in the catalog for my upcoming show at Accola Griefen, about *Ahava, Berlin*:

> Following the Nazi rise to power, the Ahava Kinderheim and its inhabitants, including Bee's mother, providentially relocated to Palestine. Situated in the former East Berlin, and also in the Mitte, Berlin's old Jewish quarter, the Ahava building was war-scarred, dilapidated and heavily graffitied when Bee came upon it. In her painting she translates

those features into automatist paint drips, mostly red and blue. Exuding a violence that is rare in Bee's other abstract motifs (even when they accompany a violent scene), these skeins and drips of paint suggest that the building itself is wounded. Standing stiffly under a plaque that reads "Ahava," the artist is a diminutive figure who looks overwhelmed by the ravaged façade, by the tortured history it represents.

Yet, at the center of the painting something else is happening. Reflected in the mirrored entryway of the ex-Ahava Kinderheim are details of buildings on the other side of the street. Or maybe some details are of the interior courtyard—the painter plays with subtle spatial ambiguity. In contrast to the paint-spattered Ahava façade, these buildings are clean and cared-for; Bee paints them with soft geometric forms and muted yellows and whites. A green-leafed tree is partly visible. Unexpectedly, Bee transforms a snapshot situation (tourist daughter standing in front of orphanage where mother lived as child) into a powerful image of hope and renewal, albeit one that acknowledges the heavy price of history. The ultimate message of this painting is legible on the sign placed just above Bee's head: "Ahava," the Hebrew word for love.

BR: I really enjoyed stopping by your studio, seeing your new work in progress. I particularly liked the new pieces where you were developing a real sense of theatricality. By using your figures, which formerly had been more of a collaged element, as characters, the painting's background became more of a stage, or set. These new paintings really work as an extension of the series of "noir" paintings. Is this an evolution in your work, or are you just examining different issues in paint?

SB: I have become very taken by the idea of theatricality and artifice. I am creating these paintings as spaces for a drama to take place. The figures are actors and actresses in a stage that I am setting up for them to play out their roles. The film stills I'm referencing are very dramatic. There is a subtle undertone that is pulling you in and pushing you out. I remain intrigued by the dangerous women and the desolate men in the film noirs. These paintings have brought into focus the power of the individual faces and bodies and their relationship to the painted ground—and also their relation to each other. I'm now emphasizing the dynamic between the figures, whether they're pressing against a windowpane or pressing up against each other. In fact, the paintings' focus is on these relationships and the psychological space and emotions that are carved out among the persons that I'm portraying.

Published March 24, 2013.
Artslant

The Grammar of Identity: Deborah Kass + Bradley Rubenstein

Deborah Kass grew up on Long Island and currently lives and works in Brooklyn. Kass is an artist whose paintings examine the intersection of art history, popular culture, and the self. She works in mixed media and is most recognized for her paintings, prints, photography, sculptures, and neon light installations. Kass's early work mimics and reworks signature styles of iconic male artists of the twentieth century, including Frank Stella, Andy Warhol, Jackson Pollock, and Ed Ruscha. Kass's technique of appropriation is a critical commentary on the intersection of social power relations, identity politics, and the historically dominant position of male artists in the art world.

Bradley Rubenstein: It is really great that you are having your retrospective at the Warhol Museum—some of your most significant paintings were your Warhol/Streisand silkscreen paintings and your Warhol project, *My Warhol*. These were seminal works from the point of view of their time, but they were also a personal way of making art. They weren't just more illustrations of appropriationist strategies, to my way of thinking, at least.

Deborah Kass: At the time I thought what I was doing was the next step in a way, in terms of appropriation and feminist critique. I used an image, that of Barbra Streisand, that was not easily absorbed into a male narrative. Or a gentile one. This is what made Barbra the person, the image, the icon, so disruptive to prevailing notions of the category "female" when she burst on the scene in the early 1960s. The idea that her otherness could be a source of power and glamour and creativity was deeply disruptive at a time when homogeneity, whiteness, Christianity, blondeness, and *shiksa* goddesses ruled entertainment. Her pride in her difference and her ambition were incredibly radical for a woman. It still is, and it still makes people uncomfortable.

BR: In many ways I saw these works as being way ahead of the curve. At that time (the mid-nineties) it was a period of what I like to call "the death of the death of talking about the death of painting"—a kind of ground zero where you could do whatever you wanted, and there wasn't big money behind "rescuing" painting or whatnot. You could make an image however you wanted. Your work seemed important because it was constantly morphing.

DK: It's the Picasso model as opposed to the Pollock model I guess. For the record, painting has been dead for over 100 years officially. It was very dead when I started art school in 1970. I thought I would be an earth artist, and I did performances and conceptual work. Was it more dead than usual in the mid-nineties? I wrote an essay for a show I organized in 1992 called *Painting Culture* and wrote, "If painting isn't open to the voice of the colonized it deserves to be as dead as everyone claims???" because women just were not supposed to paint in my generation. Photos, yes; painting, no. I thought it was absurd to blame a medium for bad politics! Male painters might have had awful politics; oil paint didn't! It's like that thing on Facebook: "Republicans don't hate women, they just don't care what they think." Old male painters just don't care what women painters think.

BR: How important was it to you to have your work read on a personal level? There is a very intellectual component, and then a biographical element.

DK: I guess as important as it is to read any artist's work as personal.

BR: For example, music is important to you and an influence for these works—your beloved divas, show tunes . . .

DK: There is that great Walter Pater quote: "All art aspires to the condition of music." I was looking for more emotional contact points than I am used to seeing in a painting—and letting the language or lyric I use and memory of a tune add an emotional and even nostalgic aspect to the visual experience of painting. Using show tunes or lyrics from the Great American Songbook brings into painting another idea of history, culture, ethnicity, and democracy that one usually does not think of when thinking about "painting." But I am looking for a point of active identification.

When I started using Barbra's profile, it was also the height of the multicultural dialogue, "the cultural politics of difference," to quote Cornel West. Identity was the name of the game, along with appropriation. But something else started to click in my head as I was continually involved in shows about "identity." I got so bored of the labeling, the collective naming. At some point I realized an unsaid aspect that no one is addressing is "identification." It's an active thing, identifying with something. Identity is a noun, something that just is, almost in a passive sense. I began to realize that when we grow up we take the world in—the music, the movies, tv, the world around us—and we identify with some things and not others. It is how we begin to define our individual selves in the world, by picking and choosing what resonates, what we identify with. To identify is active, a verb.

When I grew up, I had no sense of visual art. No one talked about it or cared about it. But I was surrounded by music. My father played the sax (and violin, flute, clarinet, etc.), and he kept a constant flow of jazz going whenever he was home. He was the son of Russian immigrants. Music was a very important part of becoming both cultured and American for immigrants. There are many descriptions of walking through the Lower East Side in the early-twentieth century and hearing music out of the windows. One of the first things Jewish immigrants did when they could was buy a piano or violin for their kids. Music was a way for the kids to become Americans. Gershwin, Berlin, Arlen—great artists who shaped the American psyche. It was, after all, the Jazz Age.

This had a huge influence on me and my understanding of what art is. For me, interpreting art was the greatest art of all, since that's what jazz is—lots of musicians doing lots of different things with one text, one melody. This was my first understanding of "great." Dizzy, Miles, Lady, Trane, Monk, Sassy, Prez . . . Black musicians were my first experience of great artists, period. My father revered these artists. So do I.

So in my house growing up, there was no high or low, or pop versus something else. To be great you interpreted a pop standard your own way. And that was literally what I ended up doing with *The Warhol Project* and again now with the "feel-good paintings."

BR: In the works that you have done with text, even more than in the image-based pieces, there is an element of Walter Benjamin. He talked about aesthetics in the mechanical age, which I think means books and writing more than pictures. He wrote that there are ages where things are "shrouded in darkness," and "it is impossible to see things as wholes." Like in the Middle Ages, we see fragments. This strikes me as relevant to the text pieces. You're presenting these bits of songs or text that trigger us to remember something and then you're painting them a certain way. I know that I have misinterpreted some of them because I didn't get the song reference or whatever. How does that work for you?

DK: I pick phrases that mean something to me. They are from music I love, mostly made before my own generation's music that really formed my consciousness. Before Motown, before rock and roll, Carole King, Joni Mitchell, Laura Nyro, Stones, Beatles, Dylan—pre sixties. The sentiment might be familiar, even if you don't know the source. If you know the source that plays into a nostalgia, you can get a sense of the sentiment. Nostalgia is a very underrated emotion.

At this point in my life I am trying to get more philosophic, but I'm still impatient with the world. I am trying to balance the reality I can't control outside me with an attempt to gain some peace of mind inside, despite the insanity of our culture, our people, the destruction of the planet and each other for no reason I can think of other than greed. So I am trying to find resonant words that help. Either they explain things to me or help me identify my own point of view. Other people and the world are more of a mystery to me than ever. When I was younger I thought I had it figured out. Man, was I way off!

BR: When we were talking earlier, I placed your work alongside Cary Leibowitz and Kay Rosen. You share Cary's sense of humor and love of pop culture. I am interested in your use of type, which is constantly changing and is similar to how Rosen uses the look of words to create the work. You said something before that was really interesting: "Content is style."

DK: "Content dictates form."—Stephen Sondheim. I couldn't say it better myself.

BR: I'm gonna take that to mean that the style of the words, the way things look, is derived from, or relates to, the bit of song, or lyrics, or whatever, that you are painting. It is kind of like listening to a song with someone else, and both people have two different movies running in their heads as to what's going on, what the story of the song is. It makes me think of Matisse's *Jazz* cutouts.

DK: Or simultaneous fantasies during sex.

BR: In the most recent show you started to work in materials outside of just painting. Sign-making media, like neon. Is it just a logical development, like, "In a way, I am making signs of a sort, so . . ."

DK: I just made a new one, *Enough Already*. Perfect for a child's room or any frustrated adult.

BR: Getting back to the retrospective, has having to look at all your past work for the catalog and everything been a really motivating thing for you? Has looking at things from the past been an inspiration to make new work?

DK: I just saw the show when it opened for the first time. It was a bit of a revelation, in that the different styles I have worked through, at first by pure instinct, make much more sense retrospectively. When all the "periods" of my work are up, it ends up being a pretty legible narrative. It felt like, "This is my life?" For better or for worse, this is exactly how I have spent the last thirty years. Just about everything I ever spent time thinking about is up on the walls.

I am going back this week to look again. I'm looking forward to that. There are a lot of paintings and color up on those walls. As a result, I am finding myself thinking about sculpture a lot.

Published January 22, 2013.
CultureCatch

Glamorama: Nicola Tyson + Bradley Rubenstein

Nicola Tyson is a British painter who lives in New York. She works in many media, including sculpture, but she is best known as a figurative painter. Tyson's figures tend to be misshapen and presented with unexpected proportions. Her work has been connected stylistically to postwar British Expressionism, specifically artists such Francis Bacon and Hans Bellmer. Tyson is also known for her photographs, which document the early days of the Blitz Kids and the beginnings of the New Romantic movement.

Bradley Rubenstein: Why don't we catch up on some of the projects you're working on?

Nicola Tyson: I'm currently exhibiting an archive of color photos at Sadie Coles HQ in London titled *Bowie Nights at Billy's Club, London, 1978* that was first shown at White Columns last fall as a White Room project. The images are presented as giant "contact sheets," digitally scanned from the original color negatives that I took when I was an 18-year-old student at Chelsea School of Art. They document the nascent London club scene, post-Punk, in the fall of '78 and feature a crop of "gender–bending," soon-to-be celebrities of the 1980s, most notably a 17-year-old Boy George. Billy's Club was a seedy Soho gay club where we gathered every Tuesday to dress up and hang out to a soundtrack of everything from Sylvester to Kraftwerk.

BR: Punk was important. You caught the moment in these photos, where it turned into something else. Like you said before, it was a scene that wasn't about the music anymore; the music just became wallpaper for a scene. Did any of this have any latent effect on your later work?

NT: Crucially, Punk had rescued me from my gender-identity crisis in suburbia by introducing me incidentally to the city gay scene—still fairly underground then too—and enabling me to adopt a comfortably androgynous look. When I say "post-Punk," I mean that by 1978 Punk had gone mainstream in the UK; the thrill and underground exclusivity were over. Most of us in the Billy's Club scene were still teens and too young to participate in Punk other than as under-age fans. We hankered for something more, new, and as exciting, and Bowie Nights were a start. What really began to develop at this point was a club scene, but to call us "club kids" in 1978 would have been anachronistic, as the notion didn't yet exist, and "clubbing" was not yet an end in itself.

The period I documented was just the first three months before the press caught on and the scene exploded. I dropped out at that point because sartorially I wasn't comfortable with this bizarre carnivalesque individualism—that was a place I would later visit in painting. By the mid-eighties, club characters like Leigh Bowery had taken this dressing up to another level and transformed it into art. My work developed from a similar interest in totally reinventing the body; I just came at it from a different direction.

The scene was full-on color, and so are my photos, which was unusual for that time. Most professional documentation, back then, was done in black and white, because the press rarely bought color photos and could only work with transparencies when they did. I see my painting palette in some of those photos now! I will begin working on a limited-edition book of the photos soon.

Back when I took those club photos, I was about to embark on a degree in graphic design, but I was thrown out by my second year for non-attendance. There wasn't yet a thriving contemporary art scene in London. All the energy was still in music, fashion, and design in the early eighties. I freelanced as a reportage photographer for the music press and drifted, experimenting, in that peculiarly British, underground, unofficial art world (before the YBAs put London on the art map), finally returning to art school in '86 to study painting. But I'm now revisiting work I made in those intervening years, between art schools; I'm about to get some Super 8 films digitized, with a view to exhibiting them, reframed, in much the same spirit as the club photos. I'm known primarily as a painter, but in truth it's only part of the story. I'm an artist in that old-fashioned sense, and one of the things I do is paint.

BR: We were talking earlier about letters you had published and how you saw them as a way of talking about your own work, without referring to it directly. It was interesting to see how the tone, or voice, of them changed over the course of a year. We published the Bacon letter back in spring of 2011, but it was different when you read it publicly a year later. Much more feeling to it, I felt. Same with the others.

NT: The first letter, *Dear Man on the Street,* was my contribution to *Readykeulous: The Hurtful Healer: The Correspondence Issue* at Invisible Exports here in New York City in February 2011. Artists were invited to contribute an open letter of complaint concerning something that irked them about "the world today" and particularly about patriarchy. Over the next couple of months I wrote a series of letters to a select group of famous dead artists: Picasso, Bacon, Manet, Gainsborough, Ensor, and Beckmann—at first just for the amusement of friends, then you published some online, then I did a reading at Friedrich Petzel Gallery in May of 2011, and gradually it became an official art piece, originally titled "Letters to Artists and Other Men." I read them again at Petzel's in October that same year, during my show, and then in 2012 at Susanne Vielmetter Los Angeles Projects and Vox Populi in Philadelphia, at which point Sadie Coles suggested I create a book of the piece.

In these occasionally ranting missives, my concerns range widely; art (my own and that of others), sexual politics (contemporary and historical), and my own biography are addressed in an absurd, pointed, and playful exercise that seeks to create a mutable framework for locating and interpreting my own work—yes—without actually discussing it directly. References and puns ricochet back and forth within each letter, as well as between them, creating meaning and obfuscation by turns. I've always resisted explaining my own work, and this became a humorous way of investigating and describing the coordinates from which my working practice has evolved.

It's different when I read them aloud. I think it helps people get where I'm coming from. I've lived in the USA for 23 years now, so the humor is kind of mid-Atlantic!

BR: And you showed your first sculptures then too. I really liked the little swan pieces, the ones in clay and bronze.

NT: Actually they are made from Crayola Model Magic, a fast-drying modeling compound for kids. They are as light as meringues! It comes in 8-ounce pouches, so they are of identical volume, including the bronze version. That was cast from a piece I made some years ago, and I picked up the bird and swan motif again for this show. It's relaxing for me to work in 3D and get away from the line. Sometimes 2D is too claustrophobic. I'm also carving now—figures from logs, chunks of felled trees, of which I have stacks upstate.

BR: I like that specificity attached to the swan project—you are limited by how much material you have. You managed to wring a great deal of empathy from those pieces. They relate to your paintings in the last show, with the little animal "familiars" in the scenes. That show was a huge leap, for me at least, in your work. You imparted a real sense of drama to the scenes.

NT: Oh, you mean the pigeon in *Figure with Pigeon*. Then there was *Figure with Sphinx* also. I guess they do represent familiars in some way. These paintings seemed to be an excursion into companionship of sorts. The images were sourced from a suite of sketchbook drawings, as usual—single figures, one per page. However, it seemed necessary to pair them up with each other, not randomly, but in configurations of complementary tension and release. The drama comes from that tension. There's nothing going on in narrative terms between the figures. They are self-contained, locked into the painterly space, while at the same time being kind of highly animated. In that body of work there was less angst (for want of a better word) than in my earlier work. I found it just didn't happen as soon as the figure had company. It became more about balancing out the energy between them—bit like in "real life"! These were big canvases for me because I have a small studio. I work in my home upstate in a spare room. It got very crowded!

BR: I found that interesting—that you were letting the viewer create the narrative, however unintentionally. You told me later about your process, creating the characters separately and then choosing and combining them on canvas. Whether they were interacting or not (especially when the two figures were humanoid), they shared the same picture plane, so the viewer can't help but fill in the gaps of the space between them. I said earlier that I was struck by how different this show was from your past painting shows (for me), that suddenly you had these creatures inhabiting a shared space. It took it to a new level. There was a sense of theatricality, for lack of a better word. I didn't read them as "real-life" relationships, but rather as some sort of artificial social construct; they became actors. I thought that this was loaded with psychological potential. The viewers projected their own stories onto them, as you left them blank enough to allow that. I think that when you say "angst" with regard to your past work, it might be a sense of isolation.

NT: That the figure be solo was vital, initially. I first started working this way—that is, painting figuratively—in the mid-nineties. In those early pieces I felt like I was conjuring up some kind of libidinal presence. I called it "the painting body"—a presence that was kind of latent in the canvas, that had to be captured. An image that was evasive, unwilling, almost unable to stay, already distorting into something else. I also felt quite reclusive at that time.

BR: You were also running a gallery at that time. How did that influence the painting?

NT: I came to New York in '89 and spent a couple of frustrating years making conceptual-type art that attempted to illustrate the compelling feminist theories I'd been studying at art school, and thus I completely suppressed an intuitive approach to art making. Additionally, I organized an alternative space (1991–94) called Trial Balloon, devoted with ironic shamelessness to women artists only, especially the emerging lesbian subculture of that time (Nicole Eisenman, for instance). It was a crazy, creative, drug-taking time in the early nineties, and a whole bunch of interesting women artists and writers got connected up there in those years. That unofficial DIY art world of project spaces—mine and others—is unrepresented in the *NYC 1993* [*NYC 1993: Experimental Jet Set, Trash and No Star*] exhibition currently up at the New Museum. A really important aspect of this time was that, briefly, it was an artist-driven instead of market-driven scene, with artists being discovered, curated, and given their first exposure by other artists.

However, I barely made any work during that time because the gallery was too much work already, and by the time I closed it and returned full-time to the studio, I had the overwhelming impulse to turn within and work in a completely "unguided" manner, informed but not directed by the feminism thinking I'd been exposed to as a student.

BR: Your work began as drawings. These are still where you cull your ideas from for the paintings. Can we talk a little about the whole process of how you turn them into paintings? You and I were talking earlier about how you saw the viewer projecting a lot of stuff into the images. Do you mean them to be read another way? I see a vein of storytelling in the paintings.

NT: I find the images initially through what can be described as intuitive free-associative drawing. Consequently the works on paper form a major part of my oeuvre. However, my desires and assorted neuroses register in the images, but they are not merely expressed; instead they're used as source material in a kind of game of anarchic invention. I use the body as a sort of playground. I articulate and map it in unlikely ways because I inhabit it. The female body, art historically and culturally—until relatively recently—has of course been colonized, articulated, and misrepresented by men. So I guess I simply work from the inside out, as my body experiences, rather than merely observing and projecting onto. I experience my body as my psychological and physical "home," a place that determines how I experience, and am experienced, on many levels beyond mere appearance. How to describe that—and indeed what "that" is—became the issue for me, and not at some conceptual distance. I needed to just speak and literally see what I had to say—begin to map that subjective void.

BR: You said last fall that you weren't going to continue painting the same way for a while . . .

NT: Lately, I have begun working on a very small-scale, painting fast with no preliminary drawing. The line, my line, had become restricting. Small because I've never had that kind of stamina or attention span to work in a sustained way on any one thing from start to finish and much prefer to work on a bunch of things at once—a group of paintings, a bit it of sculpture, drawing, painting, collage, and a lot of staring into space! God I sound so prolific, and I'm so not!

Published March 17, 2013.
Artslant

The Color and the Shape: John Paul + Bradley Rubenstein

John Paul is from Chicago and works and lives in Brooklyn. Paul's collection of poetry, *Sign Language: A Painter's Notebook*, was published by Three Rooms Press in 2014.

Bradley Rubenstein: Can you give me a little of your backstory? I know you went to Yale for painting, but you have also been a sign painter and worked in movies and TV, and you are also a musician. How has all of that informed your work?

John Paul: In St. Louis I had solid training, and at Yale exposure to cutting-edge thinking.

The St. Louis years were dominated by the importance of Max Beckmann, who taught there after the war until the fifties. His canvases were a part of a student's daily diet, lining a corridor between the schools of art and architecture.

In New Haven the lesson given was freedom!—through hard work within the canons of modern art. Jack Tworkov and Al Held were the proponents—and Knox Martin, a dynamic mind in the unlocking of intuitive power.

After a brief stint in teaching in New England, I went to California. There I met West Coast painters Elmer Bischoff, Joan Brown, and others in his circle through Yale classmate George Lloyd. The Pacific landscape was a welcome change in feeling, with a hidden benefit of being away from the hot contest of career in New York.

In 1972 I returned to New York and soon set up a studio as neighbor and assistant to Ilya Bolotowsky. My friend Larry Rosen owned an art edition press called Chiron, and I was able to meet Ilya and other famous New York artists. Larry introduced me to Alex Katz, Fairfield Porter, Jack Youngerman, Tom Wesselmann, Larry Rivers, Red and Mimi Grooms, and others. The seventies were an exciting time, and I painted both in natural and pop veins. I adored the fast brush of Alex Katz, trying my hand at figure and portrait—and some still lives in the studio environment.

By the eighties I was working in a sign shop, painting outdoor walls and billboards. This was my first commercial painting career—a different approach to the city environment, perspective, and materials. In addition to covering acres of space as a commercial artist, I worked *pro bono* on art murals with my friend and sign brother Stefano Castronovo, who was a pioneer in New York art murals (Knox, an earlier pioneer). Stefano's motif was the Mona Lisa, with drunken red eyes. It wasn't in the cards for me to attempt pop collage like Rosenquist—way too dominant and original to be a shared context. He also was going towards something very painterly but "non-painting." That scared me. I didn't want to be a total grown-up, like Donald Judd or Dan Flavin. I could even concede that they were right. Just not right for me.

The seventies was like waiting in Casablanca for the figure to return to art. When it did, that would include some old favorites like Raoul Middleman and Charles Cajori, and the landscapes of Wolf Kahn. It would also mean a return to the stuffy museum painting of the New York Academy and the English tea cups of artists like William Bailey (a fine portrait draftsman but an awful artist).

Music? That's a hobby, and if it ever gets into my work like it did for Romare Bearden, that would be natural. To play jazz means to wade or swim in a stream of heroes. There are no more exemplary artists than the players and composers of modern music. If you know a tune well enough to improvise, you have an inner reference and calm much like dreaming. Take that to the next level? Perform with others? You have to want that like the footballer wants to score a goal. It's another language structure—free but with rules. You need to know the rules. I'll always be a beginner as a tenor sax player, so I concentrate on tone and sound. It's a love interest.

BR: In your paintings there are a lot of references to late Picasso, and maybe some of Chagall's more theatrical paintings. You create these narratives that are lyrical and oblique. What inspires them?

JP: Not enough can be known about Chagall. Picasso is said to have likened him to Renoir in his capture of light. He has a delicate but unconcealed hand informed by geometry—an avid "doodler." I want my work to come out of drawing, out of the act of drawing.

I asked Knox Martin what it was like to be working in New York near de Kooning and Arshile Gorky, painting under the gun of a living Picasso in the pioneer fifties, sixties, and early seventies. He didn't go down that memory lane but was always stunned and amazed by Picasso, especially the sculpture.

In those Mosquetero paintings, Picasso is baroque—he identifies with the great Baroque painters like Rubens, Velázquez, Titian, El Greco, and especially Rembrandt, who also shared a theatrical and valiant interest in history. There are so many different ways that Picasso defies placement in categories and avoids redundancy.

Baroque? The paintings jump out at you as feats and exploits; the baffling formal solutions and graphic illusions are a circus, the metaphors invented and wrung through the shaping process before your eyes, with nothing concealed. Also noted, the freshness of the palate, the plenty and disposable quantity of the material. Working in the shop taught me to not be stingy about paint.

BR: There is a decorative aspect to some of them—probably a size thing. They look like they could easily fit into the Lapin Agile or something. You are playing with the size that used to be called "easel painting" and working in an area that the Ab Ex guys kind of opened up. Has working on large-scale projects like painting a building or movie sets given you a broader range, or have you always aimed for this kind of "bigness" in the work? There is a great sense of drama in some of them.

JP: Big canvases were the thing in the seventies, and I had a front-row seat with Alex Katz. A few remember that there was an *ad hoc* Sunday basketball game on the Canal and Thomson Street asphalt court. Larry Rosen, Herb Schiffrin, Peter Schjeldahl, Porfirio di Donna, Joe Zucker, and others played, for a season or two, a good-natured game of hoops.

In 1976 or so, Larry landed a show at André Emmerich on 420 West Broadway—all raw canvas stained with Dalmatian spots. At some point he lost interest, and I wound up with a bunch of large stretchers. I copied what Alex was doing, blowing up smaller paintings to oversize. I used French ashtrays and duck decoys, liquor bottles, any handy thing. I didn't care that people called me a copycat. Alex himself didn't quite like what I was doing. He told me to stop using that size (and elementary color) as a format and to be more personal. It took me a while to work out of that mode. I think the fun and nastiness of the eighties helped make that break.

When I was working outdoors, we would have to get up an image to fit a 14' × 48' or a 20' × 60' on a daily basis. So the idea of scale was totally blown. Actually Alex was helpful in getting me into billboards. I called him to see if I could work on his Times Square mural. He gave me the contacts.

You would have to be a scenic drop painter to know the fun of sketching forms bigger than your body, but that would be under the gun of the foreman, and the risks of mistakes are much bigger. Our mistakes were not artistic, and they could be fatal—about safety and the lack thereof. I went to work in the morning promising my wife I'd wear the safety harness, but that didn't always happen. And the ropes we were given to rig with were more likely than not threadbare and corkscrewed from age. There was something very retro about our shop.

I "apprenticed" with Louis Concha, a Spaniard of Franco vintage; my eyes were opened: how to eliminate the fuss of detail and paint "for the distance." The optical length is a factor. You can kill a portrait, flowers, or a car by overly polishing. Louis showed me shortcuts, transparencies.

So what you see in Impressionism also happened in New York. There are academic realists who overdevelop forms and meticulously explain the container of each scene. Others simplify and abandon "depth" of that kind for a more personal impact. Katz is just one good example of that. Manet, for the Impressionists.

There's another factor that plays into depth for me, and that's my vision itself. I had an accident in art school while working for a doctor, bartering room and board for service as a domestic helper. One of the duties dealt with the doctor's wife's diet cola. One day a case of bottles blew up in my face, damaging my left eye. That led to a flattening of my "space," (and other more complex mental adjustments). The idea of seeing space in 3D became academic. This was at a time when Al Held went from his aggressive icons and shapes to the start of Baroque Neo-Constructivism. I was confused, but I could see lots of depth in paintings. This is because good paintings have an underlying or concealed geometric design, not just the schematic or standardized perspective.

To get back to your question: making painting bigger is as much a risk as keeping in a timid, amateur format. I feel comfortable with the mural idea and was thrilled with the Diego Rivera show at the MoMA. It could also go back to St. Louis and Beckmann. The dynamic and psychological size of Beckmann's canvas is exponentially greater than the literal measurements. And when he gangs them up as a triptych—whoa! So if I like a theme, and it comes from a concern that belongs in my world, it can go any size. Public murals are a definite interest.

BR: You just had a solo show in Brooklyn called *Rain Check*?

JP: The title was a form of modest expectation. As a "professional" my resume has huge gaps, and I have not kept many appointments with "destiny." But so many people showed up on a dismal blustery night, my comrades from many bars, many laughs and trials in their lives—the show must go on, and I was extremely gratified.

It was fun and good practice to place a live bet on mostly current work. The umbrella series is from the last two years, all from "abstract" or imagination. The soft 6' × 11' panels were all done specifically to bend with the seventy-foot convex curved wall in the Salena Gallery. I painted all of them and two more between January and the end of February. That was like a contract deadline, and I felt pressure—not an unusual feeling in my past business of outdoor signs. So the images wandered off-theme in three out of five: *Spring Street*, the *Bathers*, and *Observation Car*. *Spring Street* is an imaginary view of the spill-over crowd at my favorite pub, the Ear Inn.

I think there are reasons why I love "making" rain happen in my work. When rain comes, there is a disruption and urgency of a most innocent kind—that's one. Also, it's an excuse to unify the figures and geometric shapes of the umbrellas with a soft diagonal bias. And maybe a nostalgia for the days when I prayed for it to rain all day. Then I could be excused from the job and make the early morning call: "Hey Joe, it's raining over here. Can I stay out today?" He'd be happy to save on the payroll, since the work was almost always outside. "That's ok, John. Stay in the house. See you tomorrow." Then I would be free to hang out in my studio with a model or go to the bar and relax. Rain meant freedom.

Published April 13, 2013.
CultureCatch

Watch That Man: Larry Krone + Bradley Rubenstein

Larry Krone grew up in St. Louis and now lives and works in Brooklyn. As a performer, he has appeared at music and art venues in New York, including Joe's Pub, PS 122, and the Whitney. Larry's costume design and fabrication for his own performances has led to the creation of House of Larréon, his line of custom gowns and stage costumes, outfitting cabaret performers, dancers, and rock singers, including Bridget Everett, Neal Medlyn, Adrienne Truscott, and Kathleen Hanna. In 2014 Krone published *Look Book*, an artist's book of his costume and fashion work.

Bradley Rubenstein: In the almost twenty years now that I've been following your work, I have always been struck by how much attention you pay to every detail, how much craft goes into each aspect of the work. With that in mind, as a link running through your various projects and series, can you talk a little about the early stuff—the dolls made out of your teeth, for example?

Larry Krone: The dolls are a great place to start. They were a breakthrough for me at a time when I quit being intimidated by the idea of art and just started making what came naturally to me. I'm a big collector of things, and I remember being so pleased with myself at being able to achieve these little objects that looked like something the Franklin Mint might produce but had a secret personal art content that would give them extra value. In this case, the secret was that the heads of these little court jester characters were actually my four wisdom teeth—cleaned, glued back together, polished, and painted so that the inverted roots of the teeth looked like the peaks of fools' caps. Each time I painted one of the teeth, I would imagine myself as the guy in the Franklin Mint commercial, putting the last hand-painted details on the ballet slipper of their special-edition Pierrot Doll, and crack myself up. After those four original dolls, they got crazier, as I indulged in themes: a witch, a mermaid, a pirate, a devil, Gene Simmons. Each costume was unique and hand-sewn from silk, and the hands and feet were cast in silver and gold from little wax carvings I did. The more details I could get on a tiny doll, the more thrilled I would be, partially because it worked to the end of making something cute and precious out of something loaded with content and kind of gross, and partially because I just enjoyed making something so ridiculously adorable.

BR: I first saw them, I think, at the New Museum, but you had been showing in New York for a while. I was still living in Boston when I met you. Can you talk a little about what brought you to New York?

LK: That New Museum show was in 1996. I was in a *Selections* show at the Drawing Center in 1994, which led to meeting you, because a Boston gallery went to the Drawing Center and put two of us—Kara Walker and me—from that show into a group drawing show that included you. As to my earlier history, I grew up in St. Louis and came to New York in 1989 to go to art school at NYU. My draw to college was the prospect of living in New York City, plus a partial scholarship from NYU that included a program that paid for a trip to Europe every year. Also, I had been supporting myself in St. Louis after high school, but my parents offered to pay my way in New York while I was in school. I wasn't interested in college or ambitious about becoming an artist at all. A career in art seemed beyond me, though I guess it was probably a fantasy in the back of my mind. I just couldn't imagine the things that I liked to do being taken seriously by the art world. But I got a lot of encouragement from my professors and some introductions to galleries once I graduated, so I was able to start exhibiting my work as soon as I was out. My parents paid for a tiny studio for me in a divided up loft on Lafayette Street, where my first studio visit was from Marcia Tucker who became a great friend and supporter.

BR: I remember being at your place in the East Village when you were just starting out on the ukulele. You had used music in pieces before, but it was country, like Dolly Parton; then you were doing covers, like "Sweet Child O' Mine," which were awesome. They were so sincere but also really funny, doing metal songs on a ukulele. When did you decide it was time to start writing your own material? You really made a complete move then, also, from an object-based way of working to performance.

LK: Well, I didn't ever really make that move away from objects, though gradually I have become less concerned with insisting to the world that the performance work is directly connected to my practice of making objects.

BR: True—I have always noted how you even hand-letter all your handbills and whatnot. You turn every aspect of your work into some kind of drawing or multiple.

LK: I originally started performing music as an extension of a still-ongoing body of work that examines male identity using country music as a model. At the time when I started performing, I was noticing that my strongest emotional reactions came from music, which—considering that someone else wrote and performed the songs—was very separated from my own reality and experiences. In the objects I was making, I was thinking about using other people's finished products as building blocks for content in my own work. (Remember post-modernism? I didn't realize it, but that's sort of what I was doing.) "Sweet Child O' Mine" and "Over at the Frankenstein Place" are good examples of me trying to use music the same way. Those songs are so beautiful and perfect as their own things, but my goal was to present them in a new way that was specific to me and my own experience in the context of Art. Also at that time, I was making drawings combining idyllic landscape photography with Dolly Parton song lyrics and writing out words to "Margaritaville" and other songs using strands of my hair.

BR: So the show coming up at Pierogi—can you give anything away or is it Top Secret?

LK: I wish I could pretend it's top secret, but if any of your readers have been in the vicinity of my Facebook page over the past few years, I'd be busted. Since about 2009, I've been making a bunch of work under the blanketed title of *Then and Now* and posting pictures along the way, shamelessly soliciting "likes" whenever I finish a piece or when I just feel especially isolated by my obsessive process. It's ironic that making this work separated me so much from the art world, because its content is really about collaboration and coming together. That's part of what's behind the title of the Pierogi show, *Together Again*. Now that I have finally allowed myself to show this work in a big way, I feel together again with the world and within my own mind.

The work in *Then and Now* combines the craft projects of mostly unidentified people with my own labor-intensive workmanship and ideas. I'm a compulsive thrift shopper, and for years before I started working on *Then and Now*, I had been buying embroidery, crochet, and needlework projects, as well as remnants and materials from craft projects whenever I saw them at a cheap enough price. In the first *Then and Now* pieces, I sewed found hand-crocheted potholders and doilies together into geometric patterns or organized color arrangements. The idea is that I facilitated a collaboration among these people, whose handiwork somehow ended up in my hands, and joined in.

As with a lot of my earlier work, there is a sense of failure and haphazardness in the final products, because the formal choices are beyond my control. For example, there's a piece called *Then and Now (Rainbow Order)* that does its best to make a rainbow from found crochet pieces culled from thrift stores in Missouri, New York, and Michigan. The pieces and yarn that I had to work with determined the imperfect rainbow gradation and irregular shape in a way that I would have had to force if I were trying to simply crochet a rainbow afghan.

The biggest deal in the show will be *Then and Now (Cape Collaboration)*. It's a huge cape I made from hundreds of found embroidery projects I'd been collecting for years. After I sewed the pieces together to construct the cape, I filled in every piece of fabric left unembroidered and exposed with sequins that I sewed on one-by-one. It took me two and a half years to make.

BR: You are working in so many different media—the obvious precedent seems like Warhol and his Factory, but your House of Larréon is more DIY . . .

LK: When I was little, my Grandma Henny used to say to me, "*YOU* are a Renaissance man! You can do everything!" It got kind of old, and I didn't take her that seriously because she was my grandmother after all. But that did kind of sink in. I can't really do everything that great, but I do like to spread myself around. And I really believe in not forcing a path for myself in my career and life. Is it savvy for me to focus so much of my attention on songwriting when I have a flailing visual art career to tend to? Not for the career, but for me, yes. And House of Larréon. Where does that fit in? Like my performance work that has always teetered over into the entertainment world, my costume and gown design seemed like an indulgence that I was allowing myself, because it was so fun and immediately satisfying. Also funny. I couldn't believe I was succeeding in making dresses that were so vulgar and ridiculous—using techniques I learned from watching Project Runway—and having them worn by such high-profile and dynamic performers like Bridget Everett on stage. The real joke in the end is that the dresses work in a totally unironic way!

To be a little "unironic" myself, all of this crossover and success in finding an audience for these different things I do feels like my dreams coming true. About ten years ago, I took a mental break from the art world, though I continued to show my work and certainly to make it. At the same time, I came out as gay and met a whole new group of people in the "downtown" music/cabaret/theater/dance world, including my fiancé Jim. There was no room in my new life for art openings or networking, as is necessary for a visual artist, and I lost art world friends. It was liberating to me that none of my new friends were associated with the art world or even had any sense of me as a visual artist with a relatively established emerging-artist kind of career under my belt. Instead, I did a lot of singing and performing with this circle of friends and was accepted that way. Really, when I started House of Larréon was when I became outed as an artist among that group. Avant-garde dance and performance people started coming to me for costume and set design, which is such satisfying work—it feels cool to imagine myself as a real modern artist like Rauschenberg or Isamu Noguchi who brought their aesthetics to dance and theater in a way that was part of their larger body of work. With this stuff, with more of my full-on Larry Krone show performances in the works, with the House of Larréon *LOOK BOOK* coming out, and with *Together Again* opening at Pierogi in November, I feel like there are no secrets left that I'm keeping in either of my worlds. Everyone knows what I do, now!

Oh, and Andy Warhol? Yes, I relate to him.

Published September 29, 2013.
Artslant

Precarious Space: Angela Dufresne + Bradley Rubenstein

Angela Dufresne is a contemporary artist who was originally from Connecticut and Kansas City and is now based in Brooklyn. She is known for her large-scale, theatrical paintings that explore narrative in a variety of ways. Dufresne is currently on the faculty at the Rhode Island School of Design.

Bradley Rubenstein: When you did the double show (at Monya Rowe and CRG Gallery) last fall, I really got the full scope of your work. I saw it as theatrical in two ways. The first, obviously, is how you draw on pop cultural references like movies and music, but the second way is how you kind of separated the work into these large narrative paintings and then smaller, almost headshot-like ones. Like you had an onstage body of work and a backstage group. There are also all the references to a history of painting; some of your works in the CRG show were almost like a weird etiology of painting.

Angela Dufresne: Ha! Agents and administrators, actors and producers . . . That was loosely the motivation behind the zooming and the panning out in the work—from the expansive to the intimate. It comes from investigating the similarities of space and time manipulations in film and paintings, at least in my imagination. The way space can expand, emphasize, or focus can be directed—scale can become narrative. All these formalities supersede actual narrative in either film or painting. The formalities of theatrical framing can provoke empathy or detachment without context. I'm very interested in empathy; detachment is so Germanic. I want to throw empathy on the table as a possibility for painting, push aside detachment, and see where things can get messy without getting stupid or sentimental.

Reference in the works occurs via reenactment—empathetic reenactments. In this way I am an actor, letting the voices of images and ghosts pass through me. I actually think of painting as a physical medium and a metaphysical medium that can converse on multiple planes simultaneously. The framing of parlors and pastorals—those two types of archaic theatrical spaces have been the stage of painting forever. I like your term etiology to describe the way the history was treated in a lot of the works, though I was thinking more that it was humanity, and not painting itself, that was the diseased entity. Certainly painters have been party to some ridiculous ideologies throughout history, but what field of art hasn't? That insanity at times leaves the field of painting looking quite reactionary, but even in those instances the actual paintings remain as amazing vestiges of real evidence, material evidence of something dreamt, lost, delusional—or delightful, utopic, sublime. Painting is what told the story. Why do people always have to blame the paint?

BR: Let's go back a little and tell me something of your background. Usually what influences an artist is kind of boring, but with your work, it seems like influence is everything.

AD: I never think influence is boring, unless someone is bullshitting how that influence plays out in the works. I mean if the artist is making delusional claims about the work conceptually, about what it's really affecting in its audience, politically or otherwise. There is a lot of theoretical influence that promotes such works, and institutions back them. For me, as a sensualist basically, influence has always been physical awe when it comes to loving works of art—first and foremost a visceral awareness that exudes from the works and causes a heightened sense of experience. Most conceptual claims made by artists are projections in my opinion. No works would happen without conceptual motivations, but great art is experiential; this involves the intellect but doesn't privilege the intellect over the sensual. I can have a similar experience at Spiral Jetty, looking at an Amy Sillman, or watching Coppola's *The Outsiders*.

I have no allegiances; all problems in art are formal when you are connecting sensually to a thing, not abstract or narrative. I think the binaries that are built into most of the discussion around visual art are ridiculous (abstract/figurative, conceptual/expressionist, relational/ transgressive, etc.), based on theories that are provincial, classist, and, dare I say, taste-motivated. Taste is important, but not good taste. I suppose my own attitudes are just as affected anyway. I think a lot of the recent slant towards "abstraction" is based on the one-percent's affection for mid-century-mod good taste, which makes a lot of recent painting kitsch—a tasteful nostalgic rehashing of a bygone era's radicalisms. Of course Oehlen felt the same way in the late seventies, so the cycles continue.

My influences tend to be women of late who I think combine the intellect and the sensual in amazing feats of synthesis. I love Catherine Murphy practically as much as my own blood kin, like I do Joan Mitchell, Carrie Moyer, Lee Krasner, Dona Nelson, Joan Brown, and Alice Neel. I was educated on scores tallied between men in history; none of this applies to me, but these women do.

My upbringing was white-collar, middle-class, suburban, non-aesthete. Our goal was to survive, be secure. The life of the senses was delegated to consumerism and faux natural sentiments, watered-down rituals and heteronormal procreative sex. None of this really worked for me. I wanted women, dirt, uncivilized joys, delicious melancholy, absurd punk rituals . . . the list goes on. To be a sensualist is radical from my point of view, and my political life seeks to support the right to such freedoms. I don't want to survive; I want to live.

BR: All your paintings are *alla prima*—one-shot paintings. You work outside or in the studio?

AD: Both, ideally. I try to achieve both anyway. The *alla prima* is a way for the paintings to equal lived experiences, to be alive, for the process and the piece to be linked as closely as I can get them. Immediacy. They aren't always *alla prima*, but they should always feel like they are happening right in front of you, like a living thing. Non-painters can't always perceive this immediacy, but anyone should be able to sense the tenuous precariousness of the space in the paintings. The gesture in the works is a result of immediacy, not a desire for a particular expression or expressionism, and a primal economy of forms needed to articulate *alla prima*.

I, of course, live for the Giotto, Mayólica plates, Chinese ink painting, and Bill Traylor—all things that can't be revised, rewound, or reworked. I love risk, the proximity to failure. I'm thinking of John Kelly's tightrope-walk performances and wondering how such stunts could be manifested in a painting. Probably not, but I like the idea.

BR: There is an interesting quote I read recently by Barnett Newman, which I think applies in some ways to your work and way of working. He remarked on how painting a picture or constructing an image was about "a taste for the infinite," a turn of phrase that reminded me of Kubrick. But he then goes on to say, "Anyone can construct a good-English-sentence kind of picture . . . The true artist is interested in painting with a capital "P." I see this applying to your way of working, in that all of the Fassbinder references or Rococo colors and such are merely things that you use as a structure so that you can just . . . you know . . . paint.

AD: Artists all start out with the classic art impulse question: what if? Johns, Kelley . . . Baldassari too. What if I painted from Fassbinder? What if I tried to relive Watteau? What if I let other people tell me how to portray them? This is a pseudo-commission-like project of portraits I am working on now. What would happen in the work, in the process? Who will I become as a result? What will any or all of the previous knowledge I've accumulated add up to, if anything, after I've lived through this present work? I don't always know who I am, or what I will be after I make a work. That's the biggest motivation, the urgency of the work. It's what keeps me working. I don't know what will happen. These what-ifs, these concepts, are the motivation for entering paintings, and what happens there cannot be contained by the initial references or prompts. It's a big sensual mess. It's what living is all about for me.

BR: I saw a short video that you made, maybe last year. Was that a new thing, or have you done more? It seemed to relate a lot to your painting.

AD: Yeah, my videos haven't been seen so much, certainly not in gallery situations or museums, but I have been making them since the late eighties. I studied video and painting—dual-majorish—at KCAI from 1988 to 1991, with this amazing Canadian artist teacher who had just gotten out of UCSD, Wendy Geller. She was a truly interdisciplinary artist; it was a miracle to find her there. Though there were great teachers there in painting, Lester Goldman for one. I actually edited on 3/4-inch reel-to-reel, if you can believe that. My practice came out of this Midwestern TV upbringing and then this modernist Cézanne schooling, media, films. Video was my portal into contemporary life. Painting was the window to history. This allowed me to occupy both spaces—let them influence each other. In a way, both brought the West Coast work and the East Coast work to my plate as a young artist. I am always vacillating between the two, though I make more paintings than videos, I have made many videos. The latest works, I think, are actually doing something equal to the paintings. They certainly challenge the paintings, force them to take more risks, perform more. I heard Mel Bochner once talk about how drawing should be the place where unforeseen possibilities get explored, integrally—where the imagination can operate unhindered. Video works like that for me, so I think of it like drawing in a certain way. It's faster than drawing a lot of the time, so more risks can be taken more quickly. I like that.

BR: You just came back from Yaddo. What were you working on there?

AD: Well, I went there with the idea of making four works improvised around the idea/genre of landscape—spaces that were classic landscape, even epic, but connected to very banal experiences of mine own. One is a car ferry ride over Lake Champlain we had earlier this summer; it was like a Harmony Korine–J.M.W. Turner painting. I wanted to try it—I LOVE *Spring Breakers*. Everything about it is contemporary, but the imagery is all sublime—truly sublime.

Another is a moon painting. I fly fish, and I am always out late into the evening, so many times the moon comes up over the river, or the yard, or the highway, and it's just ridiculous. I wanted the center of the piece to be a big black ball, an illegible explosion, a field of active chaos, with moments of clarity all around. I love darkness as a field, as a way to paint light, but who doesn't? I think all those landscape pieces are about light first, then color and space—a particular kind of organic space. There are figures, in a very Hopperesque way, meaning there's no narrative; they are just there. I had a wonderful conversation about Hooper the other night with Dawn Clements. She was on a panel about Hopper at the Whitney. Also, I wanted to work some splatters back into the works, but with a representational function to them, so I made this painting with snow. I'm very interested in snow too, like darkness—a field to work off of. I used spatters of varies hues of white and blue to make dots receding and advancing in space, to obscure things, make actual depth, sync illusion and materiality in painting in a perverse way. I was also thinking about this amazing Spaghetti Western, *The Great Silence* by Sergio Corbucci, which I highly recommend. He uses snow so dramatically, so brilliantly, in that movie. I was doing some small portrait grabs of Klaus Kinski out of the film and realized it was the snow, the space, that made the film so powerful, like the elements in Mizoguchi. I want all this in my paintings—I'm a greedy whore!

Published October 27, 2013.
Artslant

Altered Images: Gina Magid + Bradley Rubenstein

Gina Magid is an American artist, born in 1969, who lives and works in Brooklyn. Using paint, charcoal, satin, and other mixed media, she integrates contemporary images that double as ancient and well-worn archetypes in order to create layered and psychological artworks.

Bradley Rubenstein: Growing up on Long Island and being near New York City with all of its museums and galleries, did that have a big effect on you?

Gina Magid: I didn't have a ton of access to art when I was a kid. It wasn't especially encouraged nor valued in my family or in the public schools I attended. It wasn't until I was a teenager that I began to discover it on my own.

I visited MoMA sometimes. I saw a Francis Bacon retrospective that greatly influenced me. I thought they were morbidly beautiful and violent. I remember them with candy-colored backgrounds. I also read the collection of interviews between Bacon and David Sylvester, which, early on, had a profound impact on the development of my studio practice.

As a teenager I responded to the boldness of German Expressionism and Abstract Expressionists such as Franz Kline and Egon Schiele. Early artistic influences were probably Cy Twombly, Henry Darger, Basquiat, and Schnabel. I also looked a lot at Rita Ackermann, Karen Kilimnik, Richard Prince, Mike Kelley, and Elizabeth Peyton and still do. I guess I'm absorbing and being influenced all of the time by the works that I see and love. It's reassuring to experience other artists that I feel like I can relate to, artistically speaking. Others often reference Sigmar Polke, Picabia, and even David Salle during visits to my studio—I think because my use of layered and psychologically charged imagery has something in common with these artists.

BR: I remember talking with you a while ago, after seeing some of your recent pieces, and remarking that it seemed like you'd never seen a painting before. Your work somehow has a quality that is truly innovative—not innovative in a planned sense but more like really good punk music. It has an "I don't know what's gonna happen next" feel for me. I also get that looking at Clyfford Still, for example. Here is this guy who just made it up as he went along. How do you feel about that? I know you are actually a really good printmaker. You know technique.

GM: I do know printmaking technique, but I never formally studied painting. I learned from looking at art as well as from reading what artists have to say and then figuring it out for myself. I'm a process painter, in that I don't usually plan my pieces out ahead of time. I try to be as present as possible when working and to continually respond to the painting as it develops. It's a kind of meditation.

BR: Your paintings are packed with imagery. Some of it is really loaded, I think. Things mutate from one form to another. It seems like you kind of riff off the paint as you work. Can you describe how it all comes together for you?

GM: I draw from a collection of found and created images, art historical references, colors, words, memories, and ideas. Anything, really, that moves me or that I'm thinking about will be collected, brought into the studio, and may find its way into a painting. Sometimes years later it becomes relevant or I find the right place for it within a piece. The images that I use are always meaningful for me; sometimes they work as clues or fragments of language—visual language. I'm finding that I tend to return to the same imagery over and over again. Now, after almost fifteen years of painting, I can see patterns emerging.

It's difficult for me to explain my process in the studio. When it's going well, I feel like an alchemist, working with forces I can only partially control.

BR: Is it an intuitive process for you? Or do you already have some idea in mind of where you're heading?

GM: It's an intuitive way of working. This is great when it's all gelling but hard to find when it's not. I sometimes wish I had more of a structural framework to rely on. That could also be said of my feelings toward life in general.

BR: Going back to Bacon, one of the things he said about his process that seems to relate to your process: "I hope to be able to have the first instinctive kind of basic thing and then to be able to work, almost directly, as though one were painting a new picture."

GM: Well I'm not sure what exactly he was thinking there, but I can see how it might relate to my philosophy a bit. Right . . . like I don't want to ever have a formula or understand it completely. Rather, I approach my time with a kind of beginner's mind, in order to discover something new.

BR: Looking at the paintings in your show this fall, I couldn't help but note similarities of subjects or themes that you still work with; but these things had been layered differently. In some, your subjects were kind of "floaty." In others they were piled up more archeologically. Archeology actually seems to be a really great way to approach your work—seeing images piled up over time. Is this how you see what you're doing, or is it just one way of reading the pictures?

GM: Sometimes paintings end up very minimal, and other times they become layered and rich with imagery. There's not much in between. There's a painting in the show called *Making the Bunny*, which addresses this. In it, the figure is attempting to form an unruly mass into a rabbit, but it's not going very well. For me, this is an allegory of the artist's work. The figure is trying to somehow shape all of this energy into something beautiful that she can love, but it's difficult. Kind of like Dr. Frankenstein trying to bring to life his beautiful monster!

BR: You were working on a painting last fall that I really liked of a dead skunk. The painting ended up getting a pair of swans, which really changes the tone of the piece, taking it from some kind of existentially dark and creepy place to something just weird. How intentional are these sorts of things? Or is it just that you felt like adding the swans at the expense of the original idea?

GM: The original idea of the painting is still there. I painted the dead skunk from life during a residency in Wyoming at the Ucross Foundation. I began a series of roadkill paintings because I passed them each day as I rode my bike to the studio, and their presence really affected me. Living in New York we are quite cut off from nature, so encountering wildlife—both dead and alive—was a profound visual and emotional experience for me. I watched as those animals on the road deteriorated each day. It was awful. And there were always new ones. I started thinking about how animals have no idea of what is going on as far as cars are concerned, cars being just one element of this artificial world we are creating. We live so out of sync with the rest of the life on this planet.

The pair of swans at the bottom of the canvas, I added much later. They were derived from a very different cultural reference, but the painting is still about the skunk. Now the swans can add their own mystery, magic, beauty, and maybe even some love to the piece. I don't like things to be too direct or about just one thing, because that is never how I experience life. It is much more complex and layered.

Published Spring 2001.
ArtKrush

Little Q + A: Allison Schulnik + Bradley Rubenstein

Allison Schulnik was born in 1978 in San Diego, California and now lives and works in Sky Valley, California. Schulnik uses painting, sculpture, ceramics, and hand-made, traditional animation to choreograph her subjects in compositions that embody a spirit of the macabre, a Shakespearean comedy–tragedy of love, death, and farce.

Bradley Rubenstein: I just read that you had originally been a dancer, and after watching the film *Eager* it makes perfect sense. There is a real sense of choreography in it. Can you talk a little about your beginnings as a filmmaker and painter?

Allison Schulnik: I have a lot of painters in the family, so I was painting at a young age. I think everyone expected me to be a painter, including myself, so I decided to go to film school instead. I didn't really have an interest in going to school for painting. I wanted to learn to animate.

BR: Where are you from originally?

AS: I'm from San Diego—been living in LA since I was 17. Mostly I was dancing there, and of course painting and drawing. And being a general menace. But really, dance was my first love. Painting led me to film.

BR: So painting came before film?

AS: I started in the art school at CalArts because I didn't know you could apply for film school without having made a film. They told me painting was dead, which I agreed with at the time. I spent all my time in the animation classes. I transferred the following year to the Experimental Animation program under Jules Engel and loved it. After not painting for a few years, I came back to it after school and fell back in love with it. I was painting portraits mainly for many years. Then on to other stuff. I didn't make a film for eight years after school. I worked about seven years doing grunt jobs in animation studios, and also minimum-wagers when animation jobs were scarce. I tried a little unsuccessfully to get illustration work, but basically my stuff was a little too odd to ever get any commercial work. Meanwhile I painted pretty much every free hour I had. I had no social life except with Eric, who worked even more than I did. Since then it's been a split romance, fickly switching between animation and painting kind of yearly, falling in and out of love every time.

BR: I liked your last show, *Mound*, at ZieherSmith a lot; it seems like you have really developed the painterly work, and you've included some large-scale sculptures that support the film. The painting *St. Louis Man* (2013) is quite strong, both as an image as well as a sort of philosophical meditation. I wrote about that piece, and I used this quote from Sartre talking about Giacometti's work, which I think relates to what you were doing: "[His] ambiguous images are disconcerting, for they upset our most cherished visual habits. We have long been accustomed to smooth, mute creatures fashioned for the purpose of curing us of the sickness of having a body; these guardian spirits have watched over the games of our childhood and bear witness to the notion that the world is without risks, that nothing ever happens, and that consequently, the only thing that ever happened to them was death at birth." Rereading this now, I think you could apply this piece to *Eager* as well.

AS: I think you could apply that to *Eager*. I think it's freeing, not sad, to know that there is only one resolution in life. The body is what we have, to constantly learn, love, and experience all we can, despite its deformity or limitation. It's a beautiful thing.

Mound was my first show at ZieherSmith. I was super excited about the space there. It was the first time I got to fill a wall with a film projection. It really allowed the film to fulfill itself as a true moving painting. I got to create an escape, a whole experience, when it was across from the other figures in the space.

BR: Watching the film I was immediately drawn to the physicality of it—the physicality of making it, more precisely. It reminded me of Stan Brakhage's film comprised of butterfly wings, each frame handmade. You do all the stop-motion effects yourself, as well as creating all the characters. How scripted are your movies? Is there a lot of post-editing, or is it a really organic development that you leave alone?

AS: The movies are planned out. I used to think I was more free-form with my approach, but I realized I obsess over frames—fractions of seconds. I do pretty rough storyboards but place them in a pretty exact animatic. I want shots to hit on exact musical beats, to the exact frame. The free-form, organic part is the actual animation. I set up the shot, obsessing over tiny little leaves or pieces of dirt in the corner of a frame, meanwhile knowing exactly where it will be edited into the film—where the shot starts and ends in the musical phrase—but then allow the characters to animate however best their form dictates. I animate straightforward, that is, not laid out ahead. Sometimes the animation is planned in my mind, sometimes not. And then in the end I obsess over keeping all the little dirty parts, mistakes and stuff, such as hairs, thumbprints, even a clay tool popping in for one frame by accident. Those are the things that make it special and handmade, not machine or robot. In that sense, I leave it to its own nature. I rarely shoot a scene twice. I never really edit within a shot. Sometimes I shoot extra frames, but they usually end up getting trimmed off. Mostly, whatever I do first goes in the film. There are always surprises and happy accidents. I also allow myself to change whatever I want, but usually the first thought is always the best.

BR: I went back last week to sit through the film several times to try to really pay attention to the story, but the film itself kept surprising me with really tiny pieces that I hadn't noticed before, such as the stop-motion flower sequence. As I watched, I saw how the film process is extended into the ceramic sculpture. I looked at the piece with the horse differently afterward. There is a Lynda Benglis show of ceramics up now; the horse reminds me of how Benglis mixes functionality and formalism.

AS: I could see that. I like that mix.

BR: Has working in LA given you more freedom to play with such a wide variety of forms? There is also a sense of humor to your work, however dark, that reminds me of Paul McCarthy and Mike Kelley.

AS: LA probably gives you more freedom to spread out. I guess you can have more space compared to New York, but not compared to the rest of the country. I don't think I could work on one thing all the time no matter where I lived. I always need to be switching between things. You can be a loner and yet still have community here in New York. People understand space here. You can disappear as needed. Most of my friends are in the film and music worlds, which is a big chunk of the city so that's nice. And, of course, working alongside Eric always challenges me to be better and give more to my work, as he does.

BR: So, I can't resist. What is it about cats?

AS: What is there not to like about cats! They are small, furry, warm and make weird noises when you touch them.

Published April 30, 2014.
CultureCatch

More Dark Than Shark: Wesley Kimler + Bradley Rubenstein

Wesley Kimler is a Chicago-based artist, born in 1953. Kimler, is an irascible painter and raconteur, making colossal paintings as large as 15 feet tall and 27 feet wide. He is outspoken, often attacking what he views as the neo-conceptual academy of the art world, advocating artistic independence and self-reliance in painters. This stance has earned him the nickname "The Shark" for his biting commentary.

Bradley Rubenstein: I first encountered your work in the late eighties. I remember a painting of yours called *Hunters* that was quite memorable. It had the impact of something iconic, like an Egyptian stele or a Barnett Newman piece. The work that you have done in the last several decades has continued to have that effect, in my opinion, and I have enjoyed following along on your trip through painting. Let's go back, though, for a minute and fill in some of your history. You live and work in Chicago. Where were you before then?

Wesley Kimler: Alright, well, I left home when I was fourteen years old. I grew up in the old South of Market area of San Francisco, living in derelict single-room-occupancy hotels. At one point or another, I lived in them all. Desolation Row. It was pretty wild, I guess. For a time I had a room in this raw, falling-down wreck of a hotel, The Harrison. Now, The Harrison—so named because it was located at 5th and Harrison—had survived the San Francisco 1905 earthquake, but it had sunk down—half of it had anyway—so everything was slanted on an angle. It was a big hotel, wide hallways—there was an ugliness to it. But The Harrison Hotel had one great thing: an artist in residence! Doucher The Shit Spreader. I never met him personally, but oh, did I come to know and admire his work. Doucher worked exclusively in the medium of human excrement—I assume his own excrement—and when he struck, there was a brilliance to it. So large were his moves, and all-encompassing was his art, there was simply no way to negotiate past his work without being touched by it, be it a hallway, stairwell—he could do it all! And always signed "Doucher the Shit Spreader." The manager of the place posted up warning posters: "Doucher I will find you!" Whatever. I don't think so. Whoever this Doucher was, he was clearly a master shit spreader. The artist's last piece I happened to witness was a hallway installation—the passage leading to the manager's apartment—painted loosely with a thin crap glaze, culminating in a heavily impastoed shit door . . . simply stunning. Unfortunately, I moved shortly after that and never knew whether he went on, got caught, changed mediums . . . I guess I'm lucky the story ends for me on such a high note.

I didn't go to high school—I was a street kid, in other words—but what I made myself do was take music lessons during that time as I was growing up. I studied baroque flute with the idea that I could [laughs] be a classical musician. As I grew a little older, in my late teens and early twenties, I was hanging around with a lot of pretty well-known jazz musicians—some really great jazz musicians, like Joe Henderson and Woody Shaw (the great hard bop trumpet player who was a mainstay with Art Blakey for many years) and the whole crowd of the Both And Jazz Club at Divisadero Street in San Francisco, which is where I grew up. I saw how hard their lives were, so i decided to become a painter. It looked more comfortable. It seemed like it wasn't as harsh as making art in a nightclub, with all the heroin and broken lives and so forth. Of course, it's no different, but I thought it would be.

So I switched to painting and worked on my own for a couple years. When I was 20, I ended my childhood to work for an importer in Afghanistan for a couple of years. I was buying tribal carpets and *kilims* and Turkoman silver and the like—also lapis and some turquoise from Iran. When I returned from overseas, I decided I was going to paint seriously. I did it for a little while and then moved down to Austin, Texas, where I did my first year of formal study at a little art school at the Laguna Gloria Museum. I painted still lifes, seascapes, and portraiture with a woman who had gone to Pratt. She had a private art school on the side, but she taught at Laguna Gloria for all her little old lady friends, and me. I learned the basics of oil painting from her.

My next stop in art education was at the Minneapolis College of Art and Design. The students and teachers there wanted to know where I learned to paint the way I painted. I explained that it was with the little old ladies, painting their nieces and nephews and grandkids. These little old ladies, unlike your typical art school kid, know how to do something; they were there to accomplish something that took actual skill.

So for two years I did well there and was an influential student, I think. But after two years, I felt like I was done. So I moved out to the West Coast and started practicing—started painting. It's the same throughout history: what good painter hasn't been self-taught? You study, you learn, but with painting, unlike being a musician, for example, there's a self-taught element. That's what makes the induced painters individual; you get a certain amount of knowledge and understanding, and then you go and do something with it that's your own—particularly from the twentieth century on.

So I would say that, really, I did three years of formal training. I didn't get a degree, but my education came in fits and starts; I'm still involved in "the art education of Wesley Kimler," learning how to become a better painter. I'm learning as much about it today as I was learning twenty years ago.

As I developed through the years, I spent a lot of time looking at the people I like—painters who have been cast under the label of Abstract Expressionism. De Kooning was a huge influence, although I really like Joan Mitchell and some of the West Coast painters from that era, like David Park, Joan Brown, and Elmer Bischoff to a lesser extent. Also Richard Diebenkorn, of course.

I looked at all of that, but I also really liked the London school of painters: Kossoff, first and foremost, not Auerbach. Also Lucian Freud and Francis Bacon, but Bacon really is kinda like a poor man's de Kooning. He tried to illustrate what de Kooning was able to *demonstrate* with gesture and plastic invention. I'm more interested in de Kooning's level of virtuosity than the designed terror and horror of Francis Bacon.

Meanwhile, after leaving art school, I went back to San Francisco, and I lived and worked in a warehouse. I did not try to show, unlike today, where people try to show while they're still students. Back then you got to be in a museum show when you'd really earned the right to be there; it wasn't used as a promotional device like it is today. So during this time, I *practiced* for five years. I thought I had to kinda get good first, and I still feel that way. A lot of people seem to think I'm an egomaniacal type, but I doubt it. I think I'm pretty humble in the sense of who I am and how critical I am about my own work. I'm just always trying to improve. I'm seeking improvement, not perfection, as a painter. It's an ongoing journey, it's a game, and as Matt Beckman said "it's a very good game."

BR: One thing has remained a constant for you—the paint. It seems inherent to your work, which, on many levels deals with power and a certain approach to masculinity. I'm reminded of a scene in the movie *Fight Club* where the Ed Norton character is talking to the Brad Pitt character in the subway. They are looking at a cologne ad, and Pitt says that it is just surface, an advertisement for something that doesn't exist, and that the Ed Norton character represents the brutality of masculinity buried underneath the surface. Your works, despite being images, pictures, seem to try to go below the appearance of things. You're getting in the ring, so to speak, art historically, when you paint. How far off am I here?

WK: Well, you're not far off at all. The thing for me is the black-and-white drawings. With the chiaroscuro and the starkness of black and white, I'm able to get the psychological resonance that I want. Going back into my life a little bit, where the black-and-white drawings come from . . . I worked for a while as a messenger. This was, of course, in San Francisco. I rode a 1-speed, heavy bike with a basket on the front. It was grueling work at $50 a week—awful. I would go in and deliver things between these printing houses, and at the time there was a lot of chiaroscuro, black-and-white kind of work in advertising, so I saw that often. I always thought, "If only I could work in one of these places, I would be so happy." To survive psychologically in my life—which was pretty hard at the time, living in a $6-a-week hotel room and doing this messenger job all day long—I started to see everything in the world in black and white, without color. I spent weeks refusing to see color. I retreated into my imagination, never to return. Let's face it, it's more challenging to work with color; what comes so easily with black and white is not so easy when chroma enters the picture.

BR: There is a great story about de Kooning running into Pollock after his "black and white" show where he said something like, "Great show, but could you do that in color?"

WK: Beauty and color must resonate psychologically to work. It's how painting has been, what it is—Géricault, Delacroix, and so on. The color had an emotional sensibility and resonated psychological drama. But after, say, the Fauves, a lot of that sensibility got lost in the formalism of the twentieth century, in the deconstruction, but a lot was gained, also. That color in a painting should have drama wasn't the issue. The issue was whether it should be psychological or formal. The Fauves questioned that hierarchy, that sensibility, and a lot of Modernism continued in that direction-free painting from depiction, unhinged. De Kooning is an excellent example of the cognitive dissonance I'm referring to.

So where we are at now is the emotive quality of contemporary painting, of abstraction, becoming random—a mere formality at this point. I disagree. I always freight the color up in my paintings to a certain psychological state, which can make them more difficult to paint. It's a conflation of making a painting and painting a picture. If a painting has beautiful color and looks great but doesn't feel right, it's got to go back under the knife. So no, you're not far off. They are completely psychological, they are emotional, they are emotionally specific, and they are also dumb, physical, inimitable objects. They are survivors that have endured my torture chamber of a process—ha!—existing in some kind of conflicted gestalt—complicated, a concrete thinglyness, carrying enough existential traction to well up and dwell convincingly in reality. All my paintings are rafts of the Medusa! We cannot return: I think it was Joe Goode who once said, "I respect my heroes too much to imitate them." You see a lot of, like, eighth-generation Ab-Ex out there at the moment—it's very popular—and the problem, for me at least, is it is only that, without claiming any new territory. It doesn't seem terribly ambitious. Though it does seem to sell well in the whole art-as-investment scenario.

BR: The most recent paintings I have seen still have the figure as the starting point—a kind of cipher figure in a military uniform. It is obviously a reference for the battle that takes place with the paint, but do these pictures have any political reference?

WK: Yes, obliquely they do. If you look at the paintings, figuration happens in a lot of different ways in the work: some of the figures are anonymous, shadowy, people taken from those I know, know of, or have imagined; some of them are really abstract, paint people that kind of come out of the gesture of the paint; and others are quasi-realist, pretty tight. I can paint in a lot of different ways, and I do that when I make my work. It's an argument that engages me and ultimately defines what I do. When it comes to painting, I am non-ideological; I'll try anything. I'm not interested in arriving at some formal conclusion as a visual artist, as I am not wanting to confuse originality with eccentricity. I believe in working in the grand manner—in letting who I am find me.

Often the figures in my paintings are very specific people. This is the case when you see an almost photographic image. In recent works, they are from the Pacific campaign in World War II. I thought the Pacific Theater was kind of our *Iliad*. I painted pictures of war because I wanted to make works with some weight. I also wanted to make paintings that said they were about war and *were* about war. These aren't paintings like Luc Tuymans's concentration camp, where he painted an anonymous basement and then decided to call it *Concentration Camp*—"Oh, well *now* it's about WWII." My paintings don't require a title; they make no specious claims. They are not abstracted illustration of spoken language. There are specific references, geographical references: the hills and the blobs are usually taken from the island of Peleliu. There are specific people, specific battles. I don't have to name this or that for you to know what it's about. I want to cut the art talk and make paintings about war, so hopefully these paintings speak for themselves.

Additionally, I wanted the paintings to be reactionary, in the sense of me reacting against corporate and auction houses, painted to be "flipped" abstraction, against the toweringly vapid stupidity that you see taking place out there with the university art-department-driven, de-skilled painting crew. Of course they're also metaphorical in that they're about me, my struggle, and how I approach painting in a very war-like fashion. So yes to all that.

But probably the next time I paint, I might make some paintings about Afghanistan, which would make them more explicitly contemporary. The contemporary aspect to that narrative is how low we've sunk at this point. During WWII, and right after that in the 1950s, American painting and culture really hit a high watermark. Artists and critics set the agenda! Not some hedge-fund clown, dumb as the day is long, with a wad of stupid money, buying to flip in a manipulated market.

Let's talk more about painting—where I think painting is at, at least in my studio . . . When you look at contemporary architecture, when you look at contemporary literature, when you look at contemporary design, you really see their practitioners taking High Modernism—the quest for essential form through science and technology that was prevalent in the twentieth century—and running with it. I mean look at Gehry, or look at someone like Jeanne Gang, or any number of people. The real deconstruction happened after color's role was contested in the early- and mid-twentieth century with analytical, synthetic Cubism—and then there was Abstract Expressionism. There you have the deconstruction and the recapitulation of what painting could mean. But in a way, that language was laid out there, and to my thinking, never spoken.

As the advent of Pop Art came along with popular culture, art became very popular, institutionalized, and fundamentally changed to adhere to the academic footprint—a "taught career," an "art beginning," with Marcel Duchamp installed as the institutional role model. What "art practice" should be recently morphed into "social practice," all supplanting studio practice. We now have more of a desk-job, project-managerial model being pushed: "Critical Theory Concerning Social Injustice." Is there anything about this that wouldn't have Joe Stalin peeing his pants in delight? Welcome to the aesthetic gulag. It's so venal it's actually hilarious to watch. The only thing worse is when these same idiots decide they are going to tell us what "matters" in contemporary painting. The *Painter Painter* exhibition at The Walker last year, for instance—I quote Matthew Collings: "Fascinating spectacle of naive narcissists staging hostile assaults on something they clearly don't have the faintest clue about, but in relation to which they have been granted positions of great authority."

So to me, my painting is not unlike looking at a piece of contemporary design or contemporary architecture: taking the language of High Modernism, taking all that was laid out, and then taking that language, those numbers, letters, symbols, and signifiers, and firing them up. Making a living, humanist painting that employs those conceits to bring painting into today as "the enemy of the people," there to shatter their preconceptions as to who they are and what painting is. I don't see the canvas as an arena—it's more like a war zone where a lot of stuff goes down, both good and bad. It can get kind of intense at times. One person, a brush, and some canvas. It is what it is—simple, fierce, and hard to do well.

I guess my way of thinking, it's pretty old school, but considering what's out there right now, it's also oddly enough kinda radical. I'm not alone. There is some serious painting and thinking about painting being accomplished by some fairly radical inimitable individuals—in spite of and in the midst of, the institutionally driven middlebrow dystopia we inhabit. I paint in a way that feels important to me. My ideation is self-generated; my paintings are arguments both internal and external, having to do with painting, with life. The biggest disagreements I have are with myself; it's the crux of how I am creative. I'm a visual artist working in a time of visual illiteracy, looking at the best, most challenging stuff, trying to extend it in my own work on my own terms, with intellect, intuition, and the reality of my hands pushing oil paint around on a canvas. Really coming to understand how color can work, what the language of sheer plastic invention can look like and mean, or not mean. Camped out in front of one messy painting after another as a way of life, living like a savage, working in a language beyond words. As Wittgenstein once said, what we cannot speak of we must pass over in silence. That, then, is painting, at least around here it is.

Published June 8, 2014.
ArtSlant

Game Symmetry: Liz Markus + Bradley Rubenstein

The Proust Questionnaire has its origins in a parlor game popularized by Marcel Proust, the French essayist and novelist, who believed that, in answering these questions, an individual reveals his or her true nature. Below, Liz Markus and Bradley Rubenstein reinterpret Mr. Proust's concept.

Liz Markus was born in 1967 in Buffalo, New York and currently lives and works in Los Angeles. She is known for her idiosyncratic paintings that combine colorful expressionism with pop imagery. Her signature technique is saturated washes of acrylic paint on unprimed canvas. Vibrant colors diffuse and bleed into one another, creating wet-on-wet compositions that evoke '60s psychedelia as well as the "high art" of mid-century Color Field painting.

What is your idea of perfect happiness?

Being in Saint Barths with my fiancé.

What is your greatest extravagance?

Being an artist.

What is your current state of mind?

Somewhat irritated. I'm in an airport.

What is the trait you most deplore in yourself?

My tendency to crumble in the face of people I perceive as authority figures.

What is the trait you most deplore in others?

The inability to stop wallowing in their misery.

What do you consider the most overrated virtue?

The willingness to wait in line for brunch.

What is your favorite occupation?

Shopping with my fiancé.

What is your most marked characteristic?

A tendency towards worry.

What do you most value in your friends?

Being chill and understanding.

When and where were you happiest?

A beach in Malibu this March when my man told me he'd like to spend the rest of his life with me.

What do you dislike most about your appearance?

My lack of a vintage Gucci bag on my arm.

Which living person do you most despise?

Whoever popularized brunch in New York.

On what occasion do you lie?

On being introduced to someone. I pretend to be cheerful.

Which talent would you most like to have?

The ability to be born into money.

If you could change one thing about yourself, what would it be?

I'd dial down the crazy.

If you could change one thing about your family, what would it be?

I would change the fact that there's no East Hampton mansion that's been in the family forever.

What is your most treasured possession?

A certain ring I wear.

What do you regard as the lowest depth of misery?

Extreme loneliness.

Who are your favorite writers?

J.R.R. Tolkien, J.K. Rowling—I'm boring myself now.

Who is your favorite hero of fiction?

Captain America.

Who are your heroes in real life?

The people who saw that I needed it and helped me.

What are your favorite names?

Bill, Bob.

What is it that you most dislike?

Crowds.

What do you consider your greatest achievement?

I've produced an awesome body of work in my lifetime (if I do say so myself).

If you were to die and come back as a person or thing, what do you think it would be?

A double rainbow.

If you could choose what to come back as, what would it be?

I think the question is, "What does it mean?"

Where would you like to live?

A quiet place with trees AND high-end shopping.

How would you like to die?

Such a depressing question.

What is your greatest regret?

That I forwent sleep and sex this morning so that I could get to the airport in time, only to find out my flight was delayed.

What is your motto?

"Why the fuck not?"

Published June 25, 2014.
CultureCatch

The Man Who Sold the World: Millree Hughes + Bradley Rubenstein

Millree Hughes is a digital artist, born 1960 in Hawarden, North Wales, the son of an Anglican priest, and now lives and works in New York. He began making art on the computer in 1998 in New York City. He created the imaginary glam band Lummox, which he described as the pure embodiment of working-class pop culture circa 1972 in Rhyl, Wales. Following that, he starred in *Lummox: the Movie* (2014), a documentary about his band. Hughes is also known for his lenticulars, which are animated images that move in relation to the viewer.

Bradley Rubenstein: Let's start by talking a little bit about *Lummox* (2010) before we get into the new work. I thought it was hilarious, and at the same time there was a serious aspect regarding cultural mediation that a lot of your work touches on. It also came out before James Franco's Cindy Sherman show at Pace (*New Film Stills*, 2014), and all the Marina Abramović performances with Jay-Z and whatnot, so it really caught something about our cultural moment.

Millree Hughes: Thank you. I like that you put our documentary in the context of Abramović and Franco—making the artist a persona in the work in a way that comments on it.

This idea of an artist persona runs counter to the authenticity that seems to be expected of American artists. Contemporary painting is full of this loyalty to painting as an act of conviction—as being true. What horrified Pollock in the movie that Hans Namuth took of him was that it made his practice appear fake. I can embrace looking fake—well, actually, it's more that I'm okay with giving the impression that I don't really know what I'm doing. That's interesting to me. It's funny because there's a side to creating where the art becomes autonomous and doubles back on you, making you look like an idiot. Artists are very afraid of that—not being in control.

I was influenced by this great short documentary by the BBC about the making of an Anya Gallacio sculpture. She'd been given a little grant, and she used the money to make this pillar of soap on the beach at Brighton. You see her preparing and going down to the coast on the train to put the piece up. Her assistants are building what looks a bit like a soap chimney as the tide starts to come in. She's looking on thoughtfully when two men in suits step into frame. They say, "We represent the people of Brighton and Hove, and we believe you've been given £500 of tax payers' money to make this abomination! What do you have to say for yourself?" She replies that she herself is disappointed with the piece. She was hoping it would be more frothy at the bottom. The conversation is hilarious; she agrees with them that it's not a good piece, but her reasons are formal. Eventually the councilors walk away frustrated, leaving Anya staring at the piece as it topples over into the waves. I don't think she intends it to be funny. She's just responding to events. But for me it becomes a whole new artwork—much closer to what I experience as an artist. Intending something, unsure of the results. Far from the conviction, say, of Matthew Barney's opus or the Richter documentary. Perhaps that's what I understand by your term cultural mediation. The documentary made me think that I could set up the kind of situation Gallacio finds herself in, to talk about issues of theatricality and authenticity in art.

Lummox was directed by Peter Boyd McLean, and we worked together very closely to walk the line between truth and fiction. It's about the preparations for a glam rock performance I put on as part of *Art Basel Miami Beach 2005*. The director and I appear to butt heads throughout.

I'm me, playing me, but there's also this sense that Peter's trying to become me. It's a great example of Lacan's "Destructive Envy." The subject wants to replace the object of desire and in the process destroy the original. On top of that, I'm also this *Lummox* character. It's why I wanted him to be a glam rocker because in glam the artist can take on multiple personas. In *Ziggy Stardust*, Bowie is himself first, but he's also Ziggy and the character singing the song. He's even David Jones, the civilian, who became Bowie. It's hard to tell what's real in the movie; I don't seem that pleased with the end result of the performance but that's not the point. I'm not convinced by conclusive answers.

BR: You've worked in movies and videos doing scenery, and you've also been in one of Michael Lee Nirenberg's films. You cross over a lot in an interesting way with different media. Going back a little, can you talk about where you started? Were you always interested in this fluidity of mediums?

MH: I love being in Mike's movies. Slapstick, horror . . . he's a camp master!

The things I do in other media are always about the issues I have with the convention of painting and its relationship to technology. In *Lummox*, I was trying to put a figure into my digital landscape pieces. An earlier piece, *Landscape in the Figure* from 2002, is another way of looking at the same problem. I grew up in North Wales in a holiday resort called Towyn. It was kitschy, filled with caravan sites but surrounded by this daunting romantic landscape. My obsession with the conflict between nature and technology began in 1968 when the government in London sanctioned the flooding of a valley near Bala to provide electricity for cities in England. It was a real insult. The landscape is so much loved by the Welsh.

In the eighties I lived in a squat and played in a band—a post-punk band called Wow Federation and later a kind of hard-rock/theater-rock band called The Circle of Shit. Both bands were theatrical and satirical, but eventually I became frustrated. I can't really play like I can draw. In 1990 I focused on painting, although I've been creating the pieces on the computer since '98.

A lot of what I want to say in "painting" comes from gestural abstraction. You know . . . I draw with a pen on a tablet and flip it around, zoom it, stretch it, work it. Computer-made painting is very nonphysical, so a lot of the expression in the gesture has to be faked to a certain extent (www.millree.tumblr.com). I can also make the image more organic by using randomization filters. That's what's happening in my Blue-Chip Mash-Ups. They are giclée prints that combine the work of two different artists whose pieces sold for more than $1 million. I use "Displace" and "Match Color" filters in Photoshop, but without any other manipulations.

I do draw a lot though, with a Sharpie on paper. I really need to keep my hand directly involved with the image, probably because I know it's going to end up on a screen eventually.

BR: It's that crossover that lies at the heart of all of your work that I find interesting. There are a lot of artists, like Hockney, for example, who have made that transition from actual to virtual painting, who don't seem as compelling to me. It's more a cosmetic thing, rather than developing a new vocabulary in painting to work with.

The interest in interrogating the genuine through the artificial, both in *Lummox* and in your digital painting, relates a lot to what you're doing now, but we will get to that in a minute. It strikes me that much of what you do is like a visual form of Restoration comedy; you work in really high-profile art forms, yet you both satirize as well as deeply understand the things you're sending up. Is that a close reading?

MH: The satire isn't so much a critical take-down of art world shibboleths. It's more about allowing the worst possible thing that could happen to you, happen, albeit in a pantomimic way. Avant-garde theater playwright Young Jean Lee says in an interview that her starting point for writing a play was to think of the worst thing she could think of and do that. So having made *Lummox*, where I play an artist who really doesn't seem to know what he is doing. I would really like to make a follow-up movie about another "worst thing" an artist can do. Asking the critics to decide exactly what your art should look like. You're right to think of Restoration Comedy, although my favorite caustic playwright comes along a little later. It would be a remake of Sheridan's *The Critic*.

I've been working as a scenic artist on TV and movies since the eighties. Also, I'm the son of an Anglican priest, and I think there's a relationship there. In church, as with TV, I was given a privileged look at the behind-the-scenes of a highly theatrical presentation. It has probably reinforced my psychological distrust of pat constructs of meaning.

Mostly, though, I'm interested in promoting fearlessness. In the sense that artists shouldn't be afraid to make complete prats of themselves. I think the younger generation of New York artists are playing it very safe. The great shows I've seen recently are mostly made by older artists like Walter Robinson, Dona Nelson, and Judy Linhares. I've heard Young Jean Lee speak about producing alternative theater, and she says that she's not afraid to make what she wants because she sees no possibility of it making her rich. I think the hyper-inflated art market is playing havoc with the art. This is the reason I made the Blue-Chip Mash-Ups. Perhaps it's possible to remix reified artworks and make them meaningful again.

BR: This is all totally brought together in the new work . . .

MH: When I started the Mash-Ups in 2010, my idea was to pick the top ten sellers at auction of the early 2000s and mix the work together, two at a time. We used to have a gloriously horrible best-of-the-year round-up record in Britain in the late eighties called *Stars on 45*. All the Number 1s of the year would be mixed together to a click track. I wanted the sensation of having the beat on one turntable and the hook on the other. I don't draw on or collage onto the art; I displace the contours of one image relative to another and mix the colors, like pushing faders on a deck.

I soon realized that some things mix better than others. For example much Chinese art of the 2000s retains its qualities no matter how much you mangle the image, but it's so clunky and illustrative. On the other hand, I would lose all sense of a Rudolph Stingel in one pass. So I changed the rules and just took jpegs from anything I fancied on the Artnet site that had made over a million at auction in the last ten years. I began to lose interest in the integrity of the original and whether I liked that artist or not. I let the distortion take over.

BR: One last thing, and I think it kind of relates to what you said about Bowie and Ziggy earlier . . . I think that Bowie was definitely influenced by Burroughs cut-up technique of writing, and I think he ended up inventing a cut-up method of performance. Now I listen to something like "Voodoo Problems," a Jimi Hendrix/Jay-Z mash-up, and I am listening to a new song—a new song first, then pick it apart for where it comes from. You have pulled off that trick with the Blue-Chip Mash-Ups. I look at them as an image first, a new image. Where do you see yourself taking this? What are you thinking about for your next act?

MH: I like your phrase "cut-up as a method of performance." Mash-Ups and Cut-Ups break the normative flow. It makes you aware of art's tiniest parts again—and how they fit together.

I became fixated with this in the Mash-Ups. One image is used to displace the tonal highs and lows of another image. The more you displace the values into more complex parts, the closer everything gets to a granular synthesis. Almost an organic texture. A couple of the pieces I just passed repeatedly through Displace until the image disappeared, turning into a thick fractally moss. This is what stops me from fully accepting that technology is swallowing nature. The fanciful notion that somewhere at the heart of mathematics the grass is growing! Or at the very least, some kind of mold.

Texture on a recorded image connotes distortion—some kind of inability to correctly record (an ability that is not finite) an event. Online I find myself looking long at a still from a sixties performance at Judson Church or The Fall in concert in '76. The kind of camera, the film stock, and how that image has aged, all contribute to the feel. I particularly like old flyers for concerts. I've become hypnotized by images past. Nothing current has the necessary grit.

I've been wondering for some time why, even when a creative act is not reliant on corporate funding, artists and performers use already-tried approaches. Why new bands are not trying to make a new musical language or style. Perhaps the past is much more desirable than the future. Even though the seventies was filled with anxiety and economic difficulty, it looks so innocent next to our times. I can't imagine things are going to get better for us ecologically or economically. I think this fear has created a massive creative sinkhole under American culture— the feeling that with progress comes a horrible erosion and that nostalgia is integrative. But artists are supposed to try things and not follow old routes. We need to make new surfaces.

Published September 12, 2014.
CultureCatch

Game Symmetry: Franklin Evans + Bradley Rubenstein

The Proust Questionnaire has its origins in a parlor game popularized by Marcel Proust, the French essayist and novelist, who believed that, in answering these questions, an individual reveals his or her true nature. Below, Franklin Evans and Bradley Rubenstein reinterpret Mr. Proust's concept.

Franklin Evans was born in Reno, Nevada and lives and works in New York. He creates painting installations with the artist's studio as his subject. Evans is currently an instructor at Cooper Union in New York.

What is your greatest extravagance?

Around 10 AM Day 1 – Bandols before 5 and 247 paint brushes

After 5 PM Day 1 – studio A/C

AFAP – digitally printed gingham wallpaper throughout the loft

What is your current state of mind?

After 5 PM Day 1 – a surprising mental tilt

Around 10 AM Day 2 – an under-caffeinated yearning for focus

AFAP – a fixation on the myriad interplays between memory and perception

What is the trait you most deplore in yourself?

Around 10 AM Day 1 – apologetic micromanaging

After 5 PM Day 1 – my uncontrollable penchant to over-explain

AFAP – flagrant appropriation

What is the trait you most deplore in others?

After 5 PM Day 1 – a lack of curiosity

Around 10 AM Day 2 – an absence of drive

AFAP – flagrant appropriation

What do you consider the most overrated virtue?

Around 10 AM Day 1 – honestly, honesty

After 5 PM Day 1 – virtues may be overrated

AFAP – auratic juxtapositions of artwork and knock-offs

What is your favorite occupation?

After 5 PM Day 1 – making stuff, painting, exploring materially and thinking

Around 10 AM Day 2 – eating

AFAP – assistant editor of *Artforum*

What is your most marked characteristic?

Around 10 AM Day 1 – lately my eternal innocence

After 5 PM Day 1 – unfortunately my resting scowl; popularly, my RBF

AFAP – campy abjection

What do you most value in your friends?

After 5 PM Day 1 – open ears and wallets

Around 10 AM Day 2 – passion, intellect, and determination

AFAP – handmade reproductions of their family heirlooms

When and where were you happiest?

Around 10 AM Day 1 – now, today

After 5 PM Day 1 – in the interminable life loop

AFAP – Inside the White Cube in London

What do you dislike most about your appearance?

After 5 PM Day 1 – gravity's apparent power

Around 10 AM Day 2 – its general asymmetry

AFAP – my resemblance to people's art, all metastasizing into a preternaturally photogenic fever-dream cosmology

Which living person do you most despise?

Around 10 AM Day 1 – Putin and all homophobes, misogynists, racists

After 5 PM Day 1 – impossible to select just one

AFAP – an unnamed transactional choreographer, intimately dipping and reaching among bodies

On what occasion do you lie?

After 5 PM Day 1 – visits home

Around 10 AM Day 2 – whenever necessary, although usually not as well as I should

AFAP – when the distinctions between the actual and the constructed are surreptitious and *trompe l'oeil* pranks abound

What or who is the greatest love of your life?

Around 10 AM Day 1 – easy one: my life love PDY and art

After 5 PM Day 1 – PDY and art

AFAP – Schwitters's *Merzbau*

Which talent would you most like to have?

After 5 PM Day 1 – a photographic memory

Around 10 AM Day 2 – fluency in all major languages

AFAP – iconic thievery

If you could change one thing about yourself, what would it be?

Around 10 AM Day 1 – an ability to occasionally rest my overdrive

After 5 PM Day 1 – my limited vocal range

AFAP – my messy sentimental endgame investigations

If you could change one thing about your family, what would it be?

After 5 PM Day 1 – nothing, THEY ARE PERFECT!!!! Thanksgiving is a f#!&ing dream!

Around 10 AM Day 2 – the non-liberal leanings of some family members

AFAP – its formation through coveted commodities

What is your most treasured possession?

Around 10 AM Day 1 – my studio

After 5 PM Day 1 – my studio!

AFAP – my handcrafted wicker baskets collection

What do you regard as the lowest depth of misery?

After 5 PM Day 1 – meaningless competition surrounding the peddling of paintings

Around 10 AM Day 2 – how can my idea of misery compare with the experiences shared daily on NPR?

AFAP – secret cavities built into gallery ground-level spaces

Who are your favorite writers?

Around 10 AM Day 1 – Faulkner, Borges, Proust, Tolstoy, Rushdie, Richard Yates, among others

After 5 PM Day 1 – Faulkner, Richard Yates, DeLillo, Borges,

AFAP – cunning substitutes

Who is your favorite hero of fiction?

After 5 PM Day 1 – a conflation of Lady Macbeth and King Richard III

Around 10 AM Day 2 – Hero's Leander

AFAP – the haptic mnemonic

Who are your heroes in real life?

Around 10 AM Day 1 – Matisse, possibly

After 5 PM Day 1 – in descending order Matisse, Duchamp, Rauschenberg, Warhol

AFAP – Classic pickpockets

What are your favorite names?

After 5 PM Day 1 – Nina and Simone are both lovely

Around 10 AM Day 2 – Tino, Marina, Rirkrit, and Colette

AFAP – John, Carpenter, Leonard, and Cohen

What is it that you most dislike?

Around 10 AM Day 1 – the wealth gap

After 5 PM Day 1 – waking and not waking

AFAP – the tendency to revel in *trouvailles*

What do you consider your greatest achievement?

After 5 PM Day 1 – adapting to life in New York

Around 10 AM Day 2 – sustaining a daily studio practice

AFAP – my skillful toggling between materiality and immateriality

If you were to die and come back as a person or thing, what do you think it would be?

Around 10 AM Day 1 – a sprig of chervil

After 5 PM Day 1 – an eagle, hawk, or cardinal

AFAP – an under-ripe tomato

If you could choose what to come back as, what would it be?

After 5 PM Day 1 – a Duchamp-like force

Around 10 AM Day 2 – perhaps a Picasso model or a Richard Prince appropriation

AFAP – an overripe orange

Where would you like to live?

Around 10 AM Day 1 – very near The Metropolitan Museum

After 5 PM Day 1 – Gore Vidal's villa on the Amalfi Coast

AFAP – Luxembourg

How would you like to die?

After 5 PM Day 1 – slowly enough to read my own obituary

Around 10 AM Day 2 – with permanent youth

AFAP – "In a Rocking Chair"

What is your greatest regret?

Around 10 AM Day 1 – too many missed sexual and intellectual opportunities when young

After 5 PM Day 1 – not escaping Reno, Nevada earlier

AFAP – My fixation on the myriad interplays between desire and presence, memory and perception, and, more broadly, the virtual and the real

What is your motto?

After 5 PM Day 1 – hmmmmmm

Around 10 AM Day 2 – process about process

RSAP – paint up a storm

Footnotes:

Note 1: I answered every even-numbered question first around 10 AM Day 1 and again after 5 PM Day 1. I answered every odd-numbered question first after 5 PM Day 1 and again around 10 AM Day 2.

Note 2: Between Day 1 and Day 2 I read a summer 2015 *Artforum* discussion by Annie Godfrey Larmon (assistant editor of *Artforum*) of artist Alex Da Corte and appropriated language from Ms. Larmon's piece to give a third answer to each question (excluding the last question). I use the AFAP to mark these appropriations.

Note 3: For the last question I appropriated text from Roberta Smith's review of the Albert Oehlen exhibition at New Museum (*New York Times*, June 11, 2015). I use the term RSAP to mark this appropriation.

Published September 5, 2015.
CultureCatch

Shrine for Girls: Patricia Cronin + Bradley Rubenstein

Patricia Cronin was born in 1963 in Beverly, Massachusetts and currently lives and works in New York City. Her critically acclaimed statue *Memorial To A Marriage* is a 3-ton Carrara marble mortuary sculpture of her life partner and herself. It was made before gay marriage was legal in the U.S. and has been exhibited widely in the U.S. and abroad.

Bradley Rubenstein: We were supposed to have had this conversation years ago. I was looking at some notes from around 1999 or early 2000 from a studio visit with you when you had just starting making little models for your large-scale *Memorial To A Marriage* (2002). I suppose a lot has happened in the meantime, personally, culturally, and whatnot, so let's frame our talk around that piece, the work I saw last year at Ford Projects, the Dante paintings, and your most recent *Shrine For Girls*, Venice.

Patricia Cronin: I have a long history of making work that addresses contemporary social justice issues focused on gender, from lesbian visibility to feminist art history to marriage equality. So, yes, I'm always interested in making an impact both aesthetically and politically. My aesthetic strategy is to breathe new life into traditional art images and forms in time-honored materials, and to inject specific contemporary political content that compels me.

I usually subvert Polaroids, watercolor, oil paint, bronze, or marble, and sometimes I write books, but my creative process also includes ready-mades like the girls' clothing I gathered here in Venice. In May 2014 when Italian curator Ludovico Pratesi first invited me to do a show in Venice, I was working on a project about the crisis in masculinity. The constant barrage of horrific news stories about violence against women and the systemic oppression of girls around the world overwhelmed me—from the gang rapes in India to Boko Haram kidnapping the Chibok, Nigeria schoolgirls to the Magdalene Asylums in Stephen Frears's film *Philomena*. I was grappling with comprehending the magnitude of these devastating crises and felt helpless. I decided to do what artists do best—keenly observe the world around them and comment on it, much like Goya's *Disasters of War* (1810–20), Käthe Kollwitz's anti-war works (1902–35), or Picasso's *Guernica* (1937). After I visited the Church of San Gallo a month later in Venice, the subject started to shift to addressing the women and girls. I wanted to translate the horrific statistics into something concrete and emotional. By creating an installation with the remnants of what the missing bodies would have inhabited, the physicality and the materiality of the fabric reminds us of who is missing and publicly acknowledges their suffering.

BR: Looking back at the sculpture, which you and Deb are actually using as a cenotaph, I was really struck by the pathos of it—now remember this was pre-9/11 New York—in the face of an overwhelming trend toward, for lack of a better word, the pathos of pretty much everything else that was being made at that time.

PC: Actually I lived five blocks from the World Trade Center in Tribeca, so that day had a profound effect on me. Then my father died suddenly six months later. I remember working on the 53" clay maquette of *Memorial to a Marriage* in my Williamsburg studio, watching the daily firefighters' funerals with tears streaming down my cheeks. I think all the sorrow I was feeling is in that piece.

I only make art that I need to have exist in the world. Half of the stuff I make, I look around first hoping someone else will tackle it, and when no one does, it's like, okay, I'll do it. I addressed lesbian sexuality before it was chic with my *Erotic Watercolors* (1992–96), gay marriage before it was legal in *Memorial To A Marriage* (2000–02), feminist art history when it was presumed passé with *Harriet Hosmer: Lost and Found, A Catalogue Raisonné* (2009), and now the global plight of exploited girls in *Shrine For Girls* (2015). So that's why my work is usually not at the center of what is trendy. My subjects are urgent—feminist, social justice, and human rights issues. Because, unfortunately, the art world is still such a deeply conservative place, these topics aren't a priority in what has become solely an art market. I'm interested in art history, not market history.

BR: I like that. Looking at the *Erotic Watercolors* . . . after seeing your studies for the Memorial, I saw them not as ironic, as I had originally seen them, but as sincere. I know that now that seems like it isn't a huge revelation, but considering the context then . . .

PC: I was trying to reclaim my subjectivity from a male heterosexual gaze. These watercolors were objective, factually rendered from the Polaroids, and ultimately they continue to read as cool-fully sincere. Irony was never my game. In fact, I think irony is the new kitsch. I can respect it, but it's not where my heart is.

BR: More and more I've noticed, and often commented on, the banality of "cultural criticism," "art criticism," whatever . . . They have been reduced to a very middlebrow "non-judgementalizing." The term "de-skilled" has replaced "referencing" as the most fucked-out word in criticism. Sincerity in painting and talking about serious paintings seems like the last truly avant-garde reaction at the moment. How do you feel about that? Can you talk a little about the reactions to your work over the last ten years—about some of your different investigations through paint into subjects that captured your interest?

PC: Well, I think the whole de-skilling movement is kind of a disaster. Richard Serra said that all sculpture now is collage and bricolage. This is as sad as it is true. I don't think de-skilling works in medicine, law, literature, music, nor art. There's been a huge shift in graduate MFA programs. Students are taught by a succession of adjunct/visiting critics. There are fewer real classes and less skill refining and perfecting. Students are graduating with enormous debt and no skills. But on a deeper level I think it's all about fear of criticism, a kind of performance anxiety, a kind of "I can't compete, so I'll satirize" as a form of Oedipal urge. "You can't criticize my broken sheet rock leaning against the wall. Obviously I wasn't really trying" is a common refrain from students.

BR: You say that your work addresses social issues, yet you still talk about it as art with a capital "A." There are a lot of artists I can think of, like Kara Walker, who I like a lot, but who don't ever mention "art" when they talk about their work.

PC: Well, first, I love her work—did from the first moment we both showed at Brent Sikkema Gallery. But, I don't want to choose between being an activist or an artist. Obviously I'm both. Like the great author Toni Morrison said, "The best art is political, and you ought to be able to make it unquestionably political and irrevocably beautiful at the same time." It's like a protest song and a love song being the same song. Think Marvin Gaye's "What's Going On." This has always been my goal. Joseph Beuys was the first one to coin the phrase "social sculpture." I strongly agree with the idea that art has the potential to transform society. The artist who is currently working in this mode who interests me is Theaster Gates. He uses real objects, like a fire hose, to talk about racial identity and economic inequality. Is it really a fire hose? Of course. And a work of art? Yes. With *Shrine For Girls*, are they really just piles of girls' clothes? Yes. Is it really a real shrine? Yes. Is it also simultaneously an art installation? Yes. The openness of the project is its strength. Can you go there and pray? Sure. Reflect, remember? Absolutely. And is it also a work of art, secular and cultural? Yes. Is it for sale? Yes. And does 10% of my profits go to three non-profit organizations connected to the three tragic events? Yes. It's completely real and social on every level. Visitors to the show have tried to give money directly to the exhibition attendant at the church. They wanted to do something immediately. And the most poetic moment for me and how I judge success is this: We had to rope off the church one day for a couple of hours to do a video shoot/interview. A group of Indian women tourists passed by and read my signage outside which has *Shrine For Girls* written in the 14 most frequently spoken languages. They read *Shrine For Girls* in Hindi, saw the saris on the central altar from outside, went to their hotel room, went through their luggage and brought a black sari for mourning they were traveling with to give to me to add to the shrine. There was no press release in Hindi. My art communicated across national, geographical, and linguistic boundaries. THAT is how I define a successful artwork! Not how much it sells for at auction.

BR: So can you talk a little about the *Shrine for Girls*? It's a pretty complex piece, but I think you've brought together a lot of things, ideas, and influences that make it a kind of summation of your work up to this point.

PC: I LOVE that you see it that way! Shrines are part of every major world religion. Since I was creating a site-specific installation inside a de-consecrated church, and since these women and girls are missing or dead, I decided to honor them within the construct of spirituality. The history of art is the history of remembrance and memorialization, but *that* architecture, *those* memorials and monuments, are reserved for only the most powerful people—men and sometimes *their* wives and mothers of *his* heirs. I wanted to treat these non-royal women and girls' deaths with the dignity they were denied in life. I have gathered hundreds of girls' clothes from around the world and arranged them on three stone altars to act as relics of these young martyrs. Commemorating their spirit, this dramatic site-specific installation is a meditation on the incalculable loss of unrealized potential and hopelessness in the face of unfathomable human cruelty, juxtaposed against the obligation and mission we have as citizens of the world to combat this prejudice.

BR: I see a little bit of Bill Viola and Sophie Calle in it. They have also made work for churches.

PC: Artists have made art for churches for centuries, up to and including Matisse's Chapel of the Rosary in Venice, France, and the Rothko Chapel in Houston, Texas. Both are actually places of worship *and* major works of art. Recently, Sophie Calle's and Bill Viola's installations in churches have been very interesting to me. Sophie Calle's *Rachel, Monique* (2014) in the Chapel at The Episcopal Church of Heavenly Rest, New York, which was a reflection on the death of her mother, had a light interventionist touch that was really impactful. The installation allowed for the church to maintain its purpose while inserting very clever and moving conceptual video and sculptures. Neither detracted from the other, and I think it is very important to create a tight rigorous conceptual installation in a space with pre-existing specific meaning and function. Don Gianmatteo Caputo, the priest in charge of Chiesa di San Gallo and the other 199 churches in Venice, said, "The church has to bring something to the work, and the work has to bring something to the church." It's a dialogue between an historic religious architectural space and contemporary art.

Creating site-specific art for a church, a place of sacrifice and love, defeat and hope, is a daunting task and must be approached with a different kind of consideration than a show for a white box gallery. In Robert Storr's 2007 Venice Biennale, Bill Viola presented *Oceans Without a Shore*, also in Chiesa di San Gallo. It was a dramatic installation where single figures emerged toward the viewers on video screens on each altar inside the darkened church interior. Similarly, but different, in *Shrine For Girls*, natural light creates a contemplative atmosphere, drawing the viewer close to commune with each sculpture. Other examples . . . I really liked Christian Boltanski's *No Man's Land* (2010), with piles of rumpled clothing about memory. I also like Ann Hamilton's *Indigo Blue* (1991/2007), with a massive pile of folded denim workers' shirts. In *Shrine For Girls*, I wanted the specificity of the three subjects and their horrific circumstances to be legible. I didn't want viewers to poke their heads in the church, see a pile of dirty laundry, think they got the message, and walk away. But I also didn't want to hit people over the head with the content; I wanted it to slowly reveal itself. By luring my audience into the church, by elegantly arranging the chromatically rich saris on the central altar, viewers move closer out of curiosity and then notice a small framed photograph to the side—then all becomes clear. With such disturbing content, I thought it was important not to beat them up with it, but let to their own specific emotional, psychological narrative arch take place.

BR: And you have brought back the element of portraiture . . .

PC: In addition to the sculptures, there are also two-dimensional works in the *Shrine For Girls* series.

If I were to show work from this series in a vast white cube gallery space, I would want to have the paintings and watercolors of the people involved on the walls to bring together both the individual and the vast numbers of individuals who have had to withstand this unbearable human cruelty.

During the time that curator Ludovico Pratesi invited me to do this show, that the Venice Biennale selected us as a Venice Biennale Collateral Event, and that the Diocese of Venice chose our proposal for Chiesa di San Gallo, I was making these oil paintings and watercolors while I was researching and thinking about what I would do with the three stone altars.

Amartya Sen, the Nobel Prize-winning economist, wrote in 1990 in the *New York Review of Books* that at any given time 110 million women are missing. What do you do with that number once it's in your head? Supposedly Stalin said one death is a tragedy; 1,000 deaths are just a statistic. How do you get people to focus on, to care about, such a large crisis? Especially today with our 24-hour news cycle, when every day brings another catastrophe. I was also thinking about the "identifiable victim effect" and decided that painting portraits of the specific individuals would be the perfect companion objects to the piles of anonymous empty clothes. The process of painting is meditative and reflective for me. Spending the day painting the portraits of these dead or kidnapped girls is really difficult but very necessary. There is something caring about quietly applying soft paint with a brush, pouring bowls of watercolor on smooth, hot press paper. And why shouldn't these people have a beautiful portrait and be treated with the dignity usually afforded kings and heads of state?

The watercolors have a slightly out-of-focus effect, as if the subject might come closer and into focus but never does. They're out of our reach, permanently.

With the oil paintings, I've tried to use colors with chromatic intensity so it hurts your retinas a little. It should hurt to look at these paintings because the topic is so painful.

Published October 14, 2015.
CultureCatch

Game Symmetry: Bjarne Melgaard + Bradley Rubenstein

The Proust Questionnaire has its origins in a parlor game popularized by Marcel Proust, the French essayist and novelist, who believed that, in answering these questions, an individual reveals his or her true nature. Below, Bjarne Melgaard and Bradley Rubenstein reinterpret Mr. Proust's concept.

Bjarne Melgaard was born in Norway in 1967 and now lives and works in New York. He is considered one of Norway's most famous artists. He works with sculptural assemblage. In installations that include paintings, videos, virtual reality, and mixed-media works, he explores themes of substance addiction, sexuality, racism, and self-destruction. Early in his career Melgaard created controversial installations referencing subversive subcultures, such as S&M and heavy metal music. More recently his practice consists of an emphasis on expressionistic paintings and drawings, often containing text.

What is your idea of perfect happiness?

My mother

What is your greatest extravagance?

My father

What is your current state of mind?

My dog

What is the trait you most deplore in yourself?

My mother

What is the trait you most deplore in others?

My father

What do you consider the most overrated virtue?

My dog

What is your favorite occupation?

My mother

What is your most marked characteristic?

My father

What do you most value in your friends?

My dog

When and where were you happiest?

My mother

What do you dislike most about your appearance?

My father

Which living person do you most despise?

My dog

On what occasion do you lie?

My mother

Which talent would you most like to have?

My mother

If you could change one thing about yourself, what would it be?

My father

If you could change one thing about your family, what would it be?

My dog

What is your most treasured possession?

My mother

What do you regard as the lowest depth of misery?

My father

Who are your favorite writers?

My dog

Who is your favorite hero of fiction?

My mother

Who are your heroes in real life?

My father

What are your favorite names?

My dog

What is it that you most dislike?

My mother

What do you consider your greatest achievement?

My father

If you were to die and come back as a person or thing, what do you think it would be?

My dog

If you could choose what to come back as, what would it be?

My mother

What is your greatest regret?

My father

Published Spring 2017.
Sharkforum

The Sublime is Now: Lucio Pozzi + Bradley Rubenstein

Lucio Pozzi is an Italian-born American artist currently based in Hudson, New York and Valeggio sul Mincio, Verona, Italy. He studied architecture in Rome before moving to New York City in 1962. Pozzi is a painter whose painterly concerns extend to environmental art and actions. He also has created large installations, performances, and videos—one of the first single-artist exhibitions of the *Projects:Video* series at MoMA, New York. Pozzi also teaches, writes, and lectures.

Bradley Rubenstein: Painting's obsolescence as an exclusive tool for information or propaganda has liberated it from the burden of being applied to purposes other than the exploration of its own universe. You are one of a few artists who doesn't take painting for granted, but engages in it on a daily basis. How do you approach your practice with its attendant doubts?

Lucio Pozzi: I cultivate doubt because I feel that the current taken-for-granted dominance of proof and verification, of strategic clarity and resolution, is warping the exchange between artist and viewer.

When I am starting a painting, I consider it a situation, like any other mix of ingredients I may want to combine. First I set up the logistics of that which I choose to engage in: the materials, the sizes, the time. Then I decide the starting point of the operation I will conduct: the technique, the approaches, the imagery. But at all stages I make sure that none of these decisions are, for me, binding; they are only starting factors that can get transformed and get lost—even be totally contradicted during the ensuing process of making. Unpredictable doubt supplies the energy to proceed.

BR: Instead of relying on an assumption of collective criteria for art, contemporary artists choose their own individual reference points for creativity. Your works have many layers, but prominent among them, you seem to be fascinated by metamorphosis. Can you elaborate on this at all, specifically with regard to your large, mural compositions and installations?

LP: In order to avoid depending on binding rules, even those I might set up for myself, I have developed a large pool of resources—material, technical, imagistic. It's like an expanding keyboard I can play to infinity. The key to my playing it is the endless translation from one combination of elements to others. The resulting hybrids are metamorphic and never the same.

This process of translation is carried on inside every single artwork and also from groups of works—I call them families—to other groups of works. When I produce large compositions, the process of translation happens relentlessly from one part to the next.

BR: In spite of your history as a conceptual artist, you have never lost track of the importance of the artist's hand in the work. In an age that has become increasingly digital, you have managed to straddle a position that includes reproductive works (photos, prints, etc.) yet retained a personal touch that is uniquely your own.

LP: Being myself is inevitable. I think that if one does not try to predefine one's touch or modality, they will surface without the author even knowing their connotations.

What has been called conceptual art is for me the analytical starting point of my art. Enumerating the concepts, materials, and processes as ingredients underlying an operation has cleansed me of centuries-old tenets such as style. Without what I learned from conceptual art theory, I would not have been able to throw myself into further and further explorations. Without Duchamp's urinal, I would not be able to paint a vase of flowers.

Much conceptual art is now stuck in rigid denial of the subjective. By sensing it as a mere but necessary starting point, instead, I have been able to then incorporate in my process, also, factors like the touch of the hand. Many artists detail the program by which they operate. I have no program but find out what comes from my doing only after the fact. Allowing the hand its unfathomable contribution to art making injects the energy of uncontrollable psychosomatic forces into art.

BR: You have focused a large amount of attention on the teaching of art. How has this affected your own practice?

LP: Fundamentally. Because of our being bereft of commonly agreed-upon criteria in art, I have nothing to teach. This is the basis of my teaching. Thus the art workshop is a field of permanent learning for me. I don't impose, but only question and learn.

BR: If there are no common criteria agreed upon by the art community, do you believe that art can be taught anymore?

LP: No, art cannot be taught. The art school is an experiential arena where options are compared. There is no judgment, but the conversation is enriched by opinions being exchanged. These opinions are not generalities but are focused on specific conditions.

BR: You write and speak a great deal about your work and working progress. How does language define your practice?

LP: It's a collateral process. I started speaking and writing about my methodology only because I got fed up with repeatedly finding myself typecast within the obsolete canons persistently applied to the arts—the yawnful prescriptions of the new, the original, the consistent, the style, the intentions, the content.

BR: Despite the current lively discourse surrounding art making, we have generated a quagmire in our attempt to corral the content of art. In what ways do you envision an escape from the dominant practice of giving more import to the packaging of art than its content?

LP: I have a dream: that artists will take advantage of the unprecedented freedom they now have and by so doing foster a corresponding freedom in the viewers. Freedom does not mean indifference to discourse nor does it mean surrender to distraction. On the contrary, it requires a constant alert to the conditions of existence. It is rooted in a critical attention to one's innermost fabric and to the deeper potential of others. It seeks open dialogue and no conclusive answers.

BR: Would you define your art, then, as political, sensuous, or escapist?

LP: I don't define my art. I actually have no clue about what it may be. It seems useless yet indispensable.

BR: When asked why he wrote, Dylan Thomas replied something like, "In praise of God and love for mankind." How do you feel about this turn of phrase?

LP: Praise of God is a yearning for the impossible—yes, God or whatever you may want to call the dimension we strangely are able to conceive of, yet have no idea about. Mankind is me and those who walk around me: narcissus and the crowd, so fragile, so immensely diverse, a fatal attraction or a weft of mystery, misery, eruption, just being.

Published Spring 2002.
ArtKrush

Little Q+A: Erin Smith + Bradley Rubenstein

Erin Smith lives and works in Australia. She is known for her figurative, narrative painting. She has exhibited extensively in Australia and New York.

Bradley Rubenstein: It was interesting to see your work in person (at Berry Campbell, NY) after having followed you online for a while. One gets the sense of the physicality of your painting through pictures, but in person they come across far more viscerally. One of the tensions you set up in your work is the relation between a familiar image and pure gestural painting. This kind of image layering is familiar to us now; painters like Polke and Salle come to mind. But there is something in your work that is more about the passages of direct, abstract painting that remind me of Clyfford Still. I have a feeling that the painterly passages interest you as much, if not more, than the imagery.

Erin Smith: Absolutely, I enjoy both aspects. With the more abstract sections it feels like I am treating myself, to take the painting wherever I seem to feel at the time. It's very freeing and often the most exciting part. The imagery is ever-evolving throughout the duration of the painting.

Many works end up as thick, layered stories. And areas are deleted, leaving small chosen remnants to begin a new twist in the adventure.

BR: Can you talk a little about your background—what were some of your early influences?

ES: Studying and holding a bachelor of design arts from the Australian Academy of Design in Melbourne and growing up in Queensland definitely has played a part in my exploration of cartoons, advertising, and cultural references. Also, my time studying at the New York Studio School was a pinnacle for me and my practice. All of this works into the composition to give a sense of the narrative.

The importance of flux over stability throughout Sigmar Polke's work is something I've been greatly influenced by. I draw inspiration from everyone and what every day brings. I'm very energetic and highly excitable. I think somehow this comes through in the work.

BR: It's interesting that you say "narrative." Do you see stories in your work, like when you paint little scenes? Or even with some of the paintings that seem to start as portraits, do you have a story in mind when you begin, or is the narrative aspect you refer to more just the way the picture is painted?

ES: I think some work begins as a portrait, and then that portrait grows on me and I begin to build a narrative around that. Often that narrative is a complete reflection of what is happening in my world at that time. In one portrait, I felt . . . yes, this is complete. Then a number of days later he had wrestlers on his shoulders, and his hat became engulfed in fruit.

BR: There is always a tendency to try to group art into labeled categories, or trends, or whatnot. I think this is particularly true when artists deal with what was once called "appropriation" in the '80s. Now we have the mash-up in music, zombie formalism in painting, and whatever Richard Prince is doing now. Your work falls somewhere between this sort of thing, defying categorization in an interesting way. For example, your imagery isn't immediately recognizable pop icons, but kind of quirky. David Humphrey and Gina Magid come to mind as far as painters who are working in the same way. Your work seems to be more about pure painting as opposed to painting about painting.

ES: Yes, I'm not terribly great with categorization. The work is an expression of me at the time, so, often I paint over or distort an image that became too realistic. The process is of utmost importance. It's my meditation.

BR: So would it be accurate to say that the process of painting is more important to you than the art object that results? In some ways that is kind of an old-fashioned idea, with irony and whatnot being largely the current artistic currency.

ES: Of course it needs to feel right and that it is the end. Perhaps that feeling leads me to know when to stop. Like many others, it can be hard to let go and finish. It feels like you've just finished a great book.

BR: You live in Sydney and show a lot in New York. How does living there influence what you do, or is the art world so international now that regional influence doesn't really exist anymore?

ES: I'm influenced by everything. I love what's happening in Sydney and Australia as a whole. I also love New York; I love the energy of the city. I do incorporate a lot of old Australian cars in my work, perhaps as an homage to where I grew up.

BR: You mention being influenced by other mediums, like advertising and cartoons. Do you see yourself working in other mediums, like film or photography, or does your interest lie more in searching for subjects to paint about?

ES: I love digital work, however painting is where my heart is.

BR: Are you working on anything new that we should know about?

ES: I do have a number of group shows this year and plan to be back in New York. I seem to never stop painting. I hope to make something a little different this year and push myself a bit out of my comfort zone.

Published March 14, 2016.
CultureCatch

Raw Power: Brenda Goodman + Bradley Rubenstein

Brenda Goodman was born in Detroit in 1943 and now lives and works in Pine Hill, New York. She does paintings, sculpture, and works on paper. Goodman was part of Detroit's Cass Corridor movement in the '70s, a group of artists from Detroit's Cass Corridor neighborhood whose work responded to the post-industrial decline sweeping the country. She is known for her unorthodox use of painting materials and her exploration of abstraction and representation in her work, including many self-portraits.

Bradley Rubenstein: I think we should just jump right in and start with the Big Questions. We were talking about a lot of younger artists like Dana Schutz and Keltie Ferris, a whole new generation of what are being called "millennials," who I think are coming at painting from a very different angle than either you or I are. There is something about your work—and I think your show at Life on Mars Gallery illustrated it well—that really begs the question, why does art matter? How does painting relate to other disciplines? What philosophical questions can it help us with? We are, after all, alone on the planet, existentially. I don't know what you are thinking; you can't know what I am thinking. Painting is our way of communicating. Like music or literature, it is a language where we can talk using colors, lines, and shapes instead of words. David Foster Wallace said, "Art at its best is a bridge across the abyss of human loneliness." I think your work exemplifies this act of seeking to reveal things about oneself—to communicate.

Brenda Goodman: Most of my work comes from many marks I put on the surface. Then one shape pops out and starts to speak to another shape, and I just sort of put them in touch with each other until a feeling emerges and I develop it. When I worked earlier with the symbols, I created the shapes. I would have something or someone in mind and draw those shapes until one appeared, and I would say, "That's the one!" Later the marks were all from my unconscious. It becomes a very intuitive process. I am as surprised as the viewer very often because I don't know why or how I arrived at a certain painting, but what I do know for sure is it is from my gut and it's honest and real and speaks its truth. Sometimes they reveal something to me; sometimes it's not so clear. But either way something strong and emotional is being communicated.

I think I was born with a strong core. Although my childhood wasn't an easy one, that core is what I think people sense in my work. I've been in the abyss many times in my life, and I'm not afraid to show those dark, fearful, alone, and painful places in my work. I wasn't afraid either to spend years in therapy digging into my childhood. I took what resonated with me from many different spiritual practices as well. I remember a card I gave my mother when I was just 14. I wrote a note in it saying, "Instead of always criticizing my faults, why don't you ever compliment me on some good things I do, and you might find I'll change." Who says that at 14 to their mother? I've always had a strong need to express my feelings to others, and as an artist for 50 years, that's what I do in my work and my relations. I need to do this to survive, and so far I have!

I did a painting in 2013 called *Not a Leg to Stand On*. It was one of those paintings that revealed itself after it was done. There is this very large red figure whose arm and fist stretch across the entire painting, and underneath that figure is a much smaller figure that only has one leg. I looked at the finished painting and knew it was me and my mother because she was so overwhelming and controlling that I never thought I had a leg to stand on, unless I could say how I felt. Not all paintings deliver such a clear message, but this one did. I wouldn't paint if I couldn't express what I feel.

Sometimes I get tired of people thinking paintings have to deliver an explicit meaning, or any meaning for that matter. Much of painting for me is just the pure joy of putting oil paint to canvas and watching it become beautiful. For me, even when my paintings are dark, or sad, or even happy, they have to be beautifully painted. That's crucial to me.

There was a painting in my last show at Life on Mars titled *Almost a Bride* (2015). It is beautifully painted. It has all my passion for making the paint sing. For me a painting should not disappoint when you view it up close. People asked me what the painting means, and I said, "I don't really know." It just feels so right and strikes something deep inside. That's good enough. When I stand in front of a Morandi, I feel transported to another place. Some bring me to tears. Yet I have never had words or a meaning I could attach to them. And I doubt if Morandi, as he painted these bottles year after year after year, had "Ah ha!" moments of clarity and meaning each time he completed one. I think he would be pleased to know his work is communicating from another realm.

BR: Going back a minute to some of the work we were talking about the other day, one of the shows that caught both of our attention was the Jack Tworkov retrospective. There was a lot going on there—a lot of range to his work. Looking at a still life from the '40s, you made the comment that you didn't think that kind of Cezanne-influenced picture would be immediately recognizable as a "Tworkov." That was kind of an important thing to note; it used to be more common for a painter to work through a lot of ideas, styles, history—things that you don't really see today. Now, the idea of taking that much time to really practice the discipline of painting, to learn your history, is gone. What was your experience like at Arts and Crafts? How did you arrive at the way of working that we see in a picture like *The Cat Approaches* (1974) in the Detroit Institute of Arts (DIA)?

BG: It's true. Fifty years ago, being an artist was very different than it is now. Arts and Crafts was a very traditional art school. I don't imagine there are many or any art schools today where your painting teacher wants you to do months of thumbnail pencil drawings of still lifes, learning everything you can about composition. Then we were allowed to use earth colors (oil of course) for quite a while, and then finally color. We were taught how to apply paint so it "breathed." Sarkis, my teacher, would say, "Every square inch of the painting should breathe." And we were encouraged to have influences. I was so many artists through the years, and even though I was open, I sometimes wondered where "I" was in all of this. I was Dubuffet for three years. Every time I picked up a pencil, a Dubuffet would pop out. Sarkis said to me, "Stop fighting it. Become him. Look like him, talk like him, paint like him" —and it worked.

There have been many influences in my work: Van Gogh, Gorky, de Kooning, Ensor, Morandi, and Guston. I learned from all of them. There's an affinity we have with certain artists because we resonate with them. Time is different in 2016 than it was in the '60s. The desperate need to have something unlike everyone else is so strong now, and there is an urgency to do the work that doesn't allow for a slow maturation. I would go to school in the morning, draw and paint till 4 o'clock, and then go downtown to a coffeehouse, a burlesque show, or anywhere that there were interesting people to draw. Then a few hours' sleep and at it again. Sometimes I would fall asleep on a stool with a paintbrush in my hand. So for the first 11 years I learned my skills, experimented with surface and textures, and then was getting ready for something more personal to happen—something that comes from deeper inside.

In 1973 I met a well-known poet in Detroit, Faye Kicknosway, and I began sitting in on her creative writing classes. I wanted to find a vocabulary to share my everyday life—a visual diary. I wanted symbols for me and everyone in my life. I became an abstracted shape that felt like a heart to me. I was very tough on the outside and very vulnerable in the inside. I wanted more of the softer part of me to come through. Then I created shapes for everyone in my life. Much of the inspiration to do this was being in these writing classes. *The Cat Approaches* was done after I found a solid place in me where all these symbols lived. I had done some cat drawings from years earlier, and Faye loved them and wrote a whole series of poems about them. One of the poems was called "The Cat Approaches," and from that poem I did a painting with that name that hangs in the DIA. All the works from this period had a surreal quality. It was 11 years from when I started art school that a personal voice began to emerge. So to go back to your original inquiry about my history, you can see how different it is from today's art world. I feel so grateful for my early school days.

BR: We talked a little about movies and TV a while back. I think that painting doesn't live in a void and that there are other mediums that both influence painters and are also informed by painting. Are there things that you have read or movies that have either influenced you or that you think are of some importance at the moment? I think I said that there was a real sense of the theatrical to some of your paintings and that your sculpture seemed like a way to extend your painted world into three dimensions.

BG: The only times I made sculpture, which were few, were when I was in a transition with my painting. Working three-dimensionally helped mix things up. When I did the tar-cone-shape self-portrait pieces I had recently moved to New York, and it seemed necessary to do them to express how lonely and difficult that move was. I had lived 33 years in Detroit. It was my first move away from home. I did three or four of them, and I thought that the sculptures moving around a stage would be really powerful. Every once in a while I think it would be great to design a theater set, but as of yet I haven't.

I don't think I'm affected by popular culture in my work. Many artists work from that place, but I haven't. What I do connect to, though, are places and events that resonate with what I already feel inside.

When the Gee's Bend show was at the Whitney, it had a big impact on me. I resonated very strongly with their quilts, and I could see their influence in my work for a while. But more than that was an article I read that their homes didn't have any insulation, so they used *Life* magazines as insulation and covered all their walls with them. I started searching for old *Life* magazines and began cutting out pictures that personally hit me. I did a whole series of paintings around 2003 where I glued these images into the paintings.

Another example—we lived a mile from the Trade Towers, and I was on the roof of our building on the Bowery and saw a plane fly into them. I did a series of about 12 oil-on-paper pieces after that tragedy because there was nothing else I could think about. I needed to paint what I felt.

And lastly in 2006 I began taking singing lessons. Music was never part of my life and certainly not singing. Ever since a teacher ridiculed me in front of my third-grade class, I never sang a song. So it was very exciting to learn songs, and some of the early ones were Christmas songs like "Away in the Manger." Every time I had a lesson I would go home and do an oil-on-paper piece about my lesson, and some had a very personal version of the nativity scene in them. So as the world of music and voice opened to me, it also entered my paintings.

None of these examples are about pop culture. Most of my paintings come from my innermost feelings, and I make that visible through my work. But there are times when things outside of me resonate with something already there inside me, and I have a strong need to paint it.

BR: You went from Detroit to New York and lived in the city. Can you talk a little about why you moved upstate and how that has changed your work?

BG: We always came upstate to the Catskills for the whole summer. I have a studio next to the house, and that's where I painted all day—very different from the darkness of the Bowery loft. On Labor Day we'd pack the car and go back to the city. But in 2009 my partner Linda's son, Jon, died 9 months after being diagnosed with cancer. We made a decision to stay upstate where it would be more healing. We never went back to the loft again and had everything moved up here.

One of the biggest changes for me was I sort of lost my identity as an artist, which never happened before. Linda was Linda, and I was Brenda. Most people didn't know I was an artist, and if I told them they weren't really interested. So it was weird to not have my artist identity attached to me. And then there was the realization that I would disappear off everyone's screen. So I went through a pretty dark spiritual crisis in the country of what to do with my art and me as an artist. Could I settle for just painting for "me" and let go of all the many years I invested in my career? This was an abyss I had to go through, and of course I came through with the decision to go back in my studio and paint because that's what I've always done. That's who I am, a painter.

Shortly after that Michael David, a well-known painter in his own right, wanted to open a gallery in Bushwick and asked his friend, painter Joan Snyder, who she would recommend to exhibit. She gave him my name, and he offered me a show. That was 2015. At the same time I was chosen for the 2015 American Academy of Arts and Letters Invitational—a show I had wanted to be in for 40 years—and won an award for exceptional achievement. Then John Yau wrote a great review of my show at Life on Mars Gallery, and many, many other wonderful things have been happening since then—and all since we moved to the country!

Living in the mountains, though, hasn't drastically changed my work like it did for Jake Berthot when he moved upstate and his work took a sharp turn into landscape. I still come from inside me and whatever is happening in my life. When Jon died I did a series called *Troubled Waters*. It was very dark. Then three years ago I lost 70 pounds, and a shift happened inside me. I felt happier and more confident on a deeper level, and the work became lighter and more animated and even more colorful. And then recently I experienced severe sciatica for three months and couldn't do anything without pain except sit. So I did 21 small pieces of how it felt feeling pain all day.

All of those changes could have happened on the Bowery as well as in the mountains. But I think it has had a good effect on my general mood. I'm not as irritable. I don't scream at honking horns, construction everywhere, and traffic jams. We walk our dog on a dirt road every morning, looking at the mountains and all the creatures that scurry around.

BR: I really enjoyed the recent work at Life on Mars, the little pictures you painted while recovering from sciatica. Of course you were painting from your feelings, but in this case "feelings" had a double meaning, both emotionally and the physicality of pain. There was something about them that conveyed that feeling of endurance in order to make a painting. In some ways they neatly sum up your career, for me.

BG: I would say endurance is just built into my constitution. I don't do things halfway or give up easily. If I lose something I will spend hours, days, or weeks till I find it. I resolve every painting I do and won't let it leave the studio until it feels absolutely right to me. At almost 73 now, my knees and back are giving me trouble (welcome to the club), but I won't stop painting what is in my heart, and I will never retire! Anyway, have you ever heard a painter say they have retired? No . . . they just paint till they can't anymore.

Published April 4, 2016.
Artslant

Buried By Time and Dust: Michael Zansky + Bradley Rubenstein

Michael Zansky was born in 1947 in the Bronx and lives and works in New York. His father, Louis Zansky, was a famous comic book illustrator. Zansky has a massive oeuvre of paintings, carvings, sculptures, videos, and installations, including a warehouse full of floor-to-ceiling wood carvings and paintings titled *Giants and Dwarfs*.

Bradley Rubenstein: You've said that a key element to looking at your work is that you see the Abstract Expressionists as having created a break in the history of painting.

Michael Zansky: The Abstract Expressionists did indeed create a break from past abstract styles, but it seems to me a way station. One way of making a painting ended, but it opened up other ways.

BR: The thing that is most apparent is just how far you're trying to take the viewer on a trip of sorts, through a history of painting. It isn't necessarily the first thing that you would think when you walk in here, but it's there—the narrative cycles, the integration of the work with the architectural space, and how you eschew canvas for carved wood.

MZ: Take Michelangelo's Sistine Chapel—it is the illusion of how the universe is created. I stand back and I look at that as a comic strip of fifteenth-century thought—one that will get replaced by some other understanding of the universe, then another, then another. Rather than presenting some kind of systematic, Renaissance representation of an ordered universe, with *Giants and Dwarfs* the title of the series comes from the classification of stars; Red Giants are the largest, and White Dwarfs the smallest. I was expressing a largely rudderless, unstructured universe. No matter what we come up with to represent the world around us, it is always going to fall short of what the actual thing is. There is always going to be something that eludes us.

BR: And the archeological aspects?

MZ: I was thinking about Walter Benjamin's *History as Ruin*—of the layers of detritus that build up to the present. He wrote this about Paul Klee, "A Paul Klee painting named *Angelus Novus* shows an angel looking as though he is about to move away from something he is fixedly contemplating. His eyes are staring, his mouth is open, wings spread. This is how one pictures the angel of history. His face is turned toward the past. Where we perceive a chain of events, he sees one single catastrophe that keeps piling wreckage upon wreckage and hurls it in front of his feet. The angel would like to stay, awaken the dead, and make whole what has been smashed. But a storm is blowing from Paradise; it has got caught in his wings with such violence that the angel can no longer close them. This storm irresistibly propels him into the future to which his back is turned, while the pile of debris before him grows skyward. This storm is what we call progress." That was the original premise. I organized the panels, in stacks or tiers, so that it resembled some kind of archeological dig. But even though that was where I began working, it's an ongoing process. Although I'm structured, I open up and let go, saying, intuitively, "This is where I think the work should head." Wherever that may lead is open to explore, so I don't lock down the avenues of thinking at the beginning. In fact, I try to open them up, because ultimately that's what makes the work interesting for me. The abstract forms and masses of lines suggest a figure or head, and, on our own, we project qualities on this figuration. They are caught in some transformative state. I am fascinated by the unpredictability of evolution, its dead ends, and how the universe seems to unfold by the luck of the draw. I wanted to create some kind of parallel world where everything was indeterminate and constantly in flux, pulling together elements of science, mythology, philosophy, literature, and history.

BR: There is a psychological element in your work . . .

MZ: Yes. Take my drawings, for example. The power of the unconscious propels my work in particular directions. This has always been an integral part of my practice, and the intuitive nature of this process imbues it with a visceral type of integrity, where the sum of all the marks I make is an undiluted reflection of the ideas and passions that occupy my mind.

BR: One of the central tenets of the Baroque is a tendency for everything to radiate from a central point. Here you have the wood carving in the center, microscopically examined through the lenses; the carvings themselves echo this, with the radiating striations, a shorthand for crosshatching, I guess. You refer to Egyptian art with the upper and lower registers of your stacked panels, all of this giving a visual structure to a very baroque narrative.

MZ: Two artists whose work seems relevant to me here are Francis Bacon and Jackson Pollock. I wanted to combine the iconicity Bacon achieved by putting his figures in cells or endless rooms with the all-over pouring of Pollock, which was its own type of architecture.

There is also Bosch and Goya. These are artists whose works were gambling on the viewer's participation to connect the imagery. Trying to push the existing boundaries of painting plays a major role in their work. If I knew the end result, that would be less interesting. I had to go back to artists in the past to find a way to go forward with my painting. I think that the artist should ask questions, or pose questions to the audience, but the viewer shouldn't question the finished piece. The final painting should be complete, like a statement, not needing any additions or subtractions, all its pieces complete. The painted world is one that is made magically whole.

BR: There's fixed arrangement for the panels. In fact, you have such a large number of them that whenever they have been installed, what the viewer is seeing is a fraction of the total body of work.

MZ: I have over 200 panels, 4 × 8 sheets of plywood. They run over 800 linear feet. What you saw with the *Giants and Dwarfs* exhibition was about 170 panels.

BR: There is an element of theater to working on a grand scale.

MZ: Having worked for years on sets for film and television has given me a unique perspective on mass media and its relationship to painting, sculpture, video, and installation art. The sets I've worked on have been complex amalgams of all of these elements.

A movie or TV show reaches an audience in numbers that a painting will never equal. Movie theaters, TV, and the internet: these are the churches of the present. Museums are the churches of history. When I'm working in my studio, what comes to mind is how pitifully small the number of viewers is compared to the audience of contemporary media. Artists produce fetishized objects for a much smaller audience. It's hard to compare the viewer's response to the moments they spend viewing any given painting or sculpture or installation to a two-hour movie.

BR: The drawings you are doing relate to the woodcuts on a surface level; you make them using a torch, so you are essentially "carving" into the paper the way you carve the wood. They have more of a narrative quality, though, in the sense that you have a character, a protagonist, who shows up in frame after frame. You pointed out that one of the characters is your grandfather and the other his friend, endlessly battling it out. In this arena, how important is it for the viewer to understand this narrative? Are you broadening your work to include overt narrative in the drawings, or is it just that drawing lends itself to narrative?

MZ: With the drawings I used an oxygen propane torch to control the values of the line. It is done with great speed—a moment of hesitation and the flame will burn through the paper. The figures in these drawings represent elements of my grandfather and his friend, who was a blind rabbi. They would have heated arguments over obscure theological text—the absurdity of their fighting reminds me of both Samuel Beckett's plays and Laurel and Hardy. My father was a children's comic book illustrator who was always wrestling with the conflict between high art and popular culture—he couldn't reconcile the two. But in these drawings I am using the narrative elements of my grandfather's perpetual grand argument with his friend and combining it with my father's background in illustration. I am using the multi-panel format of the comic book but reinventing it like Beckett did with *Waiting for Godot*, taking elements from Laurel and Hardy films and restaging the pratfalls and slapstick humor as a tragic conflict. In these drawings the two characters are locked in a perpetual physical and moral struggle.

I don't mean for them to be a simplistic melodrama intended for a mass audience, like Batman or Superman, but a kind of drawing that questions most of art and philosophy's deep arguments, though filtered through a common vernacular form. A picture can become visually iconic in a way the moving image cannot because art objects are singular. They stop time.

BR: When you look back over the thousands of years that people have made plastic art, you find connections. For example, you can look at Egyptian art from 2,500 years ago, such as a sculpture, and it may represent a religious idea or something else, but it's still a sculpture of a cat. With film and theater that isn't really the case. There are only, say, ten or twenty classical Greek plays that still are revived with any note. Another example is Restoration comedies; they just don't have the same purpose without their context. Do you see the same happening in film and performance art now—that the relevance of your painting and sculpture is less context-dependent?

MZ: Having worked in film, I've seen its strengths and weaknesses. There is a complex dynamic at work that requires continuous and prolonged observation. With painting and sculpture, the object is fetishized, in much the same way movie stars are. Painting and sculpture are integral elements of that same enigmatic star quality. Warhol was able to combine the object and the star.

So much art, and cinema, does not convey a sense of something remarkable or compelling. It is contingent upon the individual—director, artist, whomever—to have an overarching view, which enables that individual to discuss ideas in relationship to aesthetics, culture, psychology— all of it. When I'm driving down a highway, I see reality flashing at a very quick speed; the music is on, and I'm sort of in one great concert hall. It's a fascinating thought that such a thing didn't exist a hundred years ago. You couldn't listen to music going down a highway. These cultural artifacts are now continually available to use in multiple configurations. The overall effect is one where my consciousness drifts from trees going by on the roads to any thoughts I may be having. It's automatic. It is very hard to have a continuous look at something. There are all of these constant shifts in the unconscious, both subtle ones and obvious ones. In historical film, for example, the references usually have to do with fine art of the time; and they have some idea of how people dressed, what their tastes were.

The way I see the culture now is that it is democratic. Almost any form can see the light of day. But only a handful of them will survive a cultural cutoff. The others will always be there to be mined, maybe to be used by someone else to get to a place of greatness in the future.

In conversations I've had with a friend, performance art was discussed, and he said he found it rather boring. I think it's a generational thing. It might have had credibility, but so much of that has been diluted by continual practice with a declining amount of conviction. It becomes a stylistic system that is no longer relevant for most people and lacks the integrity that was inherent in its original practitioners. This is something you see with every art movement.

Art needs a sustainability based on its own internal constraints. Much of what is happening now will fall away, overwhelmed by specific modes and styles that somehow supersede it. And this isn't always for the better.

For several hundred million years dinosaurs dominated the earth, and they were replaced by little mammals that eventually became us. I keep looking over the horizon to see if the dinosaurs are coming back. That is the history of art.

Published March 2017.
Sharkforum

Copy of A: Magalie Guérin + Bradley Rubenstein

Magalie Guérin was born in Montréal and lives and works in Chicago. She has written a book of studio writing, *NOTES ON*, in which she recounts her daily practice. She is an instructor at SAIC in Chicago, as well as the College of DuPage.

Bradley Rubenstein: I want to talk about your background and influences, but I think that there is an aspect to your work, your current work, that incorporates a lot of that, so let's start there and work backwards. Can you talk a little bit about the work that I saw at Lyles & King last fall in New York and the "copy drawings" that relate to them?

Magalie Guérin: The paintings at Lyles & King were the continuation of a series I called the Hat Project, as well as a few from the Bondage series. In a nutshell, the project started about three years ago when I decided to start every painting with the same specific shape. The original sketch for that shape came from a chair design but ended up looking more like a big cartoonish hat in two parts, hence the name. After fixing the "hat" with thick layers of gesso on 16-by-20-inch canvases, I add oil colors and build forms around and against the main shape until it all comes together. The work is abstract in nature, but it's not until I've recognized something representational in it that I can call it quits. It's an intuitive process with a lot of unknowns, which is not very easy considering that I'm a bit of a control freak. I don't really understand how the image develops and becomes final, and I'm often left feeling as if I didn't quite make these paintings. That's how the Copy Drawings came to be—as a way to repossess my own work. I decided to make color pencil drawings of the paintings, rebuilding them from the beginning, but this time with a clear understanding of where they will end up, what they look like. The image of the painting is a known fact; the drawn layers are the reconstruction of that fact.

BR: Related to this work you have a book of your studio notes. I see this as part of a larger conceptual project, like, you create the paintings, copy the work, write about the process. It seems like the OCD aspect of the project is as important, if not more so, than the discrete aspect of a single painting.

MG: The book project started as a kind of drawing exercise. I transcribed six different studio notebooks, starting when I moved to Chicago to go to graduate school, into one Moleskine book, weaving the separate entries into an achronological timeline. It took quite a while, so as I copied away I continued to write in my current journal, and the *NOTES* project was analyzed as if it were a painting. I talked about how I disliked the look of my handwriting, that I would have preferred black ink instead of blue, how I felt about the content, etc. I then copied those current thoughts into the book-object. I did two versions of it a few months apart. The second book was presented as part of an exhibit at the Glass Curtain gallery in Chicago, which was seen by Caroline Picard of The Green Lantern Press. She offered to publish it, so I made a third version of the book under her supervision—this time typeset.

BR: All of this brings to mind an article Angela Dufresne wrote last year about irony and sincerity, positing that there was "a third pill"—a reference to the film *The Matrix*—basically saying that there might be a form of sincerity that was cloaked in irony. It is a very post-meta view of aesthetics and art making. It brought to mind Charles Bukowski, who published his first book with a preface of all the rejection letters that he had collected while trying to get it published. That would have been a very meta aesthetic act—except that he had actually written all the rejection letters himself.

MG: I don't entirely relate to this; I want the gesture to have has more of an emotional resonance—a way to hang on to the work, to not let it go, to recirculate it from within. I see it as a result of a daily studio practice more than a calculated strategy. But yes, predetermined systems of production help me move the work forward. I'm more into repetition than experimentation.

BR: Before you moved to Chicago you ran a gallery, GV/AS, in Brooklyn for quite a while. At that time you were making these really interesting drawings that were both weirdly personal and something of a nod to appropriation strategy.

MG: Yes, the drawings appropriated images of famous photographs in which I inserted myself. It seemed like the most direct way for me to create images and link all my interests together: photography, drawing, and psychology. They were my very first pieces of art. Soon after that series I began to create my own environments, and the drawings became more surreal. You have to understand, I had not studied art at that time; my education came from meeting artists, running that exhibition space, and curating shows where I had to decide what I liked and didn't like based purely on taste and not any kind of understanding of art. That's how I became an artist, by looking and making. It was a slow process. It's not until I went to graduate school at the age of 35 that I had my first "critical" conversation about what I was making.

BR: I think that has been more of a strength than a liability with your work—it really does come from a genuine place, even when it seems ironic or deconstructed at times. One last question, the obvious one: What's going on in your studio now?

MG: My studio at the moment . . . well, more paintings. I'm trying a slightly bigger size, and hoping that the scale shift will make sense—still with the same process of starting the paintings with a fixed shape in gesso and building around it. I'm also making graphite drawings using a similar method of layering and erasing, which I have not done before with graphite. It's very satisfying to have found a way to translate the paintings in drawings instead of copying them. But there are a lot of new paintings I haven't had a chance to copy yet.

Published August 31, 2016.
Artslant

The Revolution Will Not Be Televised: Peter Williams + Bradley Rubenstein

Peter Williams is from Nyack, New York and lives and works in Wilmington, Delaware. He creates urgent paintings that are at once timely and have art historical resonance. His subjects include Whiteness and police brutality against black men and women in colorful canvases that unite history, biography, and allegory.

Bradley Rubenstein: When we talked last fall I thought we would discuss your work somewhat chronologically, but things have changed a lot since then, which seems to have impacted your work a great deal. Let's start with your new work.

Peter Williams: The new work has come as I've done my "research": from short blurbs on Facebook, knowledge of some of these events from the press, and books that I've read throughout the years. I am humbled by my lack of firsthand experience recently in the lives of black folks, except through the press. Life in Delaware is also humbling since I live in a Republican-lite environment. My Blackness affects how I live, but not how I survive. During the past three years the rise of anti-Obama hatred and the Alt-Right movement has begun to unfold in ways no one could have conceived, except for those we conceived as a radical Left— Dick Gregory, Farrakhan, Angela Davis, etc., to name but a few.

The incarceration of millions of young black men and women in market-rate prisons as virtual slave labor; the killing by police of this same group of young people; the exposed hatred of people of color by the white community is stressing me out. The only forum I have is through my art and my voice, and neither seems to be reaching very many people. The recent work at David & Schweitzer has allowed me to put some of the more controversial images into play.

I had received, by accident, some large canvases because of a mistake in the order I got from the art supplier. I saw this as an opportunity to explore the deaths of several young people whose lives were soiled by press reports: Sandra Bland, Tamir Rice, Michael Brown, Trayvon Martin. Several of these paintings were shown. The exploitation by the police of the lives of these individuals, except Trayvon Martin, gave weight to my belief that we are in another period: a race war, pure and simply put.

I feel that people need to come to grips with what is really happening. The Left has been very passive in this regard. We need a resurgence of the Black Panthers to awaken the community. I also feel the need to try to evolve the work and confront my audience with my feelings. One painting is called *Honey*, and it's about the consumption and cannibalism of black folks by Whiteness. The more I research the more horrified I am of the realities we are going to face as Whiteness defines the future for us.

BR: The recent Guston show at Hauser & Wirth struck me as relevant too—important for Guston's handling of the subject matter, but, also, I think he created a form of painterly political satire. Guston found in Nixon a subject really worthy of the amount of work he did. I see something of that happening in your paintings, definitely with your show at Novella: *Common & Proper Nouns: The N-Word* (2015).

PW: In the Novella show I'm responding to the realities of having to inform and negotiate with my audience a platform that allows for the development of a character (or characters). It was the first time that my passion spilled out into a manifest character, the "N-Word." His creation has been years in the making and may reflect such influences as Richard Pryor and his comedy routine about this: "Up in the sky, it's a bird, a plane, a piece of coal, a crow, no it's SuperNigga."

Often, times like this are influenced by many things including comics. But this work is superseded by the recording of the deaths, which have become a common occurrence since the advent of camera phones. One has only to reflect upon Rodney King and the image of such brutal strength of the "state." Or the horror of a man being choked to death by the police as he pleads for his life. These are the vile tactics of the powerful overlooking the raw lack of humanity. I am moved, baby.

BR: I've known you now going on 30 years, so for me it's hard to pick from various periods in your painting to talk about in depth. You did some very great paintings while in Detroit, and I've written about the one at the DIA before . . .

PW: The painting at the Detroit Institute of Arts, *Portrait of Christopher D. Fisher, Fourth Reich Skinhead*, is from a body of works on perpetrators of hate crimes in the early '90s. Young black men had gone to the wrong side of the tracks and were beaten to death by marauding white youths, primarily in New York. The piece in the DIA is the largest of these works and an attempt to open up a discussion. It was originally hung in the Dutch galleries as part of an "interventions" show. It was meant to ask questions concerning the wealthy Dutch portraits and their relationship to the slave trade. In the middle of his forehead I wrote "race war," which was considered a bit controversial at the time. Now it just seems prescient.

About this time I started to also make paintings about black stereotypes—Mammy, Sambo, etc. It was not well received in Detroit. I was considered to be trespassing over a part of history most black folks preferred not to be reminded of. I kept exploring this idea and tried to take more responsibility for the ideas inherent in such subject matter by exploring the subtle racist imagery using animals such as ducks—they manifest as a stand-in for race with thick lips and bulging eyes—and cartoon characters such as Mickey Mouse and Heckle and Jeckle, which were overtly manifested with racist stereotypes.

That lead me to the point where I really reformed my thoughts as a result of traveling abroad and seeing work manifested from its own history, in Europe—Paris, Berlin, and Madrid. Goya had a great impact on me. His horrors gave me permission to go where I needed to go.

BR: One thing that has held my continued attention with your work has been this need you have of connecting "art" and "reality," engaging with the world through your work. I just finished this new biography of Joan Didion. I have considered her work influential with regard to my own writing, but the strangest thing happened while reading about her: after 30 years of only paying attention to her work, I was finding out how anti-Semitic, racist, and self-obsessed she was. I had previously thought her style of writing, in her journalism, came from a place of political satire. Then I find out that, for example, when she wrote about the SLA and Patricia Hearst, she identified with Randolph Hearst.

I mention this because I do want to talk about your biography a bit, but I also want to ask you if you feel that it is important to know about the artist's life when looking at their work. I am pretty sure that my question falls somewhere in the artspeak category of "identity politics," but I am thinking that there is something else there too.

PW: I imagine that biography is an important asset for any critic, writer, or intellectual. The "unexamined life" is a constant thing that I am aware of. I have always felt my art was a cathartic relationship to myself. I could not as a child make sense of my family, nor the outside world. It seemed to defy any kind of logic that I could come up with. Because of the toxic relationship I had with them, I felt compelled to understand all the repercussions. In effect, I saw my relationship to the outer world as one of constant confrontation.

I seemed not to understand the simplest of mechanisms, whether it was how a clock or time worked or even why my family wanted me to be aware of certain things. That education excluded how to deal or engage Whiteness. They would leave off the idea of Whiteness and white power and would expect me to understand. I was never given answers to the questions I had and often felt their rebuke. As I engaged the larger world, it seemed that all of these rebukes were personal rather than polemical. But now I see them as related to race and class, neither of which anyone ever explained to me.

It was in the abstractions of my earliest work that two things seemed to manifest: one was a kind of interest in the originality of what I made, and the other, that people/family seemed to have ideas about what the work was about. That frightened me because I had not established in my own mind a sense of what those images meant. It seemed that people held judgments about me, good or bad. In my family if there was a judgment, it was bad because I was operating outside of a norm, and it was politically incorrect. But outside my family, whites (namely, Jewish people) seemed to be enthusiastic about what they saw.

BR: In talking with other painters, I have often found that the strongest work comes from a place of pain—psychological, spiritual, or whatever.

PW: I often felt alienated from my community as I grew and identified with the Western tradition of image making, methods, and ideals. I was quite gifted as a young artist, and I was included in exhibitions beyond my family's understanding. I suspect they were proud but did not understand what it meant in relationship to me. I was hounded by the homosexual fear and idea that to be creative you were a "fag," which I didn't know about but scared me. My father thought I had communist leanings. (I suspect he was a marketplace capitalist.) I didn't play sports, and my brothers had a violent regard toward me. So there I was, out, and I didn't even know what that meant.

I certainly felt a kind of empathy for all these attributes, even though I had no idea what they meant. I noticed in the images I made that people would remark as if they knew me, yet I was still discovering what those things meant. Abstraction was a language I could not conceive of, yet at times operated in. So I drifted to representation out of fear and desire to control what people saw—as if I could make them see me as I saw myself, a simple yet complex human being. I didn't understand all these feelings; nevertheless I was becoming the outsider. I was lucky to go into therapy at the age of 15. I found out that the darkness in my mind and work came from my family and their friends, who responded to their own understanding of who I was. I rejected them all, of course, because I was a survivor at heart.

As my work evolved, so did my sense of self and empathy for the underdog. I have always taken them in my heart and believe that I must bear witness to the events and poverty of their lives.

BR: I like that—the painter as witness to their time. It is a fact that your work will outlast you, yet your voice will still be heard.

PW: It is not my voice I feel the need to exercise but the voice of many, who remain nameless. Day in and day out they deal with, encounter, engage the horror of our current crisis. We seem to forget that the history of this country is of violating the civil rights of the "Other," be they African-Americans, Mexicans, or indigenous people. There is no heaven, only the concept that Whiteness promotes controlling the natives, as they perceive us. The ideal of an afterlife is one of the great jokes played out through religion and Christian supremacy. We look for redemption for an act we never seem to escape, our "negritude" and/or "otherness." My vision is of the history of art being able to tell the appalling story of humankind and the evils it perpetuates. Every now and then we seem to need a war or cleansing to sort things out. Why? Because we are all fallible, and the weak unfortunately are on the front lines of that battle.

It's my hope that people of color wake up and take up the battle from a safer awareness of this struggle and not go into the night unarmed or unprepared. I know I'm suggesting a horror— and I imagine it will be—however, I don't know if it can be prevented. Maybe the West, Christians, white people, and the powerful will realize what a myth they live in. However, it would be a mistake to believe in such a possibility. We just elected a jackal, capable of unknown horrors. His demeanor is that of a sinner, the way he sits inward, self-aware of his demons. I can only imagine the kind of sickness he and his comrades are preparing for all of us.

Whiteness allows this horror to be played and must take responsibility—if only through my painting. Even worse, the planet is at stake, not just the survival of humankind, and that may take millions of years to repair, if at all. I can begin to see the links and the connections as one looks at the heart of evil deeds by evil men and women.

Published March 31, 2017.
Artslant

Imperial Bedrooms: Liz Markus + Bradley Rubenstein

Liz Markus was born in 1967 in Buffalo, New York and currently lives and works in Los Angeles. She is known for her idiosyncratic paintings that combine colorful expressionism with pop imagery. Her signature technique is saturated washes of acrylic paint on unprimed canvas. Vibrant colors diffuse and bleed into one another, creating wet-on-wet compositions that evoke '60s psychedelia as well as the "high art" of mid-century Color Field painting.

Bradley Rubenstein: I want to talk about some of the recent paintings, the Trump ones. But let's frame that discussion, in the context of your work, with two groups of work that I think are important. First was your show at ZieherSmith, *Are You Punk or New Wave?*, and at the other end of the spectrum was your *Girlfriends of the Rolling Stones* paintings.

Liz Markus: Yeah, they both express the rebellious side of me. The Punk/New Wave show specifically reflected my experience of the '80s, both in high school and art school. "Are you Punk or New Wave?" was an often-heard question in high school as we tried to best understand and categorize ourselves. I think of New Wave as more conceptual and Punk as more angry. Both served as a counterweight to our preppy lives at a private, all-girls school. In the show I think of *Plaid*, the *Johnny Rotten* paintings, and *Kate-as-punk* and maybe especially *Relax* and *War*, as New Wave, though I wasn't specifically painting them to fit into those categories. My portrait of Basquiat makes a good visual bridge to the *Girlfriends of the Rolling Stones* portraits. As my Punk/New Wave paintings were a reaction to my more staid daily life in prep school, the *Girlfriends* served as a release from the stringent women in my portrait series of iconic socialites. The latter were very buttoned up and sought to appear perfect. The *Girlfriends* are sexy, powerful, and though I named the series for whom they dated, are women who are really interested in pleasing themselves rather than a man.

BR: You folded a lot of ideas into simple images. I remember being really struck by the pieces. I wrote on those paintings, and I think it is relevant to quote myself here:

Punk was about color. Puce, fuchsia, chartreuse. The colors of spray paint; the colors of cheap nail varnish and hair color. Colors abhorrent to Nature. Color represented individual choices, perhaps the last individual choice that the disempowered could actually make. The legions of those that came after missed the boat, and black became standard issue, no doubt due to the misguided apotheosis of the gormless retard Sid Vicious as the poster-boy for the movement. Liz Markus, as witnessed by her solo exhibition *Are You Punk or New Wave?* at ZieherSmith hasn't forgotten the primary role that color played in those years.

It was both color and subject matter coming together perfectly. In a similar way the *Girlfriends* pictures use period colors, like something remembered, but you weren't there then, so there is this weird immediacy combined with a sense of distance.

LM: First of all, how about that piece of writing? Really insightful about the era and my work. Yeah, I liked how punks took plaid away from conservatives and made it their own flag. *War* in pink colors is really a nod to Act Up's pink triangle in their Silence = Death posters. Using the words "relax" and "war" (both Frankie Goes To Hollywood songs) at a grand scale was actually inspired by Ellsworth Kelly's *New York, NY* painting that hung in the Albright-Knox when I was growing up in Buffalo. I love how that painting flickers between abstraction and representation. Mine failed on that score. They don't flicker. I still love them.

BR: There is also something in your work that reminds me of Schnabel—combining portraits and genre work, with strange personal references.

LM: Ah, Schnabel. I hated his work when I saw it in the 1980s. Then, in grad school in 1995 I fell head over heels for it. I love the epic scale, both of his work and his ego. He is like a wizard who can summon great forces to come together on the canvas. I think you're right about our work relating both in our variety of genre and also in our attention to beautiful and poetic mark making. I think one of the benefits of Post Modernism is our ability to sort of pick through the history of painting, cafeteria style. I insist on my right to paint whatever I want, whether it's "confusing to collectors" or not. My "side paintings" are some of my favorites. That said, incorporating portraiture with genre work with strange personal references is straight out of Picasso.

BR: There is something in your work that keeps it from being straight satire, but there is a sense of exploring celebrity, or taking the piss out of "high art" there.

LM: Yes. There was a pervasive gallows humor in my house growing up. It came from my dad. He was a holocaust survivor with a wicked sense of humor. I'm not sure he used it to get through the holocaust. I doubt it. I'm guessing he had it before and that it came back, and maybe that's what kept him buoyant and happy in the face of having witnessed a total loss of humanity.

At any rate, it's this dark humor through which I view life. I think that comes across in the work not because I'm trying to imbue the work with it but because all of my work is somewhat biographical, in that I place a high value on painting from within. In 1999 I made a wall painting with the words "It's all about how Liz Markus responds to work." I had taken the gray grid of modernist graphic designer, I think it was Josef Müller-Brockmann, and created my own modernist poster about myself. There were two identical grids on each side of a door. The only difference was that one was matte and one was glossy. I had used the vocabulary of graphic design because I was thoroughly researching it to teach myself about design for my day job. But I also fell in love with it. So it came out in my artwork. I wanted to explain, within an artwork, what it was that my work was all about. That it is my response to something, to other art, to what's around me, to being a woman, to fashion, to politics. My take on all of those things is cynical but hopeful. There is great tee shirt I have from Buffalo that I think succinctly explains my work. There is an emblem with a Buffalo in the middle, and around the circle it says "BUFFALO, CITY OF NO ILLUSIONS."

BR: Oh yeah, you can see this in your paintings of "ladies who lunch" [*Town & Country*], as well as the *Girlfriends of the Rolling Stones*. We have talked about your interest in Sargent as a reference point, but there is also some Warhol, although in the case of Sargent's portraits that isn't as large a gap as it might seem . . .

LM: For about two weeks every year or so I become re-obsessed with John Singer Sargent. I read up on his technique, study his portraits, find lectures on him, make a pilgrimage to the Met to see the work in person. Usually I become so absorbed in his genius that I lose my connection to my own work, think it's terrible, wonder how anyone bothers to paint after Sargent, lament that I wasn't born in the 19th century when I would have gotten the grand academic education that he had. It gets intense. [laughing] Then I remember Warhol and who I am, and I can go back to my own work, probably having learned yet some more from the master.

BR: Getting back to Trump, this one painting [*Rip Off* (2016), acrylic on canvas, 72" × 60"] caught me by surprise when I saw it on my Facebook feed. There was surprisingly little art that really captured my interest with regard to the election and its results. Deb Kass did a Warholian take on the election that I thought was brilliant, but then there was a lot of things that looked like satirical political art but was, well, something else. Eric Fishcl drawing clown noses on Bannon. Stuff like that . . .

LM: I had been in the middle of a series inspired by fashion when Trump won. Specifically I had just painted a model in jeans and a flannel shirt with her arms out to the side. After the election I was furious and hurt, in mourning for what felt like a death, of Hillary. I needed a place to channel the rage. So I just started to write on my canvas. Later I saw that the model is in a classic Jesus on the cross position. Though I would have never intentionally painted a woman as martyr so directly, I thought it was terribly *apropos*. I think it works because I wasn't trying to make a political painting. Those ideas tend to be lame. This one came from the same place all the rest of my work comes from.

BR: There is a key element to high satire that seems rarer and rarer . . . the idea of being inside of, or part of, something that you are willing to simultaneously love and critique at the same time. That is the brilliance of Restoration theater, as well as Philip Guston's Nixon drawings. This is something you seem to understand, and it kind of ties all of your work together.

LM: I know what you mean. Maybe that began in my Nancy Reagan portraits. Although I was using a photo of Nancy as reference, I never meant for people to recognize her as Nancy Reagan. When they did, I stopped painting her for a while. Later she fit in with my exploration of WASP culture, and I picked her up again, this time intending her to be Nancy. As I saw her face distort under my bleeding stains, I began to have some empathy for her. Often in my portraits of her she looks like she's really brittle and just barely (or maybe not even) keeping it together. Nancy was a woman who figured out how to attain power at a time when woman were not allowed access to that arena. I respect her for that. I also disagree with her politics. I don't think the paintings would have worked had I intended to make fun of her. They would have been so one-dimensional. High satire must start with some sympathy for the devil.

Published June 28, 2017.
Artslant

The Informers: Ryan Steadman + Bradley Rubenstein

Ryan Steadman lives and works in Brooklyn. He is an artist, writer, and curator. He has written for *ArtDesk*, *Cultured Magazine*, *Artforum*, *Modern Painters*, and *The Observer*.

Bradley Rubenstein: So, for background, in this series of talks for *ArtSlant*, I would like to talk to artists who are also involved in criticism or theory to some degree. When I first began talking with Andrea [Alessi, Editor for *ArtSlant*] I thought it was a pretty straightforward concept. As I thought about it more, I realized I wasn't really interested in the idea of "artist plus does something else." There are any number of "crossovers" in disciplines: Julian Schnabel is a painter and a filmmaker; Mel Bochner is a painter who has also been a good art reviewer. That's fine, but not quite the idea. Rather—using Barnett Newman, and more recently Mira Schor, as examples—I'd like to focus on artists who broaden their field through criticism, writing, curating, or whatnot. It's a micro-difference, but to me it is somewhat a measure of intent on the part of the artist.

With that as background, I want to talk a bit about some of the ways I see your work fitting into this category. First, though, can you talk a little about your background and your own work?

Ryan Steadman: Well, I went to Pratt Institute in 1998 for graduate school as a painter and have lived in Brooklyn ever since. There was a lot to learn about painting there, but what struck me most was the excellent art criticism program (Marjorie Welish, Robert Morgan), and that quickly became an interest as well, though I didn't really write until much later on, around 2008.

BR: And what do you feel was the point at which you went from making things to thinking about how making things fits into a larger picture?

RS: That's a good question. I've worked for a few galleries over the years, so I've seen how the sausage gets made (so to speak), but working at Feature Inc., owned by the late Hudson, perhaps taught me the most about a wholistic approach to art. By that I mean I witnessed a gallery being run as an art project, staffed by artists, writers, and curators. This was long before the return of artist-run spaces, yet everyone who was a part of Feature Inc. didn't seem to locate their artistic output within one simple medium or practice. It was a good energy. Sorry, I sound like a hippie.

BR: I thought that much of your work for *Observer* was really good art writing. I liked how you and Walter Robinson sort of complemented each other there. He has sort of a Restoration-period feel to his writing, while I kind of pictured you as Christopher Isherwood. The talk that you and he did where the phrase Zombie Formalism was coined—how did that happen?

RS: That was a very strange time, I suppose because of the market. I had been interested in, among other things, New York City artists who were looking back to Arte Povera for inspiration, creating abstract objects and wall works with found objects, but less with actual trash and more with product surplus. There was also an interest in how industry was coming closer and closer to mimicking the "tricks" of painting. It felt very American, I suppose. My interest culminated in a show I put together called *Ain'tings*. The irony is that, by this time, in 2014, I was already feeling pretty critical about the next generation of these artists, who produced cookie-cutter, high-turnover, and, of course, market-friendly works for a generation of copycat collectors who rated art like stocks. Though I wouldn't have termed it Zombie Formalism, I had the instinct to call out this work for over a year when Walter dropped his great piece, which many in the art world appreciated. Walter maintains that *Ain'tings* was the "legitimate version" of Zombie Formalism, and I still love most of the artists in that show. It was a great catchphrase, and Walter kept the ball rolling with opportunities like the SVA talk. (Stefan Simchowitz was originally supposed to be on that panel, which would've been fantastic.) At any rate, I think people craved a retro "fire and brimstone" critic because everything started to feel like a press release, and Walter's intelligent yet down-to-earth writing countered that. He wasn't afraid to say "I hate that." Another irony is that Walter's painting got a big critical boost after that, so he immediately started writing less! I was—and still am—maybe more objective as a critic. I honestly don't think many artists get into this with a "scheme" in mind. Artists lose the thread because of money or other reasons, but almost all of them have made *something* with some inspiration involved and a yearning to communicate something. I try to always remember that, even when I'm being very critical. Christ, maybe I am a hippie?

BR: The "aha" moment with regard to your writing happened when I read the "Gimme Shelter" piece (http://observer.com/2016/06/gimme-shelter-why-artists-are-using-abstraction-to-hide-their-faces/). This really struck me as almost a throwback to Greenberg and Rosenberg—someone looking at paintings and thinking about them on many levels—psychological, historical, anthropological. And, of course, I found myself thinking, yeah, that's how I think about painting too. It also seemed like the inverse of Zombie Formalism. First you have a "movement" of work that is bereft of aesthetic and moral value, then one comes along to correct it.

RS: Thank you. That was really fun to write. I don't know how many people read it, though (laughs). For the record, I think these kinds of "corrections" are mostly about fashion, particularly when it comes to painting where new variables are few and far between. The way I see it, certain artists, like a Sergej Jensen in 2005 for instance, make a style—something that would eventually be described as Zombie Formalism—popular through their own originality. Because of his rise in visibility and the fact that he's an excellent artist, Jensen's work inspired many, many young artists. So 5 to 10 years later, the style he helped energize was overwhelmingly prevalent, and since there are more bad and mediocre artists than there are good ones, you start seeing lots of bad examples of what you can loosely file under the term Zombie Formalism. It's not rocket science, and I don't think there's anything malicious about it—it's a natural series of events. Look at all the bad figurative painting we're seeing right now. But I think what's new is how compressed—meaning, fast—the fashion cycles have become, and you have to wonder if it's detrimental to the artworks we end up seeing.

BR: So, one of the things I have noted in a lot of contemporary painting is the use of satire as a way of conveying a political position. I think that relates a lot to much of the criticism out there too. You and Walter both captured something of that in your writing, and looking at your painting I feel that there's some aspect of that too. At a very basic level you are making unreadable books, for example.

RS: That's an interesting take. When I came out of school I started looking closely at a generation of ironic or satirical artists like Lisa Yuskavage and Sean Landers, and my own paintings were originally a paired down form of "slapstick" narratives. I would say that the current book paintings definitely court an ironic reading by simply focusing on the "aesthetic" of reading material rather than its content, but I'd like to think the paintings are as much an earnest questioning of how and why these things came to be. They're also inspired by a love of the artistic precedents that fueled some of these aesthetics, such as Josef Albers.

BR: Do you separate the ideas and subject matter you write about from your studio work, or do you see one as elaborating on another? There are a lot of topics that are easier to tackle in writing, I think, that would be difficult to address in a painting.

RS: I think as far as my writing goes, the ideas and subjects are fairly separate from what I'm pursuing in the studio. For one, the media outlet often determines what is written about, and second, I feel as if I really need to do the research and expand my knowledge base in order to adequately write about a new artist or show. That being said, I cannot help but have a certain point of view that I bring to both my art and my writing, and the work I'm writing about will often inspire my own studio process. I would say my writing vacillates between stumping for art that I *know* is good and needs more recognition, and art that feels foreign and can teach me something new.

BR: You have a show up now at Safe Gallery in Williamsburg. Can you talk a little about the new paintings?

RS: Yes, it's a two-person show with the painter Anna Schachte, who makes lively and freewheeling abstractions that riff off of letters of the alphabet. Though I've often shown my work on the wall, this show gave me the chance to really position the pieces as "sculpture" more than ever before. I've always considered the work to be a synthesis of painting and sculpture, since the canvases are painted in the round so as to further emulate books (with spines and pages), but this is the first time I've shown most of these paintings flat, and it really emphasizes all the different angles of the works. On top of that, this is the first show where I've created "assemblages" of the books. I started by simply stacking them on top of each other to highlight new color and line combinations, but that led to even more acrobatic experimentations.

Those ideas came after some talks with the artist Ethan Greenbaum, who selfishly wanted me to expose the backs of my canvases in novel ways. (Ethan often turns accidentally exposed parts of buildings into luminous and mystical objects through his own multi-pronged art process.) It was a great idea, of course, and I also happened to be very into the suspended and animated geometries of Joel Shapiro at the time, so suddenly, a few comically balanced book stacks began to appear. I think it just furthers how I've wanted to push the aesthetic focus of the book into the spotlight. I like to relate books to paintings, an art form that "died" and then had to be loved for its pure form instead of its function. The book is going through something similar, what with information moving to the internet. It's absurd that we still have all these giant, heavy books lying around, but we like them, I guess.

Published January 10, 2018.
Artslant

Game Symmetry: Hannah Kallenbach + Bradley Rubenstein

The Proust Questionnaire has its origins in a parlor game popularized by Marcel Proust, the French essayist and novelist, who believed that, in answering these questions, an individual reveals his or her true nature. Below, Hannah Kallenbach and Bradley Rubenstein reinterpret Mr. Proust's concept.

Hannah Kallenbach is a Brooklyn-based actor and performance artist whose work takes many forms, often at once, ranging from stand-up to face dancing to durational performance installations. Her current artistic interest is flaunting her grossness and connecting audiences through our universal loneliness.

What is your idea of perfect happiness?

Being able to do whatever I want to do in a given moment without financial, social, political, psychological, or physical restraints.

What is your greatest extravagance?

I am learning to not spend as much money on my work, to use more trash or found items.

What is your current state of mind?

Make make make and document all that you make be young and embrace fucking up and have fun art can be fun theatre can be entertaining life can be fun.

What is the trait you most deplore in yourself?

Self-deprivation is pretty useless.

What is the trait you most deplore in others?

Feigning interests, small talk, fake nice.

What do you consider the most overrated virtue?

Intelligence. Smart humans are so often excused for shitty behavior based on their intellect. You see it during the #metoo and #timesup movements. People attempting to excuse shitty behavior with "but he's so smart." I don't care how smart you are, how you got the social standing you now have. Do better.

What is your most marked characteristic?

I think having an identical twin is a marked characteristic of mine.

What do you most value in your friends?

Someone who will say yes to dancing at 3 a.m.

When and where were you happiest?

In Greece in sunset in the ocean on an inflatable, drunk, alone, I remember thinking I am most happy right now.

On what occasion do you lie?

Oh, I lie all of the time. Small things mostly. Especially to strangers. I'll say anything if it makes the interaction slightly more interesting for me. For instance, my name at Starbucks and Panera is Kiki. Every time I wear these pants with paint on them I bought that way from American Eagle, a stranger asks me if I'm a painter and I just agree and make up fake stories about my painting career. Sometimes I'll make up whole stories of things that I haven't done just to start conversations with strangers on the subway. I love to lie.

Which talent would you most like to have?

To be a singer. It must feel so liberating to soar with your voice like that.

If you could change one thing about yourself, what would it be?

I wish I had an incredible memory so I could write in vivid detail about my life and the things I've seen. I think vivid memory is key to being a great writer.

If you could change one thing about your family, what would it be?

That I could talk with my parents freely and uncensored about ourselves. There's so much I may never know about them.

What is your most treasured possession?

I've moved so much I really don't have that much stuff, but I wrote these hand-written notes, in detail, about each person I've ever kissed. Originally I made them to give to my "future daughters," which is hilariously dumb, maybe, but yeah, it's fascinating the details you forget if you don't write them all down. Also I love that I thought that I might have daughters one day and they'd want to know their mother as a sexual being.

What do you regard as the lowest depth of misery?

Loneliness.

Who are your favorite writers?

I'm really into Kathy Acker right now, but I also hold a large space in my heart for *Star Wars* fan fiction.

Who is your favorite hero of fiction?

A hero . . . I've always been a fan of the Sith, which I know are technically the villains. They are honest and find power in their emotions, which I always found to be a beautiful message living in a society that tells us not to get too emotional. The Sith are kicking ass using their emotions to guide them in their power. I always loved that.

Who are your heroes in real life?

So many! I'm manically listing my stream of consciousness . . . Carrie Fisher, Aziza Barnes, Jessica Almasy, most all the children I babysit, Kristine Haruna Lee, Christen Clifford, Zoë Ligon, Carolee Schneemann, Rachel Chavkin, Roxane Gay, Theresa Buchheister, Sam Pinkleton, Michelle Obama. Can I list my partner and all their parents?

What is it that you most dislike?

I dislike being taken advantage of, being talked down to, being fetishized, being ignored.

What do you consider your greatest achievement?

I am constantly seeking experiences.

If you were to die and come back as a person or thing, what do you think it would be?

I would come back as a v straight bro as pure punishment.

If you could choose what to come back as, what would it be?

But I would want to come back as a v gay dolphin.

Published February 7, 2018.
CultureCatch

Little Q + A: Rick Briggs + Bradley Rubenstein

Rick Briggs is from Philadelphia and lives and works in Brooklyn, New York. He has developed distinct bodies of work that reflect his philosophy of making art based on personal experience and out of his own working history. Briggs is a member of the American Academy of Arts and Letters.

Bradley Rubenstein: This is a great place to start, with the painting *Shotgun Wedding* (2012). It is kind of like an index of the imagery and ideas that you are working with now. It reminds me of a kind of work, similar to that of Jonathan Lasker or Peter Halley, in a way. You have organized your gestures and process.

Rick Briggs: I feel like Lasker's gestures are always in quotation marks, like he really wants that distance. I've always maintained my gesture as being more intuitive and direct, and about capturing a moment. That said, I did begin this painting with a vague idea of indexing different roller pan patterns. This happens when a relatively dry roller picks up the impression of the roller pan, which then looks "printed" on the canvas simply by gently rolling it out. But I can never quite settle on a simple approach to painting, like cataloging a gesture or texture. It seemed too detached, scientific, even. I like to make rules and then break them. Besides, I'm more invested in experimentation and transformation. That's where the round canvases and cutting into the surface and making niches showed up in this painting—something I began doing in the mid-'80s.

A funny story related to this painting is that about a year after I made it, I saw a Sarah Cain show at Lelong. She had done this installation, and one of her paintings had a roller stuck to the surface and holes cut through the canvas. I was with a friend, the painter Harriet Korman, who had already seen my painting in the studio, and we just looked at each other in amazement and burst out laughing. Here I thought I'd done something "original," and there was someone else on the other side of the country making a somewhat similar painting (in a way), and neither of us knew of the other's work. Collective unconscious? Zeitgeist? I don't know, but I do know painting is very humbling.

BR: These new pieces feel really right for the moment. After a period of "zombie formalism" and whatnot, it's interesting seeing paintings that are imbued with a kind of vitality to their gesture—an "internal architecture" is how I think I first described them when I saw them.

RB: Thanks, Bradley. Vitality is important to me. I always think of Matisse saying, if you're not ready to go into the studio, go ride a horse. In other words, bring some energy, some verve. After all, we're trying to breathe life into these inanimate objects, and that's not easy. I also like the word "internal" because I'm not referring to any external architecture, but, rather, interested in finding a structure that comes from within. *Rolled Structure* (2010) was the first roller painting and was a breakthrough in the sense that the painting had previously been made up of all these cute little areas that essentially added up to nothing. It was failing miserably, and I needed to paint the whole thing out quickly. I resorted to my house painting supplies, alkyd primer, and rollers. I knew from experience that these moments of failure are also ripe with potential for creation, and since the surface was still wet, I just kept working on it. A basic image appeared, but without the rhythm of the line, it's nothing. I've always had an affinity for the simplicity of the line paintings of Agnes Martin, early David Reed, or even Robert Ryman paintings composed of stacked, thickly brushed horizontal lines. In the early to mid-'90s, I did a series of work that essentially tried to wed the existential angst of Guston's late reductive abstract work of the early '60's with the horizontal line paintings of Agnes Martin with her Zen-like approach—a collision of approaches, to be sure. With this new linear work I felt like I had circled back to those earlier concerns. *Big Yellow* (2011) reminded me of a painter's scaffold and had a feeling of monumentality. And *44* (2014) was one of those where all the pieces just fell into place very organically, where it felt like the painting made itself. I like it when a big painting feels like a tossed-off sketch. I suppose the one that has the most kinship to external architecture would be *Space Waffle* (2011), which was perhaps an unconscious response to the anonymous corporate high-rises beginning to go up in Williamsburg. I like the idea of referring to high Modernism, but by utilitarian means.

BR: Jumping back a bit, because I think it relates here . . . Tell me about the *Painter Man* groups you did.

RB: Many artists have to support themselves with a job. My two *Painter Man* series were a darkly humorous pseudo-autobiographical narrative of my life as a house painter. I needed to tell a story and thought: here's a way to empower myself and embrace this idea of the artist as workingman. My work has always had an autobiographical aspect, but with the abstract work it had never been so explicit. It was interesting to think in terms of film, as much as art history, as a source to draw on for imagery. For example, the paintings are flooded with blood imagery, but the inspiration is as much from Kubrick's *The Shining* as any painted depiction of a martyred saint. Also, since my background had been entirely in abstraction, the challenge of suddenly having to figure out how to represent stuff was interesting. But once I'd told my story and completed those two series, I didn't feel the need to keep retelling it. I'm not interested in repeating myself, which is why I keep moving. What became more interesting to me was the idea of transforming my everyday job materials into art. I liked the ready-made authenticity and spattered surfaces of my used drop covers and the physical, material nature of painting on them. This became the through line between that work and what I'm doing now, with my inclusion of stir sticks, drop covers, paint skins, t-shirts, which, in turn, connected me back to the work I was doing in the '80s—attaching small canvases on object-like painting. It's very flattering when people tell me now how that '80s work looks so current.

BR: Your work reflects a kind of '70s aesthetic in a way. I'm reminded of someone like Blinky Palermo, who really broke down the barriers of what were proletariat materials, and gestures. He did a wall piece I saw in Germany where one wall was rolled, and one was brushed. He was basically just painting the gallery white, but the gesture—the artistic gesture—of brushing the wall compared to rolling it was an aesthetic question.

RB: I don't know that Palermo piece, but the conceptual simplicity of it seems quite poetic to me. I went to school in the '70s, so of course that time had a huge influence on my thinking. I'm thinking now of movements like Process Art, Lyrical Abstraction, and Arte Povera, for example. Speaking of proletariat materials, I think people forget how radical Judd's plywood boxes were at the time, or Burri's use of burlap for that matter. I really like that attitude of making art with whatever's at hand. In art school in the '70s, there were people making squeegeed abstraction à la Jack Whitten; I was scattering acrylic paint on raw canvas on the floor à la Larry Poons. I loved the freedom of mixing some paint in a bucket and reaching my hand in and grabbing the paint to toss. I guess the use of the paint roller is, in a way, an attempt to maintain that freedom.

The Abstract Expressionists were probably my biggest influence. I love that de Kooning and Kline worked as housepainters and that, along with Pollock, used house paint in their work. De Kooning's comment about, all he really needed was a gallon of black and a gallon of white and he was in business, really resonates. I switched to alkyd house paint from oil because I wanted to work large, and the cost is peanuts compared to tubed oil paint. Can you imagine squeezing out paint tubes to make enough paint to make one long roller mark? It's absurd. Plus, I like its ready-to-go consistency.

BR: In this one (*Black Sticks*, 2014) you touch on Pollock's *Blue Poles* (1952), and Miró, with the paint can skin. Your use of those reminds me of Frank Stella saying that he wanted the paint to look as good on the canvas as it did in the can.

RB: It's funny to think of my little painting in the context of the monumentality of Pollock's *Blue Poles*. My "poles" are simply stir sticks, which function as line, but there is a connection there. The paint skins form inside the can, and I hated peeling them off and throwing them away. They become ready-made colored circles.

I once had a teacher who claimed Pollock wasn't that important because he didn't have any followers, but Larry Poons is someone who certainly comes out of Pollock, and Dona Nelson has been pouring paint for years. You can't avoid your influences, right? The only way past is through. Miró did a lot of weird things; he may have been one of the earliest to pour paint. I'm remembering seeing some pancake-like pools he poured on paintings. I love his playfulness and the buoyancy of his work.

Stella once said, "When I open a can of green paint, I wonder why anyone would want to represent say, grass, with it—it's so beautiful just as it is." I think of Stella when I go to Janovic—I love buying a gallon of any color I want.

Published September 5, 2019.
CultureCatch

Little Q + A: Carroll Dunham: Millree Hughes × Dennis Kardon × Bradley Rubenstein

Below is a discussion following the show *Carroll Dunham* at Barbara Gladstone, April 20–June 16, 2018.

Millree Hughes is a digital artist, born 1960 in Hawarden, North Wales, the son of an Anglican priest, and now lives and works in New York. He began making art on the computer in 1998 in New York City. He created the imaginary glam band Lummox, which he described as the pure embodiment of working-class pop culture circa 1972 in Rhyl, Wales. Following that, he starred in *Lummox: the Movie* (2014), a documentary about his band. Hughes is also known for his lenticulars, which are animated images that move in relation to the viewer. His subject matter is nature and landscape realized by distant means, underscoring the difficult relationship between nature and technology.

Dennis Kardon, born in 1950, is from Des Moines, Iowa and lives and works in Brooklyn. Early in his career, in the '70s and '80s, he exhibited black-and-white cut paper pieces. He also made woodblock prints and paintings in the '80s. His best-known piece is *49 Jewish Noses*, which displays 49 noses of Jewish family members, friends, celebrities, art dealers, etc. that he sculpted and painted. Kardon writes art reviews in publications including *Hyperallergic, Art in America, artcritical, artnet,* and *The Brooklyn Rail.*

> Sailors fighting in the dance hall
> Oh man, look at those cavemen go
> It's the freakiest show.
> —David Bowie

Millree Hughes: What is it? How do I know it's good? In the old days the paper would tell you, the TV would tell you. If it was cultural there was one station that specifically dealt with that Now, unfortunately, it is hard to tell. There are too many voices vying for your attention. Which one is trustworthy? If you are an artist or a musician, an actor, or a writer, you can use your judgement. But if you're not, how can you tell, for example, if a painting is worth looking at?

Carroll Dunham has never been willing to talk about what his pistol-penis packing Puritans or his funky female figures are actually about. He has only ever talked about his work formally and how it relates to art history. How his female figures relate to Cézanne's bathers, for example. But I found myself at his last show asking "Can we talk about the assholes?"

This time is no different. Painted in 2017 they are not necessarily about the American election. Despite that, many of the paintings are of two cavemen with bushy manes and floppy dicks battling it out in the woods. I see the wrestling figures from Poussin's *Rape of the Sabine Women* of 1612 and something of the simplicity and figural dynamism of Picasso's *Figures on the Beach* of 1931. Dunham creates a great, in the middle, in your grill, physicality. He has stripped the figure back to grubby white canvas contained by a thick black line. There's a tree green and a sky blue. But after that there's not much left on your plate to eat, other than the meat and two veg.

Bradley Rubenstein: The flora and fauna are crucial here. He has painted those with a different hand. They seem more layered on à la David Salle's work than actually part of the scene. And that dog is such a weird combination of kitsch cuteness and a schoolboy reference to dogs licking their balls. It is that combination we saw with his last show at Gladstone: a Lady Godiva on a horse. There was a series of working drawings that rendered the scene over and over, until gradually you had a childlike drawing, a sort of set of notes on regression therapy, or the kind of children's drawings of nude family members where the parent is like, "Do I need to worry about this?"

But there is humor here that is both coarse and refined at the same time. There is a diptych, or two variations on a theme, of a rear view shot of testicles, and of an anus. In one the anus is on top, in the second, it is balls up. On the one hand it is an almost Picasso-like abstraction, integrating the body into the landscape, like in his late paintings. On the other hand it reminds me of an old Joan Rivers joke: "So I am in bed last night and my husband says 'Joan, your box is too tight and your ass is too loose.' And I say, 'Edgar get off my back.'"

MH: American artists frequently tell you that what you are looking at it is not what they meant you to see. Chuck Close claims that his work is about the formal language of painting, He's just been practicing on what is closest to him. They just happened to be the famous artists of the day. Vanessa Beecroft exhibited a room full of beautiful naked women in Prada heels but only ever talked about them as if they were objects. Jeff Koons is particularly good at pinning some glorious "advert bullshit" to his masthead. It's about desire! It's about beauty! Anything other than what you are actually looking at.

BR: There is something about Dunham's nudes that seem timely now. There are younger artists who deal with the same ideas, but in some cases their simple act of painting the nude is political. Noomi Roomi, a Moscow artist said:

> If we will look back at ancient Greece, for example, where homosexuality was common, we'll notice how inspirational was male's body for artists of that time. They depicted both female's and male's beauty because they didn't have any non-hetero taboos; they were opened to both genders. I guess, the problem of not drawing bodies in sexual context can be seen as that we still have this fear, we still perceive male's nudity as something "gay." Also, women do reflect on themselves—maybe that's why they paint females' bodies more often, although I don't understand why modern female artists don't explore the male as much. But, it should be noted that my art was never exhibited in galleries or on festivals in Russia because no one dared exhibit them. I only got positive responses from Russian audiences, but never got any permission to show my works publicly. Also, I was rejected when I wanted to print my books in Moscow because my art was seen as dangerous, prohibited . . . People are clearly afraid.

Dennis Kardon: Dunham's new paintings are sexual, but not homosexual. They are very much about a white straight guy trying to come to terms with his attitude towards male bodies, starting with his own, as expressed by the fact that the two figures are almost the same, so I assume they are aspects of himself in turmoil, or at least wrestling with the idea of his maleness. In the last two shows, one of which I reviewed for *Art in America*, the female body was seen as an *other*, or as a muse, and always depicted alone, so I guess accessible to artist/viewer. The paintings of trees on the other hand seemed a stand in for the male body. And they still have a formal metonymy with cocks and balls.

The history of body depictions in Western painting is usually that women's bodies are objects of desire, and men's bodies are objects of torture or competition, with the exception of Caravaggio or David. Manet's *Jesus Mocked by the Soldiers* (1865) is a great example of the different male attitudes of masculinity. In Dunham the wrestlers do not touch each other erotically, though there is a certain tenderness expressed that is just short of a caress. Penises are never erect or semi-erect.

The abundance of assholes feels to be about fear of penetration, and dominance. I keep waiting for one of the wrestlers to stick a club in one. When a lone male is lying down, the painting is titled *Left for Dead (1)* (2017), which is telling, as if abandonment is the issue, and the competition is not innocent. I did find it interesting that he eroticized men's nipples, making them erect and pink, and pretty much the way he paints women's nipples.

MH: Why are American artists so evasive about content? Why do they put something right in your face and then pretend that they don't see. The separation between content and intent that is endemic to really successful American art begins when it leaves the studio. The galleries attempt to legitimize the art. If the painting is worth a lot of money It must be on a continuum with everything else that rich people buy. It needs to be placed in history. Something is good because it's like something else that has already proved itself.

DK: I disagree with your idea about content as a visual narrative that a painter should verbally address. Content occurs in the ambiguity that a painter establishes and is something that viewers could address verbally, but it is not the business of a painter to spoil for viewers. So instead painters address their physical actions in the creating of the painting, or even the feelings that might arise, which is why the formal structure is safe to talk about. I think artists today talk way too much about content or subject matter in their work, which should be left to a viewer to try to come to terms with.

BR: The last thing I want to bring up is that Dunham is dealing with depictions of sex, and in an odd way with the sexuality of painting. I like what Mira Schor wrote:

> I would lay claim both to being polymorphously perverse, because, after all, why shouldn't painting benefit from the input of more than one sense, and also to having the very same body part, connecting my optic nerve and my hand to my sexuality, especially if sexuality is defined as not just the province of genital intercourse but as a profound life/death drive. It is in fact precisely this intersection of visuality, sexuality, and manual impulse that makes me a painter. And I would add something left out of this particular biological theory, that is, the connection of optic nerve, sexuality, and hand to intellect.

I think there is something of late Picasso in Dunham's work—that acting out or recreating sexual encounters on canvas.

DK: The day Dunham really ups the ante will be the day when one of those guys is black, and I will be interested in how he will depict his dick. All the people in Dunham's recent paintings are as white as can be; the white of the primed canvas.

MH: So stop focusing on the cocks, the pussies, and the assholes; they are in Dunham's work to get the punters in the door. Once they are there they should be looking at how the paintings are made and what other artists they refer to . . . right?

BR: Yeah, "Boys keep swinging, boys always work it out."

Published June 12, 2018.
CultureCatch

Paint It, Black: Ajamu Kojo + Bradley Rubenstein

Ajamu Kojo is from Little Rock, Arkansas and is currently based in Brooklyn. He is a painter, photographer, sculptor, writer, and filmmaker, best known for his project *Black Wall Street*. His work is primarily figurative and examines history and current events, sometimes focusing on social inequalities, exploring topics such as racism, sexism, and religion.

Bradley Rubenstein: So, just starting at the beginning, you grew up in Little Rock, Arkansas . . .

Ajamu Kojo: I did. In quite the patriarchal environment. I'm not even sure why I felt the need to point that out except that it may shed some light on who I am as a person. The men in my family were a strong influence on my upbringing. In my mind, as a child, all of my uncles were the definition of cool personified. I come from a line of educators, farmers, ministers, entrepreneurs, attorneys . . . I grew up privileged enough to never need much, yet aware the privilege could be taken away at a moment's notice.

My Pop grew up on a farm. My mama did not. My paternal grandfather was a farmer and my paternal grandma, an educator. Both of my mama's parents were educators. My maternal grandfather was a jazz and blues lover. I used to go into his man cave and listen to his 45s and full-length albums as a youth, which is what ultimately lead to my love for jazz music. We were exposed to a bit of everything growing up. My mama would enroll me and my siblings into summer arts programs, and my Pop would instill the importance of hard work. I'll never forget the summer he and my cousin Vernon got me a job cleaning school buses during the dead of summer. I learned very quickly I wasn't about that life. One summer was enough for me. Yard work and a paper route would suit me just fine!

But I digress . . .

I seem to recall discovering Miles Davis *Kind of Blue* and *Bitches Brew* LPs in the man cave. The *Bitches Brew* LP cover blew my mind. It was freaky to me. Beautiful, but freaky. I didn't see that image again until I entered college, and that's the moment I knew it was just as special to me as the music inside the album cover's sleeve. The artist's name is Mati Klarwein, and little did I know at the time, my fascination with his work would lead me to Vienna. Up to that point, I'd never set foot inside Europe.

Yes, Klarwein's works can be attributed directly to my studies in Austria. The hills and mountain regions of Austria reminded me somewhat of Arkansas. Of course the ice cream there is far better. I didn't formally attend art school under a university setting. I'm primarily self-taught, not to be confused with never having been instructed. I took a summer art course during elementary school and attended art class during high school. I've also been drawing since childhood. But it wasn't until I traveled abroad that I found myself seriously focused under academic tutelage.

BR: Before getting into your painting, you also went to film school, which I think is really relevant to the *Black Wall Street* series.

AK: It is indeed relevant. I studied film production during my undergraduate years at Howard University. I spent many hours writing and imagining what it would be like to make a living as a filmmaker. I'd been interested in some aspect of storytelling from a young age. I recall being very interested in *Archie and Jughead* comic books as a youth. That same interest later developed into a fascination for science fiction and fantasy comics like *Heavy Metal* during my adolescent years. So, yeah, the element of art and storytelling has been a part of my life since early on.

When I began taking on the *Black Wall Street* series, I knew from the very beginning that the most important element would be the story. What is it that I want to say? Why is it important? And how do I make it universally relatable?

BR: That is something that really comes out in your work, the importance of narrative.

AK: Each painting acts as a single frame out of the 24 that it takes to make up one second in film.

There were many things I experienced while living in D.C. that can be attributed to my fondness for the art of storytelling and film, but there was a very specific moment I seem to remember being directly related to the story of *Black Wall Street*. I made note of it and filed it away. I knew I'd come back to revisit the idea one day. However, I had no idea when or what form it would eventually take on.

BR: Can you talk a little about that. Not just about the series itself, but all the steps along the way. I think your process is highly conceptual in a way that is very strong.

AK: Well, I initially thought of producing a film on the subject matter, but by the time I was to give it any serious consideration, I was heavily engrossed in my career as a painter. So, I decided perhaps I could mix the two to a degree.

BR: And you do already actually work in the film business, so you are coming at the project with a lot of that knowledge.

AK: Indeed. Having worked in production years prior and now working in pre-production, I've been exposed to the broad strokes of what it takes to create a film on a professional level.

I decided to create a small-scale BTS film documentation of my process. I wanted the portraits to be personal not only for myself and the subjects, but also for the audience. So I decided to enlist the services of my comrades, fellow artists, and friends to encapsulate the spirit of the ancestors that lived before, during, and after the devastation of the Black Wall Street massacre. A good friend of mine served as the production designer. We dressed the set, which was located inside my apartment, and scheduled sittings throughout a 12-hour period. The day was catered, and once I got the last shot, everyone stuck around for a mini wrap party.

There was a lot of hard work involved, and I loved every moment. This of course would be considered the pre-production stage, which was followed by the actual production of creating the paintings, and then of course the post-production/exhibition phase of the works themselves. The payoff has been extraordinary.

BR: One of the things I find really impressive in the series is how theatrical they are, in the way, say, David is theatrical. You are taking this historical content but adding layers both physically, but also with regards to different disciplines—your photography, art direction, and whatnot. We were talking in your studio about the black pours for example.

AK: Ah, yes! The black pours. The mystery. I think what's been most interesting about the black pour element of the paintings is listening to people's interpretation of its meaning. Therefore, I don't want to give away too much during this interview. I would however like to share an anecdote about the black pours/runs which frame my canvases: I had a gentleman approach me during the opening and express how the ancestors must have guided the way in which the paint rolled down the canvas as not to obstruct the visage of my subjects. I was both flattered and amused. I didn't have the heart to tell him that I manipulated the canvas in such a way as to control the flow of the paint. But is that not part of the mystique behind art? Create the illusion and wow the audience? It makes sense why I'm such a huge fan of magic; especially sleight of hand.

You mentioned the works being theatrical, and I thank you for the compliment. I must admit, this has been one of the more challenging components to the compositions. In the past, I've embraced a more candid approach to my portraits. I enjoy cracking the veneer of my subjects so that the final result feels less contrived. And so, being that the very nature of these portraits lends itself to a more rehearsed composition, the challenge for me is finding a happy medium between that and something far less prepared. Part of that obstacle was overcome by using people I know. That familiarity was helpful. I still feel I can push even further. I'm pleased with the results, but . . . I dunno.

BR: You have a body of work going which deals strictly within a very traditional history of figure painting . . .

AK: My time abroad was spent learning a very specific technique of mixing egg white tempera and oil paints known as the *mischtechnik*. It is believed to be the closest to the formula that the Dutch and Flemish masters used in their own works. When I initially discovered the art of Mati Klarwein, I wanted to paint like him. I was schooled under the tutelage of Maestro Phil Jacobson, who was taught by Ernst Fuchs. Fuchs also taught Mati the magic technique as well.

BR: That focus on materials and sense of the history of painting is important, especially in the last ten years or so where much painting is being made that is either satirical or emphasizes the "deskilled" artist.

AK: Yea, I mean if I'm gonna be perfectly honest about it, I practice the discipline mainly because it caters to my meticulous nature. I also like the way the paintings look, not quite like traditional oil paintings.

BR: I think approaching the figure is also a political form at the moment. I just saw a piece in *New York Magazine*, a sort of discussion on the politics of painting the nude right now.

AK: Well, I just so happen to have begun a series of nudes about four years ago. I've created it mainly for two reasons: my appreciation of the human form, in this particular case, the female form; and the lack of Black nudes, people of African descent, in galleries and museums. You'd think there were no Black people deserving of being documented in this way. When you study art history, or visit museums across the globe, nudes are a major inclusion. What's noticeable is a large absence of Black people. These museum walls need some color on them, and my hope is to swamp them with Black bodies. That'll be a nice contribution to American history. Now, if that's political, so be it, but it damn sure will be beautiful.

Published June 24, 2018.
CultureCatch

Game Symmetry: Alexis Nunnelly + Bradley Rubenstein

The Proust Questionnaire has its origins in a parlor game popularized by Marcel Proust, the French essayist and novelist, who believed that, in answering these questions, an individual reveals his or her true nature. Below, Alexis Nunnelly and Bradley Rubenstein reinterpret Mr. Proust's concept.

Alexis Nunnelly is from Indianapolis, Indiana where she received her BFA in painting at the Herron School of Art and Design. She works between The New York Studio School in Manhattan and her home in Brooklyn, New York.

What is your idea of perfect happiness?

A life filled to the brim with endless curiosities and support to chase them, mutual respect, no assumptions or expectations. An ability to be in awe of what you take in and finding joy in living.

What is your greatest fear?

Regret, complacency, stagnancy; bodily: loss of function; superficially: heights and deep unknown bodies of water—so maybe that's loss of control.

Which historical figure do you most identify with?

Cleopatra, Jane Goodall.

What is the trait you most deplore in yourself?

I have an awful capability to interrupt. I spend so much time in my own head, running through 50 thoughts in one second, and thoughts tend to dissolve just as easily as they form. I actively work on this daily and often fail. I also find myself to be incredibly manic, induced by procrastination, a constant source of self-deprecating anxiety.

What is the trait you most deplore in others?

Lack of empathy, awareness, or inability to shatter the ego. Lack of flexibility.

What is your greatest extravagance?

I take my pleasures seriously: bubble baths; sun-drenched skin; decadent meals with loved ones; aesthetics; libations; crying at the stars; knowledge; giving myself space to feel good; dancing in lingerie in a candlelit room; deep, passionate love; nuance.

What do you consider the most overrated virtue?

Modesty, chastity, purity in the traditional sense. Purity of heart and character can come from setting yourself free from cultural alignment. Maybe I just think we need to reconsider what virtues our postmodern culture deserves.

On what occasion do you lie?

I used to lie so I wouldn't have to go to class. I don't really lie about that anymore.

What do you dislike most about your appearance?

Sometimes I want to be super girly and clean and put-together, but I know that is not practical to the ways that I function on most days.

What is your greatest regret?

I like to think I have none, and I don't really want to spend my time feeling that. It's one of the scariest emotions to me.

What or who is the greatest love of your life?

Resonating with something that you just can't put into words . . . Bliss. Nature. Paint. Leander Knust.

Which talent would you most like to have?

I would love to be able to speak many languages. Body language, sign language, music coding, cat, etc.

What is your current state of mind?

Hyper-aware, eager, enthused, independent, nostalgic, yearning.

What do you consider your greatest achievement?

Jumping off the cliff.

What is your most treasured possession?

Function, my knowledge, maybe my data and photos of my past, proof of my existence. I think about possession and what it means to claim something as yours.

What do you regard as the lowest depth of misery?

Drowning in emotion.

Where would you like to live?

In a bright, warm greenhouse. There's probably lots of green and lots of mirrors and lots of windows and lots of sheer drapes and lots of nooks and lots of books and lots of dinner parties and lots of art and plenty of space to paint.

What is your favorite occupation?

Mine.

What is your most marked characteristic?

Conviction.

What is the quality you most like in a man?

I like when people are themselves.

What is the quality you most like in a woman?

I really like when people are themselves.

What do you most value in your friends?

Loyalty, and I love my friends so much 'cause they all do their own thing so hard and are goofy and teach me to stay curious. My friends are the best 'cause I isolate myself a lot, and the people that know me best somehow know when I need them. It's like they read my energy.

What is it that you most dislike?

If we are still talking about friends here . . .

How would you like to die?

Gracefully and without regret.

What is your motto?

Know Thyself.

Published February 1, 2020.
Battery Journal

Physical Graffiti: Anna Ehrsam + Bradley Rubenstein

Anna Ehrsam lives and works in Brooklyn, New York. She is a fine artist, patented inventor, and a professor of art history and studio art. Ehrsam is editor-in-chief of the online and print editions *Battery Journal* and co-directs Park Place Gallery.

Bradley Rubenstein: When I sat down to start thinking about your work for this talk, I realized it has been about 20 years that I have been following it. I knew you when you were in grad school, and if I remember correctly we used to run together sometimes. Somehow that seems to be a good place to start. The thing that strikes me most about your early work in performance and sculpture was the physicality of it—in the sense that a lot of your work deals with the body as a subject or field and also that much of your work was very labor-intensive.

Anna Ehrsam: Proving and testing myself with feats of mental and physical endurance have always been part of my work. My physicality gives me the ability to shape matter, words, stone, video, and performance in a way that allows me to network and flow through ideas and material without recognizing limits. I always push beyond in my effort to explore and understand something new.

BR: This was at a time when a lot of work being made was what Chuck Close called "Staples Art," meaning that New York was expensive, artists couldn't afford large studios, so there was a lot of Conceptual Art being made from office supplies.

AE: As an undergrad in New York City at SVA I studied with Lynda Benglis, Alice Aycock, Jackie Winsor, Roni Horn, May Stevens, art history with Donald Kuspit, and other great minds to whom I owe so much. Here I discovered performance, video art, and installation and created immersive works of art with a wide range of materials such as steal, plaster, mold-making, video, performance, installation, film, as well as directing. My desire to create immersive works of art in the form of large installations was an attempt to make hermetic alternative realities for myself and others to explore. My work posed an alternative that questioned the collective cultural assumptions about gender, race, class, and power in a political and social context. I focused on issues of power and domination and the inequalities and cultural ills that I witnessed. My body is my primary tool in all of my existential and phenomenological experiments. I set up ways of exploring the physical world and embodying that exploration in the way that best suits the idea. I feel it is the artist's job to train and tune their sensory apparatus to facilitate the fullest perception, reception, and transmission of their experiential relatives in all of its subjective, object, and metaphysical complexity. Artscience is a way of exploring with an arsenal of tools, technology, and methodology that allows for the fullest range of possibilities and a distinctly existential way of being, acting, and becoming through conscious self-making.

BR: And before that . . .

AE: I was an only child who successfully passed as a boy for years. Gender and identity politics are a part of my work. Gender is enculturated and is toxic for both males and females in this culture and at large. We need new behavioral models that allow for the expression of a much more nuanced and healthy form of gender expression and fluidity. I saw clearly the pervasive cultural inequalities of sexism, racism, and classism rampant in our culture of perpetual war. This bigotry was hostile, as was the cultural climate, and I saw these influences as they were enacted by children at play on the playground. Just as I fought to defend kids on the playground from bigotry and bullies as a child, I fight today to defend against the repressive forces in culture that plague society. The playground has changed to a global field of injustice, corruption, ignorance, and war, but my mission to bring about change in the world and help overcome the injustices remains. Through education, art, and technology I strive to enact positive cultural change.

My countercultural upbringing gives me a unique cultural perspective as an outsider. As a child I perceived the adult hegemony as largely untrustworthy because they had clearly fucked up the world so royally. I knew at that time I needed to help change culture and vowed to be a champion for the underdog. I perceived the systemic, enculturated sexism, misogyny, and violence against girls, women, boys, and men as intolerably evil, and I vowed to fight back with all of my might.

I grew up in Bloomington, Indiana, a progressive international college town where Indiana University is located. Bloomington was a cultural mecca; I was surrounded by artists, intellectuals, and an international academic community. Without a TV or computer I was engaged in deep, durational thought and exploration of my surroundings in a quiet, contemplative, and complex way. Immersed in this radical countercultural environment of artists, musicians, and intellectuals, during a time of social and political unrest and foment, I was often left to my own devices, necessitating that I invent things, draw, build, even make earth works, and construct new narratives. The forest was one of my classrooms. This shaped me in important ways. I spent my time roaming the woods with my dogs, communing with trees, nature, animals, minding my mind. All the while I was painfully aware of the threat of imminent Nuclear Armageddon and perpetual war. But my world was full of art, nature, animals, peace, love, and harmony in a community of artist intellectual hippies. I lived communally with other kids and parents for a time. The adults started a daycare and a school, which is still going strong with kindergarten through twelfth grade under one roof. It's called Harmony School. I was distinctly aware of the cultural and institutional ills of the day, most of which still persist. My artwork stems from a desire to bring about cultural change.

I went to Yale for graduate school where I received my MFA and studied with the brilliant art historian and artist Johanna Drucker, along with many great artists such as Richard Serra, Nayland Blake, Jessica Stockholder, Ron Jones, and John Newman. At Yale I continued my performance, video, sculpture, and installation work. I was in Yale University's first video class, taught by Carol Scully the protege of Ken Burns, both of whom are visionary documentarians. Strangely, this pioneering class was held in the video conferencing rooms for the medical school. During my time at Yale I made several monumental works concerning institutional critique, using my body, large architectonic sculpture, video installation, and performance to explore the nature of space, architecture, and ideology. This was institutional and cultural critique from the inside of the ultra-elite bastions of power. I focused on deconstructing ideological structures, rites, rituals, and power relationships using my body as the interlocutor. I moved back to New York City after graduating with an MFA from Yale University and embarked on a large collaborative project with a fellow Yale graduate.

BR: When you did move to New York, you and your partner at that time were collaborating a lot. I remember your big studio building in Long Island City that was like a giant installation.

There was a piece you did that I saw at Exit Art, a large morphing thing, that very presciently used the World Trade towers as imagery.

AE: I make multidisciplinary complexes, connections, and ideas embodied in installations, sculpture, video, as well as cultural documents. Working with a variety of materials and technologies, I created networks across disciplines to manifest the most stimulating and rewarding experiences, while learning as much as I could about all manner of materials, techniques, and disciplines such as art history, art and cultural theory, physics, materials science, and process. If I'm not making art for myself, other artists, or museums, I am reading, going to art exhibitions, or engaged in discourse about art, culture, and politics with other artists. It was an intense immersion and an invaluable period for me as a developing artist. My early work in New York City was largely based on social political issues of power and domination. I was reading Judith Butler, Michel Foucault, Roland Barthes, Rosalind Krauss, Lynda Nochlin, and Donna Haraway, among others.

The body is imprinted and imposed upon by culture; we become gender labeled, classified, and commodified. We need new models of gender performativity and new relationships to nature and power structures. The landscape contains the idea of freedom and openness, yet it is cultivated, circumscribed, colonized, bought and sold, commodified, and exploited. My sculpture is about body as it relates to landscape, architecture, culture, and power. We are all increasingly cyborgian and have bodies without borders. In terms of physics we are all connected in an infinite web of vibrating strings, exchanging molecules with each other all the time. We are all one organism and part of the same ecosphere. We need new narratives, language, and behavior—and new ways of being in harmony with nature, animals, each other, and our environment. I am working on an app for conservation biology and ecology called Humanimal, which will promote health and wellness for humans, animals, and the planet.

BR: I have always made a distinction between experimentation in art and demonstration. There are a lot of artists who do their homework and then create things that pretty much look like homework. To experiment means you are manifesting your ideas in a material way, which sometimes works, sometimes doesn't, but requires a greater degree of risk. Both kinds of work can produce interesting results, though. An aspect of your practice does involve pedagogical sculpture, work that has specific parameters. Can you talk about how that plays out in your work as a whole—does that influence you at all? Joseph Beuys and Hans Hofmann come to mind as ones who synthesize their practice.

AE: I am pleased you asked this question. Pedagogy and social justice are deeply embedded in my work and life. I have been a teacher for 20 years with a mission to encourage social activism and critical thinking. As for social sculpture, I have created an art and cultural journal to give a context to my fellow artists and cultural producers. It is important to me to make art that has the power to expand consciousness and promote equality and cultural change. In addition to teaching and art making, I expanded my art scholarship and radical pedagogy beyond the realm of text into a living dialogue with cultural producers. I am also co-founder of Park Place Gallery, where I host and curate exhibitions that promote art, science, and technology in the service of ecology. Art is the heart, soul, and intellect of a culture, and I believe as an artist and educator it is my mission to empower others by promoting critical thinking and creative problem solving in the service of conservation, biology, and equality.

BR: So, much of your recent work explores art, science, and perception. It seems like you have moved away from that physicality in your work and maybe on to something more abstract.

AE: The body's sensory apparatus and physical phenomena have always interested me and inspired me to invent and explore new ways to experience the world, using my body as a vehicle. My interest in physics, science, technology, and my patent work are all part of my exploration of the world.

BR: You are also involved in projects with your work in education and environmental issues. At first these might seem outside of your sculptural work, but I was thinking about Beuys and his idea of a social sculpture. Do you see it the same way in your practice?

AE: I believe artists, innovators, inventors, educators, and free thinkers can change the world by presenting radical alternatives to current repressive paradigms and systems, like capitalism, sexism, and racism. I implement a radical pedagogy that interrogates the repressive ideological systems of power, domination, and control. These systems are embedded in culture and inculcated and normalized in the body politic; these repressive systems and norms are accepted as reality. My students accept these repressive socio-political economic systems and conditions as natural because they have not been taught to question authority or the norm. I use art, cultural theory, and art history to present new narratives and possibilities. I show them that language itself is plastic and malleable and that they can control it and shift ideas and outcomes to create new ideas, forms, and meaning. I teach my students to question and interrogate authority through creative thinking and problem solving, and they learn to imagine new self-empowering forms, narratives, and language, which they embody.

Art is the most fundamentally important tool for expanding consciousness and shaping intellectual growth. Through teaching I help shape, guide, and change people's lives. We could classify my creative endeavors as political art, activism, or even social sculpture. In this sense my work is engaged in a relational way with culture shifting and social praxis. Through my cultural production and mentorship I endeavor to promote change on a daily basis.

Published February 19, 2020
Battery Journal

"Bradley Rubenstein's writing opens up insights both haptic and 'meta.' It clears up our transitional ideal of the thing itself—guided like a post-Freudian notion, there exists a consciousness that includes the preconscious and unconscious mind. We are aware of the negotiated space of the creative mind and fiction of art. Rubenstein brings new ways into the constructed space of the thing we see. He is unafraid of the existence of a temporary and contemporary space that truth may exist within."
–Peter Williams, artist

"*The Black Album* is equal parts Rosalind Krauss, Michel Foucault, Charles Bukowski, and Cindy Adams. Bradley Rubenstein is the Deadpool of cultural criticism."
–Alex Thiel, filmmaker